THE CHILDREN OF
CASTLETOWN
HOUSE

THE CHILDREN OF CASTLETOWN HOUSE

SARAH CONOLLY-CAREW

WITH DIANA CONOLLY-CAREW
AND BROTHERS PATRICK & GERALD
FOREWORD BY DESMOND GUINNESS

The
History
Press
Ireland

To our parents,
from all four families
children, grandchildren,
and great-grandchildren

First published 2012

The History Press Ireland
50 City Quay
Dublin 2
Ireland
www.thehistorypress.ie

British Library Cataloguing in Publication Data.
A catalogue record for this book is available from the British Library.

ISBN 978 1 84588 750 6

Typesetting and origination by The History Press

CONTENTS

FOREWORD

It would be very hard to over-estimate the importance of this book. It mainly covers the uncharted years of the authors' family and Castletown in the twentieth century, with all the highs and lows that accompanied them.

Sally Conolly-Carew, with the help of her brothers and sister, has painted a marvellous picture of what it was like to grow up at Castletown, with the stables full of horses and the garden and greenhouses flourishing, all playing their own important role. She also makes us fully aware of the appalling difficulties that led to her father's reluctant decision to sell. Little did I think that in years to come I would find myself buying the empty house to save it from vandalism.

In 1956, soon after I married, we rented Carton from Lord Brocket as a base to find a farm for ourselves. It is about 4 miles from Castletown as the crow flies and was built in 1739 by the FitzGeralds, Earls of Kildare and later Dukes of Leinster. Midway stands by the 140ft high Conolly Folly, an obelisk built on Carton land in 1740 by the Conollys, to give employment during the Great Famine.

I shall never forget the excitement of the first time we went to dinner with Lord and Lady Carew. The governess, Miss Colls, came down the magnificent staircase in full evening dress and a fur coat! The evening was full of fun and laughter; it also helped to fuel my growing passion for architecture. My other passion was hunting, and it was not long before Diana Conolly-Carew and myself were joint masters of the North Kildare Harriers, and I was lucky enough to compete with her in cross country events.

Sally's beautifully written memories bring those far-off days to life and make them seem like yesterday. We have a lot to thank her for.

Desmond Guinness
February, 2012

ACKNOWLEDGEMENTS

My ambition was always for Castletown to relate its own story. I wanted a visitor to walk in the front door, and be able to step in amongst our cast of characters, to relive the legends, the fame, and secret family memories waiting to be told around every nook and cranny. I believe these unique untold stories will 'people' our historic house ... But read the book first!

In order for this ambitious project to come to fruition, we have needed many helpers. It has taken years of planning, digging up memories, mountains of old and new research, talking to the families of our old helpers, and of course the writing.

The main body of work has been researched (with miles of notes) by my extra-ordinary, clever big sister Diana Conolly-Carew. Without her memories and stories, there would be no book. Our brothers Patrick and Bunny have contributed, encouraged and supported all our efforts.

We have so many others to thank for their advice, support, and help, especially Charles Lysaght and Rose Angela Barone, our original planning and layout advisers.

Back in 1964, Deirdre Guinness (Mrs Egerton Skipwith) was my personal photographer, taking over 400 unique images of both the interiors and exteriors, in order to capture what Castletown looked like while we still lived there (with this book in mind).

I have had exceptional extra research help from Catherine Boylan, on behalf of her mother and historian, the late Lena Boylan; John R. Dungan MD, for help with the old castle 'Dongan Papers'; Donough McGillycuddy, for his letters to Diana; Harry McDowell, for invaluable help and support; April Mervelt, for her stories of our times; Brough Scott, for his permission to quote from his book on his grandfather, Jack Seeley; Michael Slavin, for a wonderful supply of books for my research; Chris Shaw, for older family photographs of our grandmother Catherine Conolly's time; and Carmel Locke, who has been my chief fixer and finder of long lost books, articles, and photographs.

We thank Victoria Browne for invaluable help with old Castletown furniture; Desmond Guinness for his Foreword, and for checking through the manuscript; Patrick Guinness for his view of the old Guinness butler at Castletown; Prof Dooley, for pointing us towards our publishers; and Ronan Colgan and Beth Amphlett with their team at History Press Ireland for their help and guidance.

We also wish to thank: Margaret Cummins, Anna Darragh, Mr & Mrs Aidan Kelly, Michael Kenney, Mrs Lawless, Sir George Locke, Helen McDonald, David Mercier, James Murphy, Dr Podrarg O'Snodargh, Johnny O'Neill, Tony Power, Susan Pegley, Mrs Bob Smith, Audrey Smith, Ann Stoney, and Patrick Walsh for everything.

Separately, we wish to thank Claire Hickey and all the staff of the Office of Public Works, who are responsible for Castletown now; as well as Members of the Castletown Foundation.

Lastly, I could not have written this book without the constant support and encouragement of my husband Ian Macpherson, who is my editor here.

INTRODUCTION

Invitation to Join Us ❧ *Sensing the Past*

Being the eighth and last generation of Conollys who have lived at Castletown, we are surrounded with the memories of our years growing-up as Conolly-Carew children. In this book we have tried to look back on those magnificent days as best we can; days of Grand Balls, tiaras, titles, and etiquette; of prancing horses, carriages, early cars, and donkeys, which all carried the great (and often eccentric) people to receptions, dinner parties, and balls. We look at the passing of a bygone age, and ultimately, the latter-day struggle of our parents to keep the house going.

But, above all, we want to tell you of the fun we had from day-to-day, and what life was like in those different days of servant and master, when our world was gently gilded by that inexplicably bond between an Irishman and his horse. These are the halcyon days that we would like to share with you. All is changed now, of course – for instance, our much-loved butler's granddaughter is now a Princess.

In 1938, Sylvia Carew (our mother) was the third newly married wife to take up residence during Castletown's 200-year-old history. She was treading in the footsteps of Lady Louisa Conolly, great granddaughter of King Charles II, who created the decorations in the house, who had cut the walks and rides we loved, dotted with temples, lover's byres, tea houses, and the Great Wood.

If Mother knew nothing of the colourful stories of the past, the secret castle, the gold and vermillion state coach of Speaker Conolly jangling up the front avenue, the Devil in the dining room, and how parts of the house fell down when it was first built, she could not possibly have known what the future held …

And perhaps this was just as well. Perhaps it was just as well not to know of the years ahead, when a servant's hand that would reach out of the window to hide the silver in the basement hedge; the IRA hand that threatened the gun on us all; the hand-made donkey cart, and the smoking gas-cars of the elite; the pranksters who painted the statues red in tender places; the naked grave robber; the lifeless hand of a dead butler at a Hunt Ball; the hands of lovers and trespassers climbing through the windows of the house.

How could she have known that one day, her mother (a Dowager Countess) would get down on her hands and knees to scrub the floor of the famously decorated Long Gallery? Or that a society tailor would come to watch his clothes dancing at the Ball? That loving relatives would open a coffin, only to find it full of bottles? How a barge-horse from the local canal would make her eldest son famous?

And what about our father, Bill Carew? It was a good thing he never knew that his teeth would become a cause of wonder and speculation for us, his mischievous children.

En Dieu est Tout was granted to Speaker Conolly in the reign of Queen Anne. A later motto, *Fiat dei Volumtas*, was taken by our great-great-grandfather Col. Conolly, when he changed his family name from Packenham (Longford) to Conolly, when he inherited Castletown.

1

THE EARLIER YEARS — 1860-1934

Brothers at War ❧ *Letting Castletown* ❧ *Catherine Conolly* ❧ *The Carew Sons:*
A Bachelor Life ❧ *'Burn Castletown'* ❧ *Art O'Connor*

Our great-grandfather was Tom Conolly of Castletown *(1823-1876)*, a confidante of emperors and kings, whose brother, John Augustus, won a Victoria Cross in the Crimea War. Tom spent most of his adult life trying to equal his brother's daring feats, latterly as an adventurer, buccaneer, spy and gun-runner in the American Civil War. He spent the family money, and on one occasion famously shod his carriage horses in silver to win a wager at the Great Exhibition in Paris in 1861. Yet when he died, in 1876 aged just fifty-three, he left his widow alone, with three small sons and a daughter, to cope with his debts.

By 1900 his eldest son, Lt Tom Conolly (junior), was the thirty-year-old owner of Castletown. Tom had served in the Scots Greys in the Sudan, and was now fighting in the Boer War along with his third brother, Edward Michael (Ted) Conolly, who was serving in the Royal Artillery. They both fought in three inconclusive battles at Driefontein, Johannesburg, and Diamond Hill. Young Tom was already an adventurer of note. He had sealed a personal pact with his old school friend and army colleague, Jack Seely, vowing that neither of them would surrender to the enemy unless they had been wounded. They were reacting to reports of British soldiers being overwhelmed by the Boers and surrendering all too easily.

On 10 July, the small garrison post at Nitral's Nek, held by Baden-Powell's force, was relieved by the Royal Scots Greys, together with five companies of the Lincolnshire Regiment, and two guns of the Royal Horse Artillery. At dawn on the 11th, an overwhelming number of Boers attacked the position. The garrison held out all day, waiting for the help that never arrived. By evening, ammunition

Col. John Augustus Conolly, who was awarded one of the first Victoria Crosses in the Crimean War. He was our Uncle Ted's uncle and was born at Castletown.

had run short, and they were forced to surrender the entire squadron of the Scots Greys, plus ninety officers and men of the Lincolnshire Regiment.

As they dropped their weapons, Tom Conolly remembered his vow with Seely, and decided to try to shoot his way out. He shot the Boer closest to him, but was then himself shot dead on the spot.

His act of bravado was needless, as the entire squadron was disarmed and released a few hours later. The Boers did not, as it turned out, wish to feed their prisoners. Ted Conolly had lost his charismatic, swashbuckling elder brother; and Castletown lost a favourite son.

Jack Seely later became the grandfather of racing journalist and commentator, Brough Scott, who wrote *Galloper Jack* about his friendship with young Tom Conolly, and about his grandfather's warhorse.

In 1903, the owners of large Irish houses lost their 'outside' means of support, when the income to maintain them was removed through the passing of the Wyndham Act, and the Land Reform Bill which allowed long-term Irish tenants to buy their holdings from distant landlords at peppercorn prices. Owners of estates could only keep the lands that immediately surrounded their main house, which they farmed themselves. The Act changed the fortunes of tens of thousands of less fortunate Irish families, and set them free to prosper with land of their own, but for many of the landed gentry it meant disaster.

The Government issued compensation in the shape of Land Bonds, which were to be cashed in at some later date. For Ted, all the great estates that his four times Great Uncle, Speaker Conolly, had acquired all over Ireland were gone in a stroke.

With very little money to pay for servants to care for the fabric of such a large house, Ted had little choice but to rent out the house as often as possible to wealthy tenants who invested money to keep it in good order and to pay for servants to maintain it.

Tenants were not continuous, but for the twenty-eight-year period, from approximately 1891 to 1919, Castletown was rented to Thomas F. Kelly, an Irish/American businessman with strong Republican sympathies. He claimed to be a millionaire and agreed to financially support the Irish poet, Padraic Colum, for three years.

Other impoverished writers quickly sought Tom Kelly's backing; amongst them was a young James Joyce. Joyce was living on virtually no money in Phibsboro, Dublin, and was having problems getting his writings published. On 10 December 1903, he walked the 14 miles to Castletown to confront Tom Kelly and try to persuade him to finance a weekly literary pamphlet called *The Goblin*, which he was keen to get off the ground. But a servant took one look at the rough state of his clothes and refused him entry. James Joyce had no choice but to walk all the way back to Dublin! He penned an angry letter the following day protesting at his reception, and got a telegram apologising by return, as well as a letter in the next post.[1] However, Tom Kelly did not, in the end, finance *The Goblin*, which was never published.

The second person to rent Castletown was Sir Peter 'The Packer' Parker, Chief Justice. He was so called because he is reputed to have packed in the juries at some speed.

The last was Capt. Arnold S. Wills, a soldier serving with the British Mounted Regiment, the 18th Hussars, stationed at Curragh. He was born in 1877, the son of Sir Edward P. Wills, of the Wills Tobacco Company, and between 1910 and 1911 was Master of the Kildare Hunt. He was unpopular for his tendency to dig out foxes that had gone to ground. One property owner was reputed to have pleaded for the life of a gallant fox, after a long run, but to no avail. Poor Mr Reynard was dug out, and a deputation was raised to remove Capt. Wills. He finally retired as Master of the Kildares after confronting a rather graphic banner outside Lawler's Ballroom in Naas, for the Hunt Ball; it read:

> Birds have their nests – Bees have their hives
> The Kildare Hunt doesn't want Capt. Wills.

However, Capt. Wills was good for Castletown, and made many improvements, including providing new curtains and a carpet on the main staircase. He also purchased several items of furniture, including the elegant Georgian dining room chairs[2] and, as a member of the Kildare Polo Club, he also brought the Castletown Polo Field back into play.

In 1904, Ted's older sister, Catherine Conolly, married Gerald Shapland Carew, a Tea Taster and Broker[3] in London. They had no idea that one day they would become the 5th Lord and Lady Carew, because a cousin held the title, who had younger siblings. The 3rd, 4th, and 5th Baron Carew were all of similar age (from the same generation, two brothers and a cousin), who died in 1923, 1926, and 1927 respectively. This meant that the cousin, our grandfather, held the title for precisely ten months before he died, at which point it passed on to our father, aged twenty-two.[4]

On 23 April 1905, at 28 Belgrave Square in London, Catherine (Conolly) Carew gave birth to our father, William Francis (Bill) Carew. He and his younger brothers, Gavin and Peter, lived there until they moved into 120 Tedworth Square, Chelsea, living next door to the Dowager Marchioness of Sligo, their father's aunt.[5]

Ted Conolly watched his sister's three Carew boys grow up in London, where they all attended Sunningdale Prep School; our father then went on to Wellington College, Berkshire; Gavin to Shrewsbury School, and Peter to the Royal Naval School at Pangbourne. The boys of the next generation were deliberately sent to separate boarding schools at the age of eight, because of the exploits of their father and his brothers, who apparently wreaked havoc together at their Prep School.

At the outbreak of the First World War in 1914, Ted Conolly returned to serve in the Royal Artillery. His nephew aged ten, visited Castletown on the occasional school holiday (when the house was not let), accompanied by his mother Catherine and his grandmother Sara Eliza (Shaw) Conolly (a Celbridge girl, and widow of his gun-runner grandfather Tom Conolly), and his uncle Henry Shaw and other friends.

His great aunt Lady Sligo's family name was Brown, and it was in her house that the Carew boys' mother, Catherine, is believed to have introduced her only surviving brother, Ted Conolly, to Eileen Agatha Brown in 1918. Eileen was born in 1889, the daughter of the 6th Marquis of Sligo, and was just twenty-six when she met Uncle Ted, who was aged forty-one.

As cousins, they were allowed the freedom to travel together without much comment, but when the romance became obvious, Lady Sligo is thought to have thoroughly disapproved; Ted Conolly had no money to look after Castletown, let alone a wife. There was no happy ending to Ted's story. Eileen was the love of his life and he regretted loosing her, letting everyone know that 'he could not afford to get married'. Had he led an ordinary life, without the responsibility of Castletown on his shoulders, perhaps old Lady Sligo would have given her consent in the end ... who knows! Believing that the freedom to keep your property was part of what they had all been fighting for, he returned to Castletown alone. When the house was rented, he lived in the Garden House, which had been built sixty years previously by his father Tom Conolly for his land agent.

Later, Ted returned to the main house and lived in just one bedroom, bathroom, study, and the dining room. He had a wonderful housekeeper, Roseanne O'Connor from Athlone, who brought him early morning tea, cooked his meals, and cleaned his clothes. He used to sit in solitary splendour at one end of the dining room table, and no doubt, wondered if he would ever see the days of joyous parties ever again. In the winter he huddled around a one-bar electric fire in his study.[6]

With property prices very low, he had already been forced to sell Leixlip Castle,[7] which had been owned by the family since Castletown's builder – Speaker Conolly's heir and nephew, William Conolly – lived there in the first half of the 1700s. It had been let ever since, frequently to a Lord Lieutenant, or to other various British administrators. Ted Conolly had also managed to sell some outlying acres on the estate, in order to keep Castletown going. The one luxury he allowed himself was the breeding of thoroughbred foals each year, as they brought in money at the sales. Later, he was able to race his homebred horses, and won the 1941 Irish 1,000 Guineas with a filly called Milady Rose.

One of his favourite pastimes, which he continued throughout his life, was to walk for miles across the fields carrying a long-handled thistle-cutter, chopping below soil-level and uprooting the weeds as he went. He also walked or bicycled a mile along the garden path twice a day, to feed and let out his brood mares and foals in a far field.

Two years later, he received an invitation to the marriage of his old love, Eileen Agatha Brown, to the 7th Earl of Stanhope. Manners dictated that he should attend.

So Ted Conolly, disappointed in love, lived his singularly under-funded life at Castletown.

As his sister, Catherine's, children got older, she would bring her boys to stay for the school holidays. The youngsters revelled in the magical freedom of the place, but were blissfully unaware of the show he put on for their comfort and enjoyment (hiring servants for the occasion). He had always made it clear that our father, the eldest, would inherit the house. This may have sounded exciting to a young boy, but without sufficient income to maintain the estate, there would be hard times ahead for another generation.

For the duration of the First World War, Ted had relied heavily on his Land Agent, Dease, from the nearby Stacumany, who was the father of Ted's great friend and army comrade, Ernest Dease. During this time, he let out all the fields around Castletown to his close Masonic friend, Mr Ganley. This was at a time when every piece of unused land was required to be ploughed up for the war effort. He grew corn, and managed to farm the rest of the land as quality grazing land for his sizable cattle dealership.

When Ted returned from the war, he had invaluable help and advice from Dease. He took back most of the farm and re-employed Ganley's estate workers, gradually changing the land to more tillage. While Ganley still farmed a few of the Castletown fields, he helped the finances by buying and selling cattle for Ted.

However, Ganley was not able to use the Farmyard or the Stableyard, for they were kept for the people who rented Castletown. Corn was threshed elsewhere and stored with great mountains of hay along Dongan's Walk.[8]

Uncle Ted led a busy life. Out every morning by 8 a.m. to see the workmen, he was known as a hard but fair taskmaster. His aim in life was to free Castletown from debt and to bring back parts of the estate which had been let. He lived a frugal life, his only pleasures being hunting twice a week, and going flat racing, where he was a steward.

Although he did not entertain at Castletown, he changed into evening dress every night for dinner, and quite often his great friend Ernest Dease would bicycle from Stacumany in evening dress to dine with the major. Sadly for Ted, Ernest succumbed to the exotic charms of a French lady, somewhat late in life; and Ted indignantly told the tale of how this 'femme fatale' had laid her plans to cart Ernest back to France. Although Ernest maintained he didn't really want to leave, the determined French lady was not to be denied, and Ted was left without the company of his greatest friend and ally.

As a little money slowly filtered through the system from land compensation, Ted gradually found life easier, and at last he could complete the most urgent repairs to the house. He had more time to go flat racing, where he was a Member of The Turf Club, and Steward at the Curragh. In latter years, he regularly visited Newmarket where he stayed in the Jockey Club Rooms

A constant problem every autumn were the old lime trees along the Front Drive,[9] which were originally planted there by Speaker Conolly. The farm workers remember being kept busy, for Ted would never let the Front Avenue tree branches be cut or trimmed in any way, so the men had to sweep away the fallen leaves, for all three-quarters of a mile!

Later on, when he could afford a new, more powerful car, he enjoyed driving it up and down the Front Avenue to blow away the leaves. This was very popular with the men, and they stood and cheered! It proved that cars had their uses after all – 'Marvellous invention' they said.

The estate was mainly turned to the plough, with the exception of the front and back fields. One man ploughing with two horses could turn an acre a day, (someone calculated that to be 19 miles walking) surrounded by shrieking gulls. There were usually two ploughmen working the one field. (Later, in the 1940s, a 2-furrow Ferguson tractor would do one acre in two hours.) Crops of turnips, kale, and mangolds were grown, and corn for the cattle, plough horses, and milking cows during the winter, as well as hay.

During the wintertime, the fattening bullocks were tied up loosely in stalls in the lower farmyard, as were the cows. There were also eight cart horses tied up in their individual stalls. In the winter the horses carried a thick coat and, because their heavy ploughing work caused sweat and dirt, they were half-clipped (their lower halves were clipped and the tops left unclipped, for warmth).

Everything on the estate seemed to take two men to operate. For instance, both the clippers and the mangles were two hand-operated machines; the latter being circular choppers which were used for turnips, mangolds, and chipped straw (chaff), and provided the daily diet for the cattle and the cart horses in the farmyard. To this was added oats, which required both large crushers from the stable and the farmyards.

The daily diet for the horses in the stable yard was usually a combination of crushed oats, damp bran with Corenda, and cooked barley, which looked like cornflakes and was used for conditioning. They were given fewer oats to eat if they were too excitable, and their diet was sometimes supplemented with turnips and carrots from a big clump in the farmyard. There was also a salt lick on the stable walls.

Since 1916, the Republican Movement in Ireland had grown in determination, and in 1922, the Troubles erupted into armed conflict. Many of the great houses, which had previously escaped Cromwell and/or the economic decline, were targeted by the Republicans, seen as the symbols of British oppression. This included the Carew family house, Castleboro, in Wexford.

The Republicans often travelled in posses at night and were armed with flares; always using petrol to start their grim bonfires.

Occupants of big houses posted lookouts at night, shut their shutters and bolted their doors; but once they were targeted they could do little to protect their homes, except to argue their case. They dared not leave them empty, for this would be a certain invitation for arson.

One night Ted Conolly received news that a large group of Republicans were marching up the front drive of Castletown, armed with their flares. Uncle Ted watched from his study window as they gathered by the farmyard, where an accomplice on the estate had stockpiled petrol cans. Opening his front door, he invited the posse into his small study, just off the front hall, and argued, and argued to try to save the house. He pointed out Lord Edward FitzGerald's (founding member of the Republican Movement) association with house, and that it had been built by the Irish Government for one of Ireland's greatest politicians, Speaker Conolly (a story the family has always believed), who had been born a true Irishman. He also made their aware that the Conolly family were still in residence, and that the house had never been English-owned.

The gang did not want to listen to reason, and were intent on creating enough of an inferno to destroy the house. Fortunately, at this moment, Art O'Connor burst in into the room, and persuaded them to change their minds. Perhaps Art O'Connor was the only man a Republican posse might listen to. Certainly, the only reason Castletown still exists today is because of its purebred Republican connections.

Mr Art O'Connor, was a 34-year-old local hero, who brought the name of Celbridge to countrywide attention as one of the best-known Republicans in Ireland. Born and raised on his father's farm 2 miles away, at Elm Hall, Celbridge, he had stockpiled smuggled rifles, and armed the first Celbridge Volunteer Group in 1914. By 1916 he was one of the leaders of the National Resistance Campaign against the enforced conscription of Irishmen. He went on the run for two years, while the Irish newspapers gleefully reported his narrow escapes; these were often effected on a bicycle, or by being spirited away from under the very noses of the Authorities by family and friends, after delivering rousing speeches against the British Rule. Disguised as a drover, he was finally spotted at a cattle fair in 1918, and arrested by a police sergeant from Celbridge, who knew him well.

In 1918 he joined De Valera and many of the Irish Resistance leaders imprisoned in England. While in prison, Art and some of his colleagues were elected to the Irish 'Dail' Parliament, and he became Shadow Minister for Agriculture; following their release, his party came to power. In 1921 his tirade against concessions being given to the English over the Independence Treaty, helped to raise the country to armed struggle once again, in 1922. 'Damn your Concessions, We want our Country.'

Shortly after he had saved Castletown, he was recaptured and imprisoned, variously in Mountjoy and Kilmainham jails in Dublin. He became a *cause célèbre*, going on hunger strike for fifty-three days, and forcing the authorities to release him. After his release, Art helped DeValera found the breakaway Fianna Fail Party.

Retiring from politics in 1932, he practiced law, which led to him being appointed a Circuit Court Judge for Co. Cork in 1947. When he stepped down as a judge, he was described as a warm-hearted human being, who was a friend to everyone, including Ted Conolly who delivered an address to him and was photographed congratulating him on his retirement party.

2

FINDING A BRIDE

Our story really begins with a letter of reprimand:

> *Castletown*
> *Co. Kildare*
> *1934*
>
> *Dear Bill,*
> *I have received some news of you in Bermuda! I really think the time has come for*
> *you to settle down. What you must do is to find yourself a girl of splendid fortune,*
> *come and live here, and secure the future of Castletown.*
>
> *Ted Conolly.*

What an ultimatum!!

At this time, our father had been in the British Army for twelve years, with the Duke of Cornwall's Light Infantry (DCLI), having joined straight from school, via Sandhurst. He was a good athlete, and had been the army's Number 2 high hurdler.[10]

In 1926, his father had become the 5th Baron Carew, but only held the title for ten months before he died; our father became the 6th Lord Carew the following year. In 1931 he was appointed ADC to the Governor of the beautiful Protectorate Island of Bermuda – there were girls and parties galore, and reports of high jinks and the spreading of wild oats, which eventually reached the attentive ears of his uncle Ted Conolly at Castletown. (Somehow he managed to leave his own mark on Bermuda, being remembered as the instigator of the first Fire Engine for the capital, Hamilton; and for the fire hydrants still in evidence along Front Street.)

How would he begin his search for his heiress? At the time, it was popular to marry an American girl. It was often said that wealthy Americans liked titles and enormous houses. But it was our father's youngest brother, Peter, who found him the right girl; she turned out to be a fair Scottish lass.

Peter, a serving naval officer, had stayed at Thirlestane Castle, Lauder, Berwickshire, several times between 1934 and 1935, where a certain willowy, fair, blue-eyed Scottish girl lived. She was a considerable heiress through her mother and her grandfather, J.J. Bell-Irving (once chairman of the old trading company, Jardine Matheson of Hong Kong).

Lady Sylvia Maitland, a daughter of the 15th Earl of Lauderdale, was just twenty-one when she first met Peter Carew. Her brother, Ivor, aged nineteen, was heir to the Lauderdale title. Sylvia had a mind of her own, having been unofficially engaged to the son of a local Scottish family, but had suffered the heartbreak of seeing him killed in front of her as he rode at Kelso Races. It was only much later in life that she spoke of the tragedy; and only shortly before her death in 1991 did she explain the reason for her constant refusal to allow her older daughter Diana to ride in point-to-point races.

In 1936, when our father, now Lord Carew, returned from his ADC duties in Bermuda, he met the grieving Sylvia Maitland (our mother), and must have offered his own particular brand of compassion and understanding. They had much in common, sharing a love of riding, shooting, fishing, tennis, and all winter sports. Both were stylish accomplished riders to hounds, and their official engagement photograph was taken posed on their hunters at a meet in Lauder. Mother, at such a young age, was a renowned shot and fisherwoman, having some of the most abundant salmon fishing in Scotland at her mother's family house, Makerstoun, on the Tweed, near Kelso.

Mother had grown up with parents who were equally sporting. Both she and her mother, Ivy, were the picture of elegance, riding side-saddle to hounds together over the most challenging of English hunting country in Leicestershire, as well as with the local pack of foxhounds, like the Lauderdale and the Duke of Buccleuch's Hounds.

Both Sylvia and Ivy were renowned skiers – and this was in the days when you skied the hard way; manoeuvring long wooden skis uphill, with animal skins covering the skis to get a grip when ascending (and long before ski lifts were introduced). Ivy did the Cresta Run several times when she was newly married (it was later judged to be too dangerous for women), as did her husband, the Earl.

Tennis competitions at a high level (long before the days of professional players) were part of the summer season, and groups of friends would stay in seaside hotels in towns such as Frinton-on-Sea, and joined in the annual competitive tennis matches. There was a family double, around 1932, when our mother's brother Ivor, qualified and completed at the Junior Wimbledon competition; her father, Ian, played in the doubles competition at Senior Wimbledon.

The Earl of Lauderdale and the Earl of Dundee, two of some of the oldest titles in Scotland, have the honour of carrying the two Scottish flags, the Saltire and the Lion of Scotland before the Monarch on State occasions. The Lauderdale family name is Maitland, and throughout the Middle Ages, the Maitlands owned much of the Lammermuir Hills between the River Tweed and Edinburgh.

In 1250, the original Thirlestane Castle at Lauder was a strong hill fort (the ruin is still visible 2 miles south east of the present castle), on a strategic route 25 miles south of Edinburgh, built to guard against any invaders from the south. It was owned by Sir Richard Maitland and his son, who fought for both William Wallace, Regent of Scotland, and for King Robert the Bruce. Legend also recalls that the father successfully repulsed a fifteen-day siege by the forces of King Edward I of England (Edward Longshanks).

The present Thirlestane Castle was built, in 1590, of pink sandstone, by Sir John Maitland, 1st Baron Thirlestane, Lord Chancellor of Scotland to King James VI, who later became King James I of England at the union of the crowns. His older brother, Sir William Maitland of Lethington (1525-1573), had been Secretary of State and a devoted friend of Mary Queen of Scots (James I's mother).

The Chancellor's son was created the 1st Earl of Lauderdale, and his grandson became the first and only Duke of Lauderdale. He had been captured at the Battle of Worcester by Cromwell and kept under sentence of death in the Tower of London until he was released in 1659 at the Restoration of King Charles II. He was created a Duke in 1670. He became an advisor and personal friend of Charles II, and the 'L' in the CABAL (Clifford, Ashley, Buckingham, Arlington and Lauderdale) cabinet.

The Duke virtually ruled Scotland for the King, and became extremely unpopular. He enlarged and embellished the castle, intending it to rival Hollyrood Palace in Edinburgh.

With the Duke having no son, the Dukedom was lost, and his younger brother inherited their father's title of the Earl of Lauderdale (which it has been ever since).

Ian Maitland, the 15th Earl of Lauderdale (1891-1953), our grandfather, was an arch practical joker. He was the son of the 14th Earl, Colin, and his musical wife Gwenny Vaughan Williams (a cousin of the composer Ralph Vaughan Williams (1872-1958)).[11]

Ian had some success composing music; we remember the excitement when one of his pieces was played on the radio. At school, Ian was a renowned long jumper, holding the Eton record of 21ft. He was an all round athlete, but later on in life suffered from a chronically weak heart.

He joined the 3rd Battalion, Queen's Own Cameron Highlanders, and was married in 1912 to twenty-year-old Ethel Mary Bell Irving, known to her friends as Ivy.

He served as a Major in the First World War (1914-1918), and later was appointed ADC to the Viceroy of Ireland in 1915-16 (and 1918). During that time, he lived with his wife and two-year-old daughter, Sylvia Maitland, at Viceregal Lodge, in Phoenix Park, Dublin, where his son and heir was born (1915), and where the new baby was christened Ivor after the Viceroy, Ivor Viscount Wimbourne.

Many stories have passed down from their time in Dublin, mainly relating to Ian's constant practical jokes. Perhaps it was the golden era of daring jokes, the more outlandish the better – one enterprising fellow of the time inspected The Fleet as the Sultan of Zanzibar; the same prankster drilled a hole in the middle of Piccadilly, in London. He put a screen around it, and left. It stayed there for days, causing untold nuisance, before anyone thought to ask questions.

Our grandfather was very proud of a realistic-looking faux dog mess he often kept in his pocket, in case that he might have the opportunity of embarrassing a pompous host. Once, whilst he was staying near Ascot for the annual Races, an unfortunate butler, carrying a giant silver salver of drinks, spied the 'dog mess', and satisfyingly dropping the lot. Ian discreetly bent down, picked up the offending object, and replaced it into his pocket.

In later years, he would take great delight in organising the whole army of eleven children on our summer holidays. He equipped us with saltshakers and sat us down outside different rabbit burrows near the castle – the fields were infested with rabbits. 'If you put salt on the white bob tail, you can catch it.' There a bribe of sweets involved and we would sit for hours, quite certain that a bunny would hop by! His constant sense of fun infected us children, and has left all of us with a mischievous turn of mind.

They say the Irish can laugh at themselves. What would the world be like without Irish jokes? There were some well-known hosts whose delight was to tease their guests, and if you accepted their invitation, you knew you were in for a good evening. The late Earl of Meath used mechanical means. A favourite trick was with a wind-up, long-legged spider, which he set off down the centre of his long dining room table, sending glasses and mustard pots flying, and all the ladies into shrieking disarray.

We had the impression that our Grandmother Ivy, Ethel Mary, Countess of Lauderdale, was most definitely un-amused by his antics. In later life she could be quite severe, though she was widely respected.

As a young wife, Ivy was very keen on hunting. She had no official job at Viceregal Lodge, so spent her time organising the hunting and the horses for the household. They had the pick of the British Army horses at their disposal, as did every other officer and his spouse.[12]

For local meets, the horses would be led by grooms – often riding one and leading two (most of the riders out hunting would have a second horse). At meets further away, the horses would go by train from the station near McKee Barracks, beside the Liffey. In Meath, there was a well-known meet at Kilmessan, at a small railway village in the middle of superb hunting country. On non-hunting days, many rode or drove out into Phoenix Park, or to a small indoor riding school at Collins Barracks, or the larger one at McKee Barracks.

Ivy was a remarkably strong-minded person. She had a business brain from a very young age, because of her father, J.J. Bell Irving. Having no son, he brought Ivy and her sister Marda up in the world of stocks and shares. Even the most unlikely circumstances were often turned to her own advantage. On one occasion she bought a most unusual coloured kitten for about 6 pence. She kept a careful note of the costs of feeding it, and sent it to be shown in the regular cat shows around the country. It would be put on the early morning train in its basket, and returned late at night with its prize ribbons. She achieved her aim after a while, and sold the rare coloured cat to someone in the USA for £100, making a profit of £80.

Bill Carew eventually proposed to Lady Sylvia Maitland, she accepted, and they were married on 3rd June 1937, at St Margaret's Westminster, with her twin cousins John and James Ormerod as pageboys, and a guest list straight out of *Who's Who*. He was thirty-two and she was twenty-four.

We, their four children, have inherited the sporting genes that were later channelled into serious competitive events, and seemed to have passed on those genes to the next generation. We all eventually represented Ireland, in eventing or show jumping.

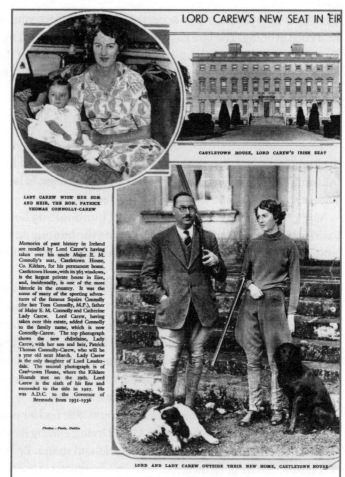

LORD CAREW'S NEW SEAT IN ÉIR

CASTLETOWN HOUSE, LORD CAREW'S IRISH SEAT

LADY CAREW WITH HER SON AND HEIR, THE HON. PATRICK THOMAS CONNOLLY-CAREW

Memories of past history in Ireland are recalled by Lord Carew's having taken over his uncle Major E. M. Conolly's seat, Castletown House, Co. Kildare, for his permanent home. Castletown House, with its 365 windows, is the largest private house in Éire, and, incidentally, is one of the most historic in the country. It was the scene of many of the sporting adventures of the famous Squire Connolly (the late Tom Connolly, M.P.), father of Major E. M. Connolly and Catherine Lady Carew. Lord Carew, having taken over this estate, added Connolly to the family name, which is now Connolly-Carew. The top photograph shows the new châtelaine, Lady Carew, with her son and heir, Patrick Thomas Connolly-Carew, who will be a year old next March. Lady Carew is the only daughter of Lord Lauderdale. The second photograph is of Castletown House, where the Kildare Hounds met on the 29th. Lord Carew is the sixth of his line and succeeded to the title in 1927. He was A.D.C. to the Governor of Bermuda from 1931-1936

Photos.: Poole, Dublin

LORD AND LADY CAREW OUTSIDE THEIR NEW HOME, CASTLETOWN HOUSE

Our parents' arrival at Castletown with baby Patrick. Their precious wedding gifts and furniture were transported to Castletown on the back of the garden produce lorry. (Courtesy of *The Tatler*, 1938)

In 1938, exactly nine months and six days after their wedding, the new Lord and Lady Carew produced a son, Patrick Thomas, in London. Within three weeks of the birth of his son and heir, Father complied with the original Conolly family edict, drawn up in the late 1700s, that all who lived at Castletown should retain the name Conolly. Though his title was still Lord Carew, by deed poll both he and his children would now be named Conolly-Carew. (This was the second time the Conolly name had been adopted by the family of a female inheritor – through his mother Catherine in this case – the first being the Packenhams in the 1800s.)

By the autumn of the same year, our parents moved into Castletown with baby Patrick.

WAR TIME

In 1938, when Mother arrived at Castletown as a young wife, with her six-month-old son Patrick, she could have no inkling of what lay ahead of her. Perhaps she got an insight when it transpired that all her precious goods and chattels were rattling along on the back of the farm lorry.

As they drove up the broad Front Avenue between the heavy boughs of the untrimmed, heavily scented lime trees and swept into view of the house, over thirty servants and estate workers were lining both sides to greet them. Uncle Ted Conolly welcomed them at the top of the steps, and the housekeeper ceremoniously handed over the enormous bunch of keys (though, later, she was asked to take them back until the new mistress of the house found her feet).

If Mother required some of her prized possessions that night, she would have had to wait, for their mountain of luggage was being unloaded into the stables as the farm lorry was needed to load up with turnips and potatoes for the early morning market (the Haymarket) in Dublin the following day.

One of the first major changes came at the start of the Second World War in 1939, when the entire kitchen wing was given over to a girl's orphanage school, including the old kitchen. A new kitchen, pantry, servants' hall, and wash room were fitted out in the cellars of the main house, directly underneath the dining room area, which enabled a small pulley lift to ferry the food to the table while it was still hot.

The wonderful old kitchen (now used as the tea room) had an old range, impossible to keep in repair, with an outdated Elsen chemical toilet beside it. Previous generations had coped with relays of liveried running footmen, carrying hot dishes and food out of the old kitchen fifty yards along the narrow curved corridor, before they turned left, up the stone back stairs, into the pantry, and through to the dining room.[13]

Mother got used to the Conolly way of not using the front door, except for important guests, or on very fine days; the house was cold enough without the unwelcome draught. The main back door, leading from the drawing rooms, was opened very rarely. The most used door was the 'shute', an enclosed Victorian stairway, built from the ground floor down to the stable yard. (It has now gone, deemed out-of-keeping with the house.)

In later life, Father somewhat resembled Capt. Mainwaring in the television comedy series *Dad's Army* – down to the glasses, the moustache and an occasional strut, but with a heart as big as a lion. He was short, portly, a stickler for detail, and had very small feet. Mother was taller, and would consciously 'bend down a bit' when a photographer was capturing them on film together. Our mother was very good-looking, and retained the same willowy figure, intense blue eyes, and short, fair curly hair for most of her life; but very occasionally she unconsciously did slightly ridiculous things.

A Christmas shopping list was written on a roll of Bronco paper, for the very good reason that it was the only paper to hand. The list was undoubtedly written 'on the hoof' while visiting the various cottages to find out the families' urgent needs for Christmas. The shop assistant not only had to keep a straight face as she unrolled the list (all the tenant's and worker's children on the estate had a present each – some families had as many as eight children), but the words were difficult to decipher on the toilet paper. The unfortunate assistant had to fetch the supervisor; you were *not* allowed to giggle at a valued customer.

She once inserted an advertisement for a cook, in later days when everyone doubled up in their jobs; it was picked up by the tabloids as a weekly funny: 'Lady Carew requires a Cook, plain cooking, can bring own horse.' She was indignant that anyone would think the horse might be on the menu!

In 1939, a year after our parents moved into Castletown to live with Uncle Ted Conolly, the Second World War broke out, and Father left to rejoin his regiment, along with many Irishmen who joined up, even though Ireland was a neutral country.

Fears and rumours spread that Hitler would tread all over Ireland, using it as a stepping-stone to invade England. Some elderly owners of grand houses hastened to bury their silver in their 'ha-ha's (stone-faced ditches). As the war dragged on the owners died off, the servants dwindled, and some of the hiding places have never been found.

Many sons, having survived the war, returned home to find the cupboard bare, and the wine and whiskey cellar empty as well. If the butler wasn't to blame (they were renowned for being excellent 'tasters') it was almost certainly the fault of the grandmother who had steadied her nerves with a few hot toddies at night – every night for four years. There was nobody to point out that the crates of vintage whiskey had been deliberately laid down for the future. Certainly, at Castletown, there was a Pipe of Port kept in the cellar opposite the kitchen, which followed the tradition of families to give this gift to an eldest son upon his twenty-first birthday, for him and the next generation to drink after he inherited the house.

Mother's greatest friend was Lady Athlumney.[14] She was a merry widow who had married a much older husband with a fast reputation. Born in Australia, she was scooped up as a young girl by her Irish Lord, hoping her money would prop up his estate at Somerville Co. Meath.

However, the story that fascinated us concerned the last will and testimony of Lord Athlumney. When he died, he left her the house, which was then to be passed down to her older sister's son. But there was a problem; the older sister did not have a son, although everyone knew she had had a fling with the old Lord (her brother-in-law) at an earlier date. (Was she getting him to pay alimony for an illegitimate son who did not exist?) Considerably later, a son *was* born to Lady Athlumney's sister. He was Quentin Agnew, and he eventually married our Scottish cousin, April Drummond.

During the Second World War, Mother kept her horse with Lady Athlumney, and twice a week, motored over to her house using her charcoal-burner car to hunt. Lady A. was slightly impetuous by nature, and would continuously ask her horse to jump impossible fences, until it refused to go. Mother had to change horses with her friend, with instructions not to spoil hers too. Having regained the horse's confidence, they swapped back again. Tragically, Lady A. suffered from a heart attack while she was swimming, and drowned in her own pool, where she was found later by a mutual friend, Peggy Nolan, who had gone into the house to change.

Mrs St John (Peggy) Nolan was a champion rider, swimmer, and trainer. She won the Dublin Grand Prix on a horse called Swastika Rose, owned by the Swastika Laundry, based in Dublin. In those ever-practical wartime years, during the winter months, the horse pulled the laundry cart all day, every day, for miles around Dublin. Peggy and the horse also came third in the London Olympia High

Jump, reputedly clearing 7ft 6in. Peggy trained racehorses before the days when ladies were permitted to be licensed trainers; her groom held the licence, yet she trained innumerable winners, and (years later) won the Irish Grand National with Zonda in 1959, which also finished third in the Cheltenham Gold Cup in 1960.[15]

Alma Brooke, the forthright daughter of Lady Mabel Brooke, from Pickering, Co. Kildare, was another great friend, who preferred to ride astride. This was a changing era, when daring ladies could opt *not* to ride side-saddle.

Just after the war, a dance was held in the Celbridge Mills in order to raise money for the Red Cross, and tickets were sold to win a thoroughbred filly donated by Lady Brooke. Mrs Young (sister of Art O'Connor) bought the last two tickets for 6 pence each. She won the horse, which was bred to win a classic race, and she trained it to pull the family trap for many years. It proved ideal, she said, as it was quiet and very brave in traffic, and never tired. Eventually, urged by Lady Brooke to breed thoroughbred foals from the mare, Lady Brooke bought the progeny from Mrs Young, and most of the horses bred from the filly went on to win races in England.

Lady Brooke, grand as she was, was not averse to a bit of first-class bartering at Young's Garage during the difficult days after the war – she often filled her car with petrol and paid for it with a pound of tea.

Later, Alma Brooke became godmother to me goodness knows why, because she loudly declared that children should neither be seen nor heard!

Later in life, Alma lived in England. When she died, her clothes were being cleared out and bundled into bags to go to the local charity shop. Luckily her maid walked in. 'Stop! Stop!' she cried in a panic, 'All of Miss Brooke's jewellery is sewn into the bottom of her skirts!'

That episode was recounted to Diana when she sat next to another of Alma's goddaughters at a party. The girl was wearing a superb set of pearls, which she proudly showed off, declaring them to have been inherited from her godmother, having been rescued from an evening skirt.

Life in Ireland during the war went on as usual, with no food rationing, although fuel for cars was not readily available for private individuals. People simply re-commissioned their old pony and dug out their old traps from dusty barns. Some managed to convert their cars to run on charcoal, though they were slower and fairly unreliable and many thought the charcoal cars not worth the bother. They snorted and snuffled along on their tortuous journeys, all the time dispensing largesse, in the shape of great dollops of dust and black smoke, behind them as they went. It was enough to make the hardiest pedestrian beat a hasty retreat.

There were still lawn meets of the Kildare Hounds at Castletown, where Mother was just as likely to ride a sturdy Connemara pony, as a high-blooded horse. Indeed, she came to love the hardiness and bravery of these miniature horses, and bred from one of her own Connemara mares. Later, she became a judge of Connemaras in the British Isles, including the mecca at Clifden, in Connemara. To this day, the Lady Carew Cup is awarded to the champion two-year-old filly. It is regarded as one of the most important awards in the international competition world.

Mother was often hunting both astride and side-saddle and the biggest danger to all side-saddle riders happened to her while she was out hunting in Cork; her horse tripped and fell over hidden tree roots. When astride, the rider can 'bale out', jump clear of the saddle when the ground looms large, but in a side-saddle, with both legs on one side, you are riding with a tall pummel between your legs and you cannot jump off. Mother fell, trapped in the saddle, and broke her back on a protruding tree-stump. She cracked her spine, and never rode again.

However, she was extremely fortunate not to sever the spinal cord, though it was crushed and painful for the rest of her life. She made light of it, but usually discreetly carried an easily folded blow-up cushion to sit on wherever she went after that. Over the years, she got through many different cushions, for each one eventually felt its age, and developed a small hole ...!

In 1940, news of the war was worrying, but at least our father was still alive. Then came the evacuation from Dunkirk, and the amazing flotilla of thousands of small pleasure-boats from England, sailing across the channel to rescue the British Army.

There is a description of father as he waited at Dunkirk, from a recent book *One & All*, a history of his regiment, the DCLI:

One of the most vivid memories of an officer of one of these companies was of the almost unbelievable coolness in danger of Capt. the Lord Carew, sitting outside the farmhouse doors reading The Times *newspaper, apparently oblivious to the mortar bombs falling around him.*

He was badly wounded on the beach, before the evacuation, though presumably he was not reading the newspaper at the time.

4

A WARTIME VISIT

There was a joke in our family that each one of us was born nine months after father had a leave from the army; and it turned out to be true. Patrick Thomas was born in 1938, Diana Sylvia was born in April 1940 (a statue of Diana, the Goddess of Hunting, in the Long Gallery), and Gerald Edward Ian (Bunny) was born in December 1941.

I was not yet on the scene when Mother's parents, Ian and Ivy Lauderdale, came to stay at Castletown for the first time in 1943.

It was unusual to travel in the middle of the war and how different life was in Ireland! Grandmother Ivy wrote several fascinating impressions of what she saw. Here follows some extracts taken from those impressions.

They flew from Liverpool Airport on a small aeroplane, where all eleven passengers had both themselves and their luggage carefully weighed, in case the plane was overloaded. Then the powers that be must have lost their nerve, for they proceeded to throw their rule-book straight out of the terminal window when they were confronted with the formidable Earl and Countess of Lauderdale with 32kg too much luggage. Obviously, unwilling to order them to unpack their noble drawers all over the airport floor, a diplomatic compromise was reached, with the passing of a 32 shilling fine, naturally intended to lighten the load on the plane. It was all very civilised, nobody jumped up and down. (Perhaps the pilot saw there was no overlarge person on his plane.) They then had to go through a very stringent security procedure, requiring all the *other* passengers to be both stripped and searched (but not our grandparents; presumably the Earl and Countess were thought safe enough); every lady had her handbag removed and tipped out; every case was opened and investigated; and even a proposed trip to the cloakroom was thwarted by a soldier saying it was out of bounds for the Dublin flight!

The Countess recalled:

> *The plane has 6 seats on each side of a passage, like the inside of a motorbus, but not nearly so wide. It was all blacked out, and you saw nothing. We took off, and the noise of the engines was terrific. I plugged my ears and read the paper. Very smooth. After an hour, we felt a bump or two. 'Crossing the coast,' they said. They landed and taxied right up to the steps of Dublin Airport terminal. 'Like a motor at one's front door!'*

The luggage and passports were retrieved within five minutes. Mother met her parents, driving a large black car, which turned out to be one of those unpredictable conveyances converted to run on charcoal, with an old-fashioned carnivorous boot opened from the top. It was comfortable enough inside – although unpopular outside! Everywhere the car went, one had to be sure there was somewhere to buy charcoal, or they needed to carry enough charcoal sacks stacked somewhere in the car to keep filling it up. There was also a small tin of paraffin and a very dirty rag to light the charcoal if and when something went wrong. Large lumpy sacks led to uncomfortable rides for unimportant people, like children!

Buying extra charcoal in Dublin on the way, the travellers arrived at Castletown, who noted:

> *It seems very odd indeed, being in a country not at war, and one realises how much things have changed over with us, but the change has been so gradual, that perhaps we haven't noticed it so much. But when suddenly returned to a country untouched and unaltered in most ways, it is queer. Food is plentiful, but dear. Lunch at Castletown was lamb cutlets, peas, French beans, stewed fruit, lashings of cream, and heaps of sugar. To follow was biscuits and cream cheese. The plates were changed for each course, in the old style.*

In those days, instead of watching television, reading, or even knitting, as they might now, the chief indoor pastime was to play Bridge, which they seemed to indulge in at any time of the day or night. However, 'indulge' is not quite the right word, because, like everything else in their lives, Bridge was played fiercely competitively (which put off us girls). Grandfather Lauderdale was reputedly brilliant at Poker, and played for high stakes in the great gambling club, Crockfords, in London.

From the perspective of the youngest child, there seemed to be a marked lack of charitable understanding in the comments they flew at each other when they played at home, like, 'Why did you bid Two No Trumps – you *knew* I had 3 Spades!' and, 'That was very bad play!' and 'This is too much ... you must bid properly!'

Throughout their lives, one or two tables of Bridge were set up in the cosy sitting room (Lady Louisa's boudoir) when there were guests. This room was beside our parents' bedrooms.

Mother was pronounced a good player, Father was average, and poor Uncle Ted was judged 'not good, but lucky with his cards.'

The Countess again:

In the afternoon we went with the children to the garden. They are very friendly and attractive, particularly Diana (aged three) and the younger boy Gerald (aged one). Diana is very pretty, but not a bit like Sylvia, she has more formed features, and later I think she may be more like her other grandmother, old Lady Carew; she has Sylvia's hair, and blue eyes. Gerald is a very hefty contented person. Patrick (aged five) is excitable and nervy, but very intelligent and tall.

We walked around the garden, the children scrambled to give us strawberries, raspberries etc, which they had squashed in their hands in their excitement!

The garden was wonderful. Tremendous range of hot-houses, with mostly tomatoes; out of doors, there are acres of all sorts of fruits. They keep 6 gardeners, and make gross sales of about £2,000 worth of produce per year. There is a lorry here that delivers to the Dublin Market. Fruit is more expensive than England, raspberries 2s to 2s 6d a pound, instead of 1s 2d in Scotland. The tomatoes are also dearer, but the rationed fruit, such as grapes, peaches etc, are cheaper.

After tea they played Bridge.

We were told with joy that 'Tonight Is Bath Night!', and one suddenly realised that there is no hot water in any tap except on Saturdays, otherwise it is all boiled in a kettle on the electric cooker. (There is no anthracite available for the lovely Essen cooker in the kitchen.)

Everyone goes off early to celebrate their bath, and we come down to dinner at 8.15 p.m.

After dinner, came yet another few rubbers of Bridge.

On Sunday, we walked down to the church at the front gates, and Patrick came too. There is an amusing sort of parson taking the service. His text was, 'Ask, and you shall be given.' He is very Irish, 'And saye well, that naught be misleading; you must ask within reason; for instance,' he continued, 'Professor Joad said the other day that when he was a boy he sat for an exam. There were 200 boys, and ten places, and he prayed to God to give him one, and he didn't get it, so he has never believed in prayer since ... Well, I ask you!!' shouts the parson, and all the congregation were either startled wide awake, or retreated into fits of laughter. I don't know if that was the effect he wished to make.

Patrick sat next to me and was very good, changing his book very often to make certain he had the right one, and when we recited the Creed, he gave a deep curtsey several moments after us.

After lunch we got to see the horses and mares. Uncle Ted shows us the lovely foals, a yearling, and a three-year-old, for which he has refused £1,000.

There were three mares, Sylvan Queen, who had been given to Mother by Uncle Ted, on her wedding day; Fair Sylvia, daughter of Sylvan Queen; and Fair Jean. Sylvan Queen was the eldest mare, by Abbey Wood out of La Neuvaine; she had won races in England, and was a very successful dam, breeding many winners, like Shelton Abbey and the stallion Prince of Blenheim, which was exported to the USA. Fair Jean had been the favourite for the Irish 1,000 Guineas, and came 4th. The youngest mare won in Ireland as a two-year-old, ridden by Mick Kennedy, and became a dam of eight winners herself.

It began to rain on the way home, so we came in and played Bridge; and again after tea.

A dinner party for twelve was planned for that night; the dining room was laden with silver and glass, and reminded Ivy Lauderdale of the pre-war days.

No baths, so we dress dirty. When we are almost ready, I see a very strange vision approaching the palatial front entrance, over which is my bedroom. [Lady Lauderdale always slept in the last bedroom on the first floor, on the far right side of the front steps.] It is a diminutive donkey, drawing what appears to be a box on wheels, and sitting in the box is a man in full evening dress (white tie and tails); this is the first dinner guest. He told me afterwards that he was very proud of the cart, having made it himself with the front wheels of an old motorcar.

Next to arrive is a cyclist, who is also in evening dress. He parks his bicycle at the bottom of the steps; all this some ten minutes before the party is due.

We all assemble and wait for the remaining five, who are said to be joining together and hiring the only taxi in the county. Very late, they arrive looking crushed and crumply, but in tremendous spirits. We have sherry by the gallon, and then move in to dinner.

Soup, boiled salmon, roast chicken with sausages and bacon, meringues, and stewed fruits, with a savoury to follow (our 6th course), fruit (grapes, peaches etc), port, and then liqueurs!

After dinner, they played three tables of Bridge until well after midnight.

Having arrived with no little difficulty, nobody has any intention of not having their full value. At 12.30, the man who owns the donkey goes off to the stable yard, where it is pitch dark, and presumably gropes about for his donkey amongst the horses. Whether he ever gets home or not – nobody ever enquires, or minds!

So, nobody gets invited to meet Colin and Ivy Lauderdale, unless they can play Bridge; it does not seem to matter to anyone if they run around the estate after an unwilling donkey, or get themselves upended in a ditch on the way home!

In the basement area, there is a very good store cupboard,[16] *lined with big wooden cupboards and shelves, and even plenty of space for the spare linen (bedclothes). It is plentifully stocked with quantities of jam. There are only a few things they cannot get here, one being mustard, and soap is very short (it does not matter, they don't have a bath every day), also tea is rationed to half an ounce per week. The lavatory paper is the queerest brown and very thick. There is also a larder there, facing the front of the house, with*

*wonderfully cold marble shelves lining one side; these are filled with meats
ready for cooking, each covered with a sieve. There are also great urns of
coddled eggs standing on the floor; all the vegetables and fruit freshly picked
from the garden that day, awaiting preparation; and cheeses. (Sylvia insists
that everyone has to cut off the mouse walk on the sides of the cheeses before
they help themselves! It didn't look too nibbled.)*

 *We go to see the poultry, ducks and geese. The butler's wife takes care of them,
they are very well looked after, but she does not appear to know a cockerel from a
pullet, even when almost grown up. I am sorry to disappoint them in the fact that
most of the young birds are cockerels.*

The butler's wife was Mrs Murphy, who collected the eggs for both the house
and for her own family. These eggs were mostly for daily consumption, but
a great number of other eggs were bought locally and stored for cooking.
They were coddled (preserved) in big china containers with water-glass,
called 'crocks'. Mrs Young also sold cockerels for the Castletown table from
her thriving Government-supported business, rearing and selling chickens
behind the new Young's Garage on the Dublin road. This site had previously
been a forge.

*We start for Dublin at 2 p.m. The car grunts and snorts down the drive and
almost stops. We get out and poke the fire, which is a sort of stove hitched onto
the luggage grill at the back, and burns charcoal. The car does not improve much,
and we 'chink chink' into Dublin at about 15mph. Nobody minds, and we are only
thankful it is just a bit faster than the pony and trap.*

 *We get to Dublin, and find the shops are very prosperous looking. A fruit shop
with oranges and bananas in the window seems an extraordinary sight. These
were once everyday fruits to us, but now they look like some curious and rare
specimens!*

 *We do a bit of shopping, and go to the cinema to kill time while the car has an
overhaul.*

 *At six o'clock we tentatively try the car again, and find it is going splendidly,
and we sail home in half the time it took to come.*

*We went to our second dinner party in two days, given by Sir Francis and
Lady Brooke (neighbours who live 6 miles away). He is Master of the Kildare
Hunt.*

We sit down to a most sumptuous meal, soup, salmon, roast chicken, trifle with lashings of cream, savoury and dessert, accompanied by sherry, champagne, port and liqueurs. The dinner was very excellent, and dished up in complete pre-war grand style, in fact, never have I seen such a meal since those days.

After dinner, we play Bridge; and then comes a snag ... There is a snag in every home ... this one is the light. Apparently, they have their own electric plant, and are only given 5 gallons of paraffin to work it for three months.

So, we play Bridge with only one electric bulb suspended from the ceiling of a large room. It is very dark (my opponent revoked in Trumps!). We play until 12.30, and the car flies us home again.

Ian and Ivy met some of their old friends from his ADC days at Viceregal Lodge, Phoenix Park:

We are off to see Rosie [Lady] Headfort[17] at Headfort House for the whole day (lunch, tea and dinner). Sylvia is doing a cattle deal with her. We allow two hours to do the journey of 43 miles. The car is well stoked-up, and we go at a good 30-45mph, stopping at Navan to buy non-couponed gardening gloves.

Rosie lost her husband recently, but she is delighted to see us, and is in good form. The party includes Mrs Cross, Mrs Irmay, General Hickey, Dorothy Pearson, and her granddaughter Olivia Taylor; eleven of us altogether.

Arriving at 12.45, they squeeze in yet another rubber of Bridge before lunch, before tea, and after tea. One of their numbers repeatedly makes bad mistakes but Rosie does not scold her!

After a hot lunch, and just a 'little' cold supper, which had soup, fish soufflé, and a choice of six main dishes from a groaning sideboard, three cold chickens, two different hams, cold sirloins of beef, cold lamb, and salads. An extraordinary sight! We had nothing to drink but cider or water.

Directly after dinner, we pile into the car, the charcoal is produced from under the back seat; it is in a huge sack. The fireplace at the back is filled with coke, and it is poked from the bottom, after that another poker is produced with a wet rag tied on the end. This is put in a very smelly can of paraffin, which has been resting under our feet. After pulling it out of the can, a match is applied to it, and thrust into the charcoal container, and left to warm up.

After about five minutes we get in and start. It begins very slowly, and we chunk off from the door at about 5 mph; everyone waving and laughing.

This pace continues until we begin to go downhill, and after a few miles it warms up until we get home at last at 11 p.m. It takes quite a little longer than the journey there.

We start off for Sallins station, where the 'race special' from Dublin stops. We have numbered seats, and the journey takes about twenty minutes to get to the Curragh. The train runs right up to the siding at the back of the stands; a very nice course. What strikes me is how few people there are, and only a handful on the other side of the course. We go to the Turf Club Stand with Uncle Ted.

After a huge lunch, we go down to the Paddock for the Irish Oaks. There are some lovely fillies. The favourite won, and I won the Tote Double! But the winnings were only £2 16s for a five-shilling ticket (so few tickets sold).

We see a few figures from the past, people who were once young and attractive, are now old and grey, amongst them Dermot McCalmont, fat, grey and elderly; Dickie Wyndham Quin (now Adare), much the same. McCalmont's new wife is very nice looking, and said to be a very good rider. Her father was there also, Nicholls the polo player. There were no less than eight races and the last at 6.15, after which we get back in the train and return.

I am giving Patrick a new pony, because theirs died, and we have answered an advertisement in the Irish Times, *via a box number.*

The woman rings up, and she appears to live in Dublin, so we arrange to go and see the pony. It happened to be next door to Col. Joe Hume Dudgeon's place near Kingston; so Sylvia asks the Dudgeons' daughter, Kay, to come with us and ride it.

We call for her, they have a very nice place with an outdoor riding school, a veritable miniature Grand National course is in the paddock, and in the drawing room a collection of bandages and bridles being patched.

We find the road, but it is not where you would think a pony could be kept. However, we find the right house, it is very small. We go through the sitting room and kitchen to the back where there is a tiny garden, about 10ft square, and a pony draped in a week's washing, which is hanging on the line.

There is no way out of the garden, except through the house; so the pony is led through the kitchen and sitting room and out onto the road. The girl gets on it and tries to go up the street, but the pony is very nappy and won't go.

'Take it the other way, the way it likes to go', suggests the owner. However, we decide it is not quite what we want, so depart with apologies and go back to Dudgeons, who telephone someone in Castleknock, who says he has a white pony – 'Just the thing!' It is almost on our way home, so we arrange to call.

We get there and find a tiny cottage. We go around to the back of the house, and never have I seen such a sight; babies in boxes, children with no clothes mixing in and out amongst chickens, ducks, and geese. The garden is minute, and we pass through into a field where there are two ponies and a donkey.

The man does not even try to catch the white pony, instead he proceeds to chase it; we all start to chase it! Three other people appear to spring up from nowhere and chase it. At last we get it in a corner near the garden, but it charges through a wire fence and tumbles into the garden all amongst the children. The wife rushes out, and chases it out again! It jumps quite a big fence and emerges somewhat cut from the wire fence.

It is a very attractive pony. We ask its age – 'Don't know', comes the reply.

'Has it been ridden?' – 'Don't know; but sure ... but sure ... it would be a grand ride.'

'Has it been in harness?' – 'Don't know, but there is a harness being made.'

We cannot work it out. The price he wants is £30, so we go away and think the pony probably isn't his at all.

We have spent a week at Castletown. Sylvia drives us to Dublin Aerodrome, which is beautiful, the best airport anywhere. There are tremendous buildings, and a very comfortable lounge etc, bigger than at Liverpool. There is a much bigger aeroplane waiting, and when the bus comes from Dublin, there are about eighteen other passengers. It seats twenty-one, and is much more comfortable with very soft and luxurious seats, and a silencer on the engines, so there is very little noise (not like the one we came in).

We get to Liverpool in about an hour, and so ended a very happy trip to Eire.

Signed,

Ivy Lauderdale.

Running around during a hectic week's visit to Castletown, and inspecting every nook and cranny with great energy, Mother's parents also took the time to get to know the individual staff.

However, one thing Ivy never mentioned: There was a girl's Orphanage School taking up the whole of the left side of the servants wing, for the duration of the war. They slept above the old kitchen.

You would think she would have heard or noticed these children, until we realise that Ian and Ivy Lauderdale were quite used to these arrangements – they had a school of 100 girls living above them in their own home in Scotland during the war. It was what you did if you had the space.

In this case, the Bird's Nest School was thought preferable to a detachment of the army, which was the alternative. Castletown's sister house, Carton, was reported to have sustained major damage to the inside fabric of the house, from an army unit being billeted there at the same time.

The soldiers billeted at Carton were quite a talking point, as they pedalled a wide area, patrolling on bicycles because of the shortage of cars and fuel.

With the servants' wing now acting as a school, all the male staff were re-located in apartments over the stables, in the bachelor's wing; and the females lived on the top floor of the main house, near the nursery and schoolroom.

During this period, the three Conolly-Carew children loved their seaside holidays each year, at Malahide or Blackrock, where they often stayed in an old railway carriage beside the beach.

5

1944-1950s

Father had rejoined the DCLI the year after Dunkirk, and in 1944, now promoted to the rank of major, he landed in France on D-Day, and was one of the first wave to reach the outskirts of Caen.

He was called away from the impasse around Caen, under orders to take over the Command of a Regiment of the Hampshire's. But his jeep was blown up by a mortar bomb; he was seriously wounded for the second time, and repatriated to a hospital in England.

While his slow recovery continued, the relief at Castletown must have been great, especially as Mother was expecting their fourth child (your author) Sarah Catherine (Sally) (named after her Conolly grandmother and great-grandmother) was born in November.

From the age of five to eight, her brother Patrick went to his first school in Lady Louisa's old school building behind the church, where one wonderful teacher, Mrs Bracken, and her assistants, grappled with 100 children of mixed ages, from five to fifteen; an inconceivable feat now, when you think that they only had two schoolrooms.

Mrs Bracken was the gamekeeper's wife at Castletown. They were a wonderful couple and lived in Lady Louisa's cottage in the Woods (where Louisa entertained her guests in the 1700s and 1800s) which was renamed the Gamekeeper's Cottage. It was a single-story house with a veranda located in an enviable position in a clearing in the Great Wood, which the Brackens filled with spring flowers and flowering shrubs. The inside of his cottage was typical of the Estate houses – it had a small entrance hall, where you turned right into a big sitting room, with one front window. Straight on led through to a small kitchen, and to the back door. Bracken's main bedroom was on the left, with two smaller bedrooms on the other side.

Riding past the Gamekeeper's Cottage was a dark experience, it used to make our ponies shy away from the sight of pegged-out animal skins, hung there as a deterrent to other vermin. There were weasels, great black crows with wings stretched out, like separated black fingers strung along the fence, and rabbits too.

Bracken was a tall gaunt man, and his trademark was his pair of large-sized gumboots. You could hear him coming around a corner, as his wellies flopped loudly against his rather spindly legs. He had a habit of carrying a loaded shotgun (broken open, making it safe), which caused us children some awe. We often watched him striding through the Great Wood with his gun, a vision that would have no doubt put the fear of God into any poacher.

Each week he cycled with fifteen dead rabbits strung across his handlebars, all destined for the kitchen table at the big house; enough for rabbit pie twice a week.

Another indelible memory he left for us, was when he and his gun were caught when a heavy iron gate swung back on him, and he shot his toes off! When he got back from hospital, he continued as before, with no fuss at all – he just got a new pair of wellies, and they flopped even more.

The country ways of anticipating the weather seem lost nowadays, even though much farming and game-keeping used to rely on it.

Both Bracken and the farm workers had their own folklore for weather forecasting; nuggets of wisdom they sometimes imparted to us in passing, with a 'Good morning Miss ... rabbits are out too early ...' Some of these folklores:

1. If a gamekeeper, on a warm day, sees a rabbit out at the wrong time of day, he could confidently predict cold violent storms.
2. Cones from the fir trees are open for good weather the next day, and closed for bad.
3. It would be a good day when we could hear the trains from the local Hazelhatch station.
4. Cart horses growing thicker coats earlier than normal, indicated a harder winter ahead. If they were restless in the field, there was wind, rain or a storm coming.

5. When a cow tries to scratch its ear, or lies down in the middle of the day, it means a shower is very near. When it clumps its side with its tail, look out for thunder, lighting and hail.

An economic experiment to raise young pheasants was tried out for two years, though it was to proved too costly and the idea was dropped. (This was long before the days when estates could charge £1,200 a day for each 'gun'.)

Bracken used the small three-cornered field, which was at the top of the vista on the right, near his cottage. Pheasant eggs were bought in, and broody hens were borrowed from all around the local countryside for a small fee. Another estate worker, the young gardener Johnny O'Neill, helped Bracken with the hatching, feeding, and rearing of the young pheasants in coops. They were released two or three months before the shooting season, and fed every day.

The numbers of these young ones added to a fair stock of wild pheasants already in the estate, and provided extra birds for shooting parties in the late 1940s and early '50s.

The guests ('guns') ate a hearty lunch at Castletown, with lots of wine to assist their aim in the afternoon. The Beaters had a sumptuous meal cooked by Mrs Bracken in her house; her pies and cakes were renowned, with plenty of Guinness to ensure that they might beat the right bush after lunch. It was not difficult to find beaters!

Because the cottage was tucked away deep within the Great Wood, and furthest from the road, it was one of the last estate houses to get wired up for electricity by the Celbridge electrician, Tom Shortt.

Years later, Mrs Bracken had her eye on the fine white two-storey Garden Lodge, occupied by the Farm Manager. When he left, she got her heart's delight. However, she regretted the move later on. The historic little Gamekeeper's Cottage in the middle of the Great Wood, was never lived in again, and has since been destroyed.

After convalescing for the second time, Father took many months to recover from being mortar bombed. Eventually, he was passed as fit enough to return home to further recuperate, and gradually took over the reins of the estate once again. Almost at once, he was asked to become a leader of the National Farmers Association. Upon hearing of this plan, President de Valera sent for him, and with great courtesy, advised Father that it was unwise to become involved. He explained he might become a political tool, and the President considered there was a chance he would become fodder in the middle of the current debate between the landlords and the farmers; for our father was both. Obviously, De Valera did not want an anti-landlord movement to start. So, Father sadly ceased to be involved; but he always remained an admirer of the President and his own particular brand of diplomacy.

At home, the renovation of the estate cottages went on all through Father's tenure. A Leixlip tenant, Mrs Farrelly was paying 4*s* 6*d* for a week's rent. In turn, her house was renovated. It needed major repairs, a new roof, electricity, toilet etc. Her family came to stay in the wing at Castletown while the work was done.

That Christmas Mr and Mrs Farrelly and their four sons, Bunny, Michael, John and David joined in the present giving and fun around the Christmas tree in the Front Hall. The family remembers it still. But, she was a worrier, and asked everyone if her rent was going to rise. The poor woman worked herself into a state about it – she need not have worried, Father wouldn't raise her rent. And so, little by little, rent book by rent book, the estate finances started to loose ground.

Over a period of time, it became apparent that the expenses shown on the farm accounts were far too high; when compared with previous years, the costs were rising dramatically. Only now, with our in-depth questioning of the families of our old farm workers, can we be certain that there was serious mischief afoot. There was theft on a regular, organised scale. Fat calves were being removed at night from the fields, and replaced with cheap substitutes; even a slip road was built, so a wagon could enter the farmyard without being seen from the main house. This road was innocently approved, but apparently led to animals, fodder and some equipment being taken at night. By the time something was suspected, years later, the damage to the farm accounts was beyond repair.

Father loved to walk in his fields in the evenings, always wielding Uncle Ted's favourite long-handled cutter that uprooted thistles as he went. He had a map in his study that showed which fields were due to be laid down to oats, turnips, grass, wheat, and, as always, four acres of potatoes. All the hay, straw and oats for the horses were home grown.

At times there were thirty-plus horses on the estate: Thoroughbred mares and foals; other mares and foals, and their youngsters; three-year-olds out at grass, being 'broken in'; four-year-olds in training (to be sold); promising young show jumpers; hunters (some used as hirelings); show ponies and jumpers; eventers (usually away with Patrick); cart horses (eight cart horses, and later down to two) and one donkey (as Barrymore's companion).

Though Mother's aim was to buy unbroken young horses, and sell them a year later as trained jumpers, hunters or show horses, they were expensive to keep.

There were wages for a head groom; a girl groom; and two trainee assistants and at least one boy to help with the 'mucking out'.

There was shoeing every six weeks for each adult horse; feeding three times a day (if stabled; once a day if out in the winter); hay and straw by the barn-full; bridles, saddles, head collars, ropes and rugs to be constantly maintained; transport; entry fees for competitions and homemade practice show jumps to be painted and maintained for the grass arena at the back of the house, to be painted and maintained.The list was endless!

It had been way back during the First World War when one of the Castletown fields was ploughed-up for the first time for at least 300 years, in aid of the war effort. The plan was to plant potatoes. This field was situated below the ha-ha at the back of the garden, facing the Front Avenue (where the new houses are now), and it was found to be full of broken bricks and brick dust. The plan was abandoned, and thereafter it was called the Brick Field. This is where we believe the old sub-standard soft Irish bricks were discarded during the building of both Castletown House and the garden wall. Some believe that better Dutch bricks were used instead.[18, 19]

Various walls in the house were exposed from time to time, during repairs, and special interest has been taken in Mother's bedroom wall (Lady Louisa's Bedroom), which provided the evidence that proved our dining room (situated directly below) had originally been built as the two rooms of Katherine Conolly's Suite, where she had her own downstairs bedroom, sitting room, dressing/sitting room, and probably her personal maid's room.

Lady Louisa strengthened her bedroom wall to allow for the removal of the middle wall immediately below it; thus opening up the existing dining room. This was an engineering feat, which is described as a 'timber stud and brick noggin wall'. It holds up a very heavy section of the house.

Certainly, in the early days, bricks were unwisely used above the roof level, both for the two giant chimneys (reputed to serve twenty fireplaces each), and for the backing of the parapet balustrade.

Almost as soon as the house was built, after 1729, a section of balustrade in the north eastern corner collapsed, and it is thought that one of the chimneys fell at the same time, for both showed signs of being rebuilt with better bricks. At the rebuilding stage, the inside of the balustrade was finished slightly differently, leaving clear evidence to this day of the damage.

The concentrated weight of the two chimneys has caused considerable structural movement over the 240-year history of the house, and endless consultations for every generation to cope with.

6

1950s Estate Workers

The O'Neills ∽ *The Garden* ∽ *To Market* ∽ *The Hay Bogies and the Boys* ∽ *The Mooneys* ∽ *Anderson and the IRA* ∽ *The Vines* ∽ *The Farm Bell* ∽ *The Farm Children's Memories* ∽ *Singling* ∽ *Chief Estate Worker and their Families.*

Much of this book must be dedicated to the totally remarkable O'Neill family at Castletown, who have uniquely served the estate, on the land and in the garden, for nearly four centuries – between the years 1580 and 1963.[20] We believe that they should be officially recognised and celebrated in the annuls of Irish rural life.

Dongan, Earl of Limerick,[21] gave the O'Neills land opposite the front gates, near the old ford, across the river. They fought for King William at the Battle of the Boyne, and, instead of pay, were rewarded with further land on the back avenue, beside the deer park wall (alongside the new entrance drive).

When Speaker Conolly purchased all the lands around Castletown from the Dongans, he was busy creating his own big estate, and managed to include a lot of the small landowners around, including the O'Neills.

To Johnny O'Neill, we owe many of the memories from down the generations; of how Speaker Conolly used the (current) farm buildings as his house; how the tall square-ish shed on the right of the farmyard used to be a mill; how an original dovecote in the lower farmyard was taken down to make a round silage pit; how there were deer in the walled deer park (beside the new entrance), presumably with a higher wall around it; the O'Neill grandfather saw cricket played in the Cricket Field until 1900 (near the Maynooth Lodge) and saw polo being played in the Polo Field (on the right of the new drive).[22]

His grandfather, born 1820, ran and made the house gas, for lighting. The gas house was in the outer kitchen yard, and had a large tin water container behind a tall wall and a large door.

When we were children his father, Harry O'Neill, was one of the gardeners and a charmer. He worked on the estate for fifty years, ending up as under head gardener, with seven others working in the profitable 10-acre market garden, which contained vast glasshouses heated by solid fuel and had tall chimneys running up the 20ft high walls. The chimneys can still be seen today beside the old garden Gate Lodge, which is now the lovely extended home of Mr and Mrs Aidan Kelly. The 10-acre walled garden itself is long gone, swallowed up by the new houses that stretch from inside the front gates.

Harry O'Neill was responsible for the vital hothouse boiler, and for keeping the giant yew hedges clipped (some 20ft high), the lawn cut, and the front yew trees trimmed (which were meant to be conical-shaped, but were a bit off centre). He trimmed the front hedge; attacked the fierce Pampas grass clumps in between the yew trees; trimmed the vines; decorated the church; and kept the four stone plant containers filled with geraniums (these were outside the back door, looking out towards Conolly's Folly).

Harry O'Neill married Roseanne O'Connor, Uncle Ted's housekeeper, in around 1924 and had a son, Johnny O'Neill. Mrs Crookshank was Ted Conolly's next housekeeper and was a relation of the head gardener's wife.

The 10-acre garden was divided in half by a 20ft yew hedge with arches, which two men with rustic scaffolding of planks and ladders, used to clip using only hand shears.

The entrance end was the market garden, for flowers grown on a commercial basis, as well as the great glass hothouses that contained out-of-season indoor fruit, which included two of the oldest vines in the world. These also provided the house and the church with decorations. Beside the entrance, along the wall to the right, was an asparagus bed. This became too labour intensive, and was unable to produce a big enough crop to make it viable. Beside it, between two paths, was a large triangular rose bed, which was Mother's particular favourite, and the bed next door was a mass of sweet peas.

The myriad of paths had ankle-height box hedges on either side, with rows upon rows of geraniums planted along all the borders. The long main border was opposite the Garden House; it had tall flowers at the back of the bed, like wonderful white and yellow gladioli, tall white daisies, proud mauve lupins, and silvery giant globe thistles (good for flower arranging).

The far end of the garden was where the main vegetables and fruit grew for the Dublin markets; and apple and pear trees were trained along the high red-brick walls.

Patrick, Diana and Gerald as young children in the 10-acre walled garden.

Twice a week, the garden Bedford lorry (one of the first in the district) was driven by Mr Cummins to the Dublin Market. It carried fruit and vegetables, including the high earning out-of-season produce from the hothouses. In the early days the noisy lorry was quite a novelty, and the village children used to wave as he passed.

We also grew daffodils along the garden avenue and in the garden itself. We would pick thousands of them, tie them up in bunches of a dozen (two leaves to each bunch), place them heads-up in long boxes, and sent those off to market as well. We were rewarded with a very minimum wage for an hour or two's labour; something like a penny every ten boxes, just about enough to buy a gob-stopper in the sweet shop the next time we rode through the village.

Mr Cummins' daughter, Margaret, provided many stories for this book, and currently looks after a much-loved neighbour, the genealogist Harry McDowell, who lives in the old Vicarage, now called Celbridge Lodge (a house built by our Shaw great-granduncle).

During the weekend evenings, in the 1940s and '50s, the local lanes and by-ways were a sea of bicycles as the young men of Celbridge peddled their way to the odd X-Road Dances where they spend the night dancing reels and jigs to the accordion; there were also the more formal dances in the nearby small town of Maynooth.

When they were courting, they carried the girl side-saddle on the bicycle bar in front of them. It must have very uncomfortable for miles.

Johnny O'Neill and his friends peddled everywhere, and later he never saw the need to learn to drive.

In our early years, young Johnny and Tom Mooney drove the heavy cart horses with their wooden wagons attending to all their farm duties, as well as aiding their constant removal of rubbish from the house, farm, and garden, which was carted to a place that was not easy to see in the main wood, buried, and well covered.[23]

They also drove the horse-drawn hay bogies (wagons) in the days when the hay was forked up into many round pointed piles, about 5ft at the base, and 8ft high. Flat bogies carried one haycock each, and were driven with caution, losing as little hay as possible while going through the gateways, along narrow woodland tracks, and over bumpy fields. These horses needed much respect, for they had feet like cement-filled soup plates. They would bury your toes into the ground if they trod on you.

We loved to hitch a ride on the flat bogies when Johnny and Tom drove them empty back to the fields, having already delivered their loads, one haycock at a time, into the hay barn in the stable yard. We stuck a dry stalk of hay in the corner of our mouths like they did ... very grown-up!

Patrick, Bunny, and Diana would ask the two men if they could take one rein each to drive the wagons. However, one year things got out of hand; returning from boarding school, and feeling adventurous the two boys ambushed poor Johnny and Tom, grabbed the reins of a horse each, and had a race! The problem was, the bogies were not empty at the time, and they had full loads on board. They lost most of the hay racing through the gateways.

Tom Mooney worked on the farm, and kind-hearted Mrs Mooney worked in the house all on her own in later years, when there were few helpers; she seemed to fill every domestic role all at once.

At first, they lived on the top floor in the old housekeeper's rooms at Castletown, but moved to the Front Gate Lodge, in the one furthest away from the Maynooth road (in total, there are three lodges there).[24]

Mrs Mooney was responsible for the front gates and would come running out of her house at any hour of the day or night, at the sign of three toots on the horn, in order to open the heavy iron gates.

One of the stories about those gates came after a family friend, Nick McDermott, took April, the girl groom, out one evening. After a 'short delay' in the yard, he drove back down the avenue to find the gates locked. He hooted his horn, but not three times, so no one opened up. He eventually managed to get out by another gate.

The Mooneys' daughter, Helen, now Mrs McDonald (an old playmate of mine)[25] remembers listening to the dreadful sounds of a night-time winter storm, with the wind clanking the great chain and lock against the bars of the gates, a fearsome noise.

The head gardener, working with his team of eight, was Anderson, a Scotsman with a Scottish wife. He had spent his young years at Summerhill, in Co. Meath, and had joined up and served in the Army Medical Corps during the First World War. After 1918, he returned to the Summerhill gardens.

One day, in 1922, when the owner of Summerhill was due home the following day, Anderson, the butler and the cook were sitting around the kitchen table when the IRA marched up to the front door carrying torches, obviously intending to set fire to the house. This was happening all over the country. The three staff fled out the back door, and hid amongst the laurel bushes while the house burned down.[26, 27]

There were three remarkable features in the walled garden: the giant yew hedges, 20ft high; the red-brick walls, built the same as at Speaker Conolly's old house at Rodanstown; and most especially, the two vines, which were reputed to be established from the same source as the celebrated Hampton Court Vine in England (which claimed to be the oldest and largest in the world).

The Castletown vines were planted in the mid-1700s, by Lady Louisa. Both the Hampton Court and the Castletown vines were reputed to have started off as cuttings taken from Valentine's Park in Essex, which now no longer exists.

Our vines hung heavily from the roofs of two greenhouses. They were about 70ft long, and about 6ft around the base in the 1950s, and had wooden supports for their heavy rods. They were retied and trimmed each year in the autumn or early spring, it was a very long job.

Sadly the Castletown Garden and its vines have gone forever ... underneath the foundations of a hundred new houses. The Garden House still stands in the middle of it all, and, until recently, acted as a nursery school.

For a time the beautiful old-brick hexagonal potting shed, a unique little building, which had been greatly prized by the family served a new life as a paper shop. However, although it was preserved as a listed building, this too has now gone – pulled down by a builder in the middle of the night. He had been ordered to restore it.

Johnny Mercier worked alongside Tom Mooney on the farm, and his son, David, remembers what daily life was like for the estate workers. They came each day on bicycles, from every direction, some peddled slowly and deliberately, while the youngsters pumped their bikes like they were riding in the Tour de France, swaying from side to side. They converged on the farmyard, to be there for the deep resounding tones of the farmyard bell, which rang out at 8 a.m., and could be heard miles away around Celbridge, Lucan, Kilmacradock, and along the local by-ways. Strangers without clocks, set their daily routine by it.

To the farmhands, and to us, the sonorous tone of that bell simply marked the start of our day. As children, it signalled to us the hour we must forsake the heavenly warmth under our eiderdowns, when we must fling on something, anything would do, and brave the cold corridor in our scramble to form a disorderly queue at the bathroom door. There were only two toilets and bathrooms on our floor, one at each end of the house. (Hence the need for chamber pots on cold winter nights.)

The bell rang twice in the middle of the day, to mark one hour for lunch, when the bicycle armada swept back and forth down the drives once more. The final bell was at five or six o'clock, depending on the season, to mark the end of the working day.

Why was it that nobody knew the history of the farm bell? All Harry Mercier understood, the man who rang it each day, was that there was an old creaky door leading into a small bare stone space with a bell rope, which he pulled. Our family had heard the bell every day through the generations, but they had quite forgotten there was a castle there!

Way back in 1722, Speaker Conolly was known to have sat for hours in the ruined bell-tower to watch his new Castletown being built. Later, he deliberately planted trees to screen the ruin from the beauty of his brand new Palladian wonder. And so it stayed hidden until now.

Eighteenth century visitors simply did not see it, or at least nobody mentioned it; except in one line in Speaker Conolly's notes, when he initially planned to incorporate the castle yard (the farmyard) into the building plans for the present Castletown. But it could not be done, mainly because the castle and its courtyard were in a sunken area (possibly scooped out for an original Motte and Bailey castle, some time after the Norman Invasion?).

We, the Conolly's, only found out about the existence of the castle, the original Castletown (hence the name), a few years ago, at about the turn of the millennium, thirty-five years *after* we left. Extraordinary to say, but our father, never knew it was there.

During harvest-time, David Mercier remembers the farm children running from the village for miles to outlying hayfields. They brought their fathers' lunches where they worked, forking the hay high into the air onto hundreds of hayricks like tall beehives.

Children and parents were allowed to collect fallen firewood around the estate, at any time, but never to cut down a tree.

When the men were out late in the fields in the evenings, at 4 p.m., their children assembled in the milking shed in the farmyard, where there were fifteen hand-milked cows. Usually, there were two children from each family to carry home a large lidded tin can, with a big looped handle, full of milk with a goodly lump of freshly churned butter. A small sum came off their pay each week to pay for this, but it was given free to those with large families.

During the summertime, when the heat was up, we would see the estate children trit-trotting home along the avenue in front of the house, without shoes. Each child did own a pair of cheap plimsolls, but the rubber bottoms stuck to the hot tarmac; so they were told to save the shoes because they had to wear them to school.

In the wintertime, when it grew dark early, the children remember walking back down the front drive to Celbridge, with its giant overhanging trees, creaking and complaining mournfully in the wind; 'spooky' is the word they still use to describe the experience. They may have been impressionable children, but the ghost of the White Lady on the drive was ever present in their minds, and the Devil was not far behind. 'Hurry or the devil'll get ye,' they whispered to each other by way of encouragement.

As early summertime appeared, there seemed endless hand 'singling' the fields of potatoes, turnips, and mangles. Rows of workers knelt on hessian bags, thinning and weeding as they worked, leaving the width of their large hand between the young plants.

Later, the back-breaking tasks continued, when the mature vegetables had to be pulled up, topped and tailed, and thrown into a horse-drawn high-sided cart. They were then either stored in a pit, or stacked in the old mill on the farmyard, and then covered with straw. An elderly worker would sit on sacks all day, sorting and chitting potatoes; some for the house and the rest for the twice-weekly market garden run to Dublin.

CHIEF ESTATE WORKERS IN THE 1950S

Ploughman	Bill Green
Gamekeeper	Bracken
Groom	Paddy Walsh
Steward	Hill, followed by Tony Roberts
Head Gardener	Anderson
Herd	Finlay, followed by Larry Kelly, then Tom Losty
Garden Foreman	Harry O'Neill
Gardener	Johnny Gleeson

THEIR FAMILIES

Bill and Maureen Green lived in Green's Lodge (Batty Langley Lodge).

Bill (junior), Andy, Mrs Abel, and Mrs Power moved locally to Celbridge, and Straffan nearby.

Paddy Walsh lived in the East Wing of Castletown.

Bracken lived in the Gamekeeper's Cottage in the Woods, with his wife, the school teacher, his son, and daughter, Rosemary.

Hill, the steward, his son Gordon and daughter Irene left Castletown, and took over as caretaker for the *Evening Mail* in Parliament Street, Dublin; and later moved to McKee Avenue, Finglas.

Anderson, head gardener, retired and left to run the Orchards.

Finlay, the herd, lived in the Herd's House in Kilmacradock. His brothers worked at Donacomper, across the river. His son Jackie lived in Celbridge; and Sidney worked as a secretary with the Shaw Group, and later qualified as an accountant.

Larry Kelly, the herd, lived in the Herd's House after Finlay.

Later, Michael and Marlin moved to Celbridge and Maynooth; Tommy joined the Army; and Peter went to England.

Tony Roberts was appointed steward after Hill. His brother was steward at Killadoon, on the other side of Celbridge.

Harry O'Neill's family worked at Castletown for nearly 400 years. He was foreman in the garden, and retired and died in the West Lodge (Maynooth Lodge) on the Castletown Estate. His sons Johnny and Harry (junior) now live in Lucan and Dun Laoghaire.

7

1950s Family Life

After our maternity nurse, Margaret McCloughlin, left, the person who had the most influence on our youngest years was Maura Sloan, our dear nursemaid-cum-nanny, who was no stiff harridan. She was trained by experience, as she said, rather than at any official nanny school. She came to Castletown in 1947, and joined the housekeeper, Mary Smith, and the under-nursemaid Nellie Nolan, living on the top floor.

All the children and their helpers occupied the top story. Maura slept with me; and Diana had a small corner dressing room to herself. Pinned above her bed was a colour postcard with the rhyme:

> The little lanes of Ireland
> Were never designed or planned,
> They're just mysterious pathways
> That lead to Fairyland.

The nursery had its own pantry; next to the open play area (which occupied the line of middle windows looking out onto the front of the house). We had built-in cupboards hiding our baby necessities. There were the childhood remedies like syrup of figs, Iodine, germoline, Friar's Balsam, white liniment, nasty cough mixture, Dettol, and sticking plasters that needed changing every day because they were not waterproof. There were clothes, potties, and our great brass and tin hip bath. Every evening, one of the workmen, Bob McGuire, carried buckets full of hot water all the way up the stairs to fill the hip bath.

The boys had metal screws and nuts, with the long arms and angles of their Meccano Sets, with wheeled cranes and impressive red string to haul any unwary cars or toy boats about. If they were not fighting in the corner, the boys usually found some mischief. They were always daring each other to do deeds that made my ears flap, like climbing around the narrow ledge, high up in the hall. I fear, occasionally, I told on them. (They never did walk along that ledge, thank goodness; but we have since learnt that our Uncle Ted had risked doing so when he was young!)

The children's bedrooms all looked down over the back of the house. Below them was the small back door (on the kitchen yard side), which we called 'Pray Shut the Door' (from a permanent notice attached to it, presumably because it caught the prevailing wind).

As we grew up, inside this door was where we kept our much-used bikes. We virtually never used the formal back door in the centre of the house, which led out from the drawing rooms.

From out of our bedroom windows, we could look down on the small steep slope (leading to the garden path below), where in later years, we all piled onto one bike for an extremely painful landing at the bottom.

Beyond the path, we could see the oval-shaped, grassy horse-jumping arena (which had once been Lady Louisa Conolly's personal garden). We could see the great monkey-puzzle tree beside it, and Diana's favourite copper beech, which was struck by lightning. Ever afterwards it stubbornly repelled all attempts to be cut, sawn, or blown-up in order to remove it. 'The influence of Old Nick,' the farmhands said, and they refused to touch it again.

We looked over the ha-ha, across the back field to the Great Wood, and through the clearing, specially cut so we could see Conolly's Folly in the distance (where the young Lady Louisa Lennox lost her heart to Thomas Conolly in the 1700s).

So, Nanny Maura provided love and tender care, and sorted out the rights from wrongs in our broadening horizons. In an age when parents like ours expected only a dutiful peck on the cheek from their children, morning and evening, we were extremely lucky to get the comfort and love from our nanny. If we are relaxed and happy individuals now, we owe much of it to the start she gave us.

Patrick and Bunny aged twelve and eight, always scrapping, took their energy away to Preparatory Boarding Schools at Elstree and Heatherdown, in England,[32] during term time. Diana and I, aged ten and five, had our own discipline, with a strict timetable of lessons at home with the governess, Miss Colls, just like any school.

You might think we could do what we liked, but school hours were never shifted; there was no hunting field during the term-time, even at the weekends. The timetable of lessons took up most of our days (though our exercise period in the afternoon was usually spent on four legs, not on two, exercising a pony).

On hot days we were allowed to swim (accompanied) in the river on a sandy bank with flat rocks, not far from the church. This was where Miss Colls nearly got swept away by venturing too far out into the fast flowing current. This area became unsuitable when an outlet pipe from Celbridge was installed, so we moved further down, near to where the large stream from the lake flows down into the river. We were never allowed to swim beside the old ruined Bathing House (like our ancestors did); the water was too deep.

Though Diana and I often played on summer evenings with a group of workers' children outside, we were not allowed to play inside the house. In fact we were forbidden to go below stairs. We only occasionally played with neighbours at weekends.

What did we lack? Maybe it was the camaraderie that goes with team sports, netball, girls' games etc. Perhaps such a protected education could have left us oversensitive to criticism, which you had to take with spades at a school, with its rough and tumble of teasing, jealousies and friendships. However, records show us that the education of children at Castletown was similar to most noble families, and remained much the same down the centuries. The boys were sent away at eight to boarding schools, and the girls were tutored at home, which relied heavily on the multi-talents of their tutor (or governess).

In Lady Louisa's day, specialist teachers were brought in, like a French Master, and Dancing Master, Arts, and Music Master.

With the age of the motorcar, Diana and I were occasionally driven to their weekly dancing classes at 120 Lower Baggott Street, Dublin; our strongest memories were of a sea of bicycles, with cars having to thread their way through the mostly two-wheeled traffic. However, more frequently we were accompanied by Miss Colls, and paid the fare on the green double-decker CIE number 67 bus (9d for an adult), which stopped at the end of its line outside the Castletown gates. They alighted at McBerneys by the river, and got another bus for the last leg – such excitement!

We were taught ballroom dancing, and we wondered who decided we should also do Greek dancing? (For poise, they said!)[33] A lady thumped the piano, and Miss Catt conducted her class of mostly girls. Once a year, she hired the Gaiety Theatre, and we all had to perform in costumes that were completely over the top. Everyone dreaded it. Diana was once one of a group of doubtful fairies. After one dress rehearsal on the large stage it was clear that the cleaning lady had not turned up that week, because all the fairies were covered in what looked suspiciously like soot.

For some reason, poor brother Bunny was roped in to be one of the furious Four-and-twenty Blackbirds Baked in a Pie. A very grumpy pie! (They must have needed extra boys). Later, we asked the formidable Miss Catt to come to tea at Castletown, but unfortunately her bloomers fell down on the front doorstep. With an anguished cry, she retrieved a large handful of the offending drawers, and the butler respectfully ushered her to the loo for major repairs. We were all duly informed of poor Miss Catt's disaster by a loud stagewhisper in Mama's ear from the rather deaf butler.

To this day, we are left to ponder on our memories of this incident. Did the ever-ready butler produce a safety pin? Did Mama fish about in her sewing kit? Maybe Miss Catt herself had come prepared for any eventuality? Or perhaps she had had to take them off. We were never told.

Alas, we never did put paint to paper for anything like art. The ability to draw a little, would have been far more use to us. We had French lessons at home, with the odd visit by a French lady for *conversatione*, to improve our French accent. 'Yoooo vill speeke in Francaise' she would lisp in terrible English, to try to get us chatting in French around a table at mealtimes. Some hope!

THE CHILDREN'S TIMETABLES AT HOME

Breakfast	8.30 a.m.
Lessons	9 a.m.
Lunch	1 p.m.

After lunch we had a half-an-hour's rest,

Piano lesson	2 p.m.
Ride	2.30-4 p.m.
Change for tea	4.30 p.m. (with Mother in the Dining Room, if she was at home.)
Half-an-hour's prep	5 p.m.
Supper	6 p.m.
Bed	7.30 p.m.

The schoolroom was located in the last two rooms on the top floor, on the left side of the house. It had been equipped in the 1800s by Col. Conolly for his many children, with double doors, with a space of about 3ft in between. The outside door was lined with green felt, presumably to drown out any distressing noises of chastisement! There was plenty of space for desks, a globe, a blackboard, and lines of books and paper in shelves and pull-out drawers.

Miss Colls had taught two other families, including the Shirley's at Lough Fea (where there was a herd of white deer). She was kindly and strict, though we were constantly glancing out of the schoolroom windows, wishing we were out there cantering about the fields. She was a superb pianist, and taught us every day after lunch in term time. We learnt to sing in tune, how to practise our favourite hymns, how to read music, and to play the piano to the beat of a metronome. Most of these were perquisites to passing our frequent music exams in Dublin. We progressed up the grades, and became competent enough not to mind playing to others on the grand piano in the hall (whether they wanted to hear or not was another matter!). Our most avid listeners were our brothers, who constantly demanded the dulcet tones of the Harrow School Songs, banged out at full pitch to their satisfaction and vocal accompaniment.

Of an evening, alone in her room, Miss Colls sat in front of her coal fire, with Jumbo, her Peke dog in a basket at her feet. She was wedded to her beloved old Bakelite wireless, listening to her favourite Beethoven or Bach concerts, played at full tilt.

At first, we were not much trouble to Miss Colls. She was our font of knowledge, our key to outside life (how others lived seemed to fascinate us).

We were once talking about measurements, comparing our own adolescent vital statistics, when we pushed the tape measure cheekily in her direction. She simply said, 'forty-four all round' and packed the offending article back in her desk. After we got around to talking of the statistics of a young actress called Marylyn Monroe and such, forty-four all round seemed impressive to us. A comparison to Marilyn Monroe was not exactly fair. She was not tall, and wore a cardigan (which looked as if it had been washed in boiling water) pulled across her like a bandage, around her ample 'tum and things'.

Her pet Peke didn't like our beloved cocker spaniel Chunky, and we became very weary of it, but she treasured its scrunched-up nose. When it was old, and needed some fresh air, she pushed it all the way to the garden and back in our old double pram, usually with the double hoods up, to keep the rain off.

We taught our ever-patient Chunky to perform tricks to order and we rode our ponies every afternoon with a pony girl, except Sundays. There were frequent horse shows at weekends.

We were not allowed to hunt, except in the holidays, and we often played with workers' children around the stable wing and around the little spinney outside the stable yard.

As the years went on, our lessons became increasingly hysterical, because we had to learn to shout at her. She had become increasingly deaf. At the same time, Father had trouble with his hearing and so the shouting came in handy.

The boys would come back from boarding schools, and practise their newly acquired swear words on their gullible younger sister, who, in turn, executed a test drive with them on Miss Colls, who was usually fiddling with her hearing aid. This contraption was one of the old type boxes, carried around in the hand, with a long flex, dividing in the middle and leading to plugged-in ear-pieces. She was always fiddling with the knobs on the box, which would usually produce whistles, from which she would back up, as if kicked by a mule. Most often, Miss Colls would give up and prefer to carry on with us yelling at full pitch, but occasionally she did manage to 'tune in'. Of course, this success was only known to us when she furiously exclaimed, 'I'm not *that* deaf!'

On we went, shouting our lessons along, until one week, when she tried inserting a new battery and proceeded to have a disastrous run of success with her ear instrument. Oh dear! The Harrow School swear words! Even if she had been manipulating a larger recording machine, she could not have heard our brother's new line in swear words any better that day. (They were mostly 'b' words, usually with literal meanings one could not have guessed.) It was not the boys who copped it in the neck, it was your author (the youngest) who stood for hours between the schoolroom doors as punishment – my initials are still scratched there!

We had coded phrases that we used at any time of the day, between us children, which sent us into helpless giggles for no sane reason. One of the most infantile of these, was in plain English: 'You-dirty-looking-thing-you.' This phrase was picked up by mistake on Miss Colls' hearing aid and it sounded like a personal attack on her dignity. It was always me, the youngest child, who was heard, almost as if she only tuned into the childish pitch of 'station Sally', and nobody else.

As a matter of fact, she was extremely kind, and had both our respect and our love. But the consequences of misbehaviour were grave. In 1957, Miss Colls was retired, and as the youngest I was sent to boarding school at Brondesbury-at-Stocks, in Herts.

Comparing the two educational systems is interesting. When I went away to school, at the age of thirteen, I found I had no catching up to do in the various subjects, except for the impossible Art.

Miss Colls had encouraged us to read books for enjoyment early on in life, so our shelves were full of the coloured sets of fairy story books, old animal favourites, like *Black Beauty*, and many children's classic historical novels (adaptations of *The Scarlet Pimpernel*, *The Man in the Iron Mask*, and Sir Walter Scott's *Rob Roy*). This gave both Diana and I an enduring love of books. The reading bug was soon taken up with considerable gusto, with repercussions when practised sitting upon a pot!

Lights out time, immediately after our prayers, was strictly kept. We were expected to go straight to sleep, for we were given no beside lights, but Diana who managed to get hold of a torch, would clamber out of bed, and sit for hours reading on her 'throne' (china pot), because she would have an excuse if she was caught! One night the pot cracked and she sat on the jagged edge, and was badly scarred. There was consternation, a lot of blood and a great many stitches. The pots were inspected, and bedside lights were allowed after that.

But life was not all nursery maids and governesses, the family did get together every evening in the first floor sitting room (next door to our parents' bedrooms), where the scene could not have been more domestic. Mother would be darning Father's socks, using an old mushroom-shaped wooden tool as she sewed around the heels. She darned his socks every night. (I used to idle away the time in a bit of a muddle, trying to work out how many feet, how many socks, how many holes per sock? Perhaps every sock had a hole for each toe?) Father would sit and read the newspaper, or be writing at the desk, which was an exact copy of Lady Louisa's from the eighteenth century (Its matching display cabinet was beside it).[35] We often spread ourselves out on the carpet, playing cards (Snap, Racing Demon, Canasta, or all sorts of Patience), or sticking photos into albums, and always jumping up to help Mother thread her needle. I was fascinated by her inability to get the needle and the thread anywhere near each other. (Now I do it myself!)

Every Sunday morning we went to the church at the end of the drive. In term-time, the pupils from the Collegiate School for Girls (a hotel in recent years) walked up the length of the village street in a long crocodile. Because we sat at the front, and because father looked straight down on us as he read the lesson every Sunday, we had little chance of much mischief. However, the organ was a constant problem to those who should have had their minds on religion. It required a small boy to climb into the restricted space at the back, and noisily wind it up with a handle while it was still playing.[36] It clattered around and around, like a pebble in a bucket. We had to sing loudly. Being small, the boy's arms got tired; a pause would ensue in the middle of a hymn, and an air pocket would get released, the organ would burp, and off we would go. At least it kept us amused.

Nowadays, we still come back for family christenings, weddings, and burials in the church that Lady Louisa helped to build. The buildings behind it are where Squire Conolly kept his bear and his hounds; where Lady Louisa built Ireland's first ever School of Industry; and in more recent times, it was a primary school for many years.

At mealtimes we ate on blue willow-pattern plates with Nanny, and later with Miss Colls. We were expected to finish what was on the plate, and occasionally Miss Colls encouraged us with a *bonne bouche*, a special treat covered in cream. If Mother was at home, we had tea with her at the end of the Dining Room.

There were lots of holiday parties at Castletown and at neighbours' houses; and, as we grew older, there were dances in private houses.

The adult mealtimes were: 9 a.m. breakfast; 1 p.m. lunch; and dinner at 8 p.m.. All the food was served up in the dining room on the best ware, crested 'C' family silver dishes and plates.

For breakfast, Father and guests helped themselves to sausages, bacon, different sorts of cooked eggs, and sometimes there was kedgeree[28] or smoked haddock, all served up on covered dishes on the hot plate on the sideboard.

The tradition, as in many households, was for breakfast to take at least an hour, and to be eaten in complete silence. A selection of newspapers was on hand to be folded noisily and propped up against a tall saltcellar, or more inconveniently, the cut-glass marmalade jar. An occasional grunt of, 'Could you pass the butter?' was acceptable.

The lady guests could choose to be served by a maid, with breakfast in bed on tall trays; or they would join the gentlemen guests in the dining room.

In the nursery, there was porridge in the winter; with warmer weather bringing corn flakes and delicious rich creamy unpasteurized milk that was fresh from the house-cow that morning.

Family lunch and dinner were more formal, with the butler and pantry boy waiting at table.

More intimate meals were usually started with homemade soup, liberally laced with Father's favourite sweet sherry – delicious. Guests were often treated to Mother's favourite cheese soufflé for their first course.

We had fish every Friday, and Mother had such an obsession about having the fish bones removed before serving, we used to wonder who had choked in the past. The biggest treat was for the occasional large fresh wild salmon, usually caught by friends or family on holiday in the west.

As children we savoured our Sunday lunch, when there was a tableful of big appetites after the walk to church and back. We made worthy inroads into a large joint of roast beef with all the trimmings (or our own roast lamb in season), which appeared in different guises over the following two days; cold on Monday, and shepherd's pie on Tuesday.

The firm favourites for the rest of the week were roast or fricassee chicken with mushrooms, and rabbit pie twice a week (their long furry bodies hung from the larder ceiling).

Sometimes there was a fruit pudding; apple or pear charlotte from our own stores, with breadcrumbs on top and a jug full of fresh creamy custard; or maybe rhubarb or gooseberry fool. There was always fresh fruit in season: peaches, strawberries, raspberries, grapes, apples, and pears from the garden, and oranges brought from the market.

In the evenings, a savoury dish was often preferred instead of pudding. This would be a dish like Devils on Horseback – bacon rolled around prunes, cooked lightly in the oven and served on toast. The very name seemed to be invented for us, because Castletown had its very own mounted Devil's Story.[29]

No meal would be finished without a mound of our favourite homemade cream cheese, which was served up alongside orange-coloured cheddar. The harder cheese was much maligned, for Mother insisted on cutting the outside slice away every day, accusing it of being got-at by the mice, despite the fact it was always carefully covered in the larder.

We had tea informally around the smaller table in the corner, with scones and a cake, and soft-boiled eggs on a hunting day.

Dinnertime was always punctual and formal, even if it was only the family. Our parents changed into smart clothes every single evening. Grandmother dressed up too, wearing one of her two wigs, which appeared to live most of their shaggy life dangling on baubles on either side of her bedroom mirror. (Her day-time headgear was a chicken hat for outside tasks, and a better hat for Sundays.)

The grown-ups were loudly summoned to the dining room table by the resounding clang of a gong, rung with such gusto by the butler that he might have been starting a boxing match.

But, it wasn't *all* formal; Father's delight after dinner each evening was to reach for a squeaky yellow duck, which was kept over the fireplace in the dining room. He would then call Diana's dog, Dotto, and Patrick's two Labradors on to the front steps, squeak the duck and set off hysteria among the dogs, which usually ended in a dog-fight and furious members of the family trying to extract their dogs.

Originally, the postman came to the house five separate times every weekday, and three times on a Sunday. But the late 1950s, it was brought only once a day by our postman at about 9 a.m. on his bicycle, with the letters in a wicker basket in the front of his handle bars and parcels strapped to the back.

He parked it at the bottom of the front steps and rang the door bell. Murphy, the butler, received the letters and laid them out in personal piles on the central hall desk. Sometimes this arrangement was a bit too public for growing teenagers. If we were lucky, Murphy could be cajoled into hiding important letters at the bottom of the pile, away from grown-up eyes. We knew he was on our side.

There was quite an art in hiding behind a pillar in order to pounce on our pile of letters before our father got to them; after all, he had seen the postman coming through his study window. School reports arriving caused much nervous tension in the house. But we were not allowed to touch those.

In our day, the postman seldom took back letters to be posted; there was nearly always someone going into Celbridge later in the day for the chemist, some stores, or petrol, who would post them.

THE POSTAL SERVICE

Mondays to Saturdays

Arrival	Departure
8 a.m.	7.15 a.m.
8 p.m.	5.30 p.m.
--	7.15 p.m.

Sundays

Arrival	Departure
10 a.m.	4 p.m.
--	7.15 p.m.

Everyone was used to the house being very cold, and we put coats *on* to dash from room to room along freezing corridors.

There were fires in guest bedrooms, the governess's room, the sitting room, and in Father's study (and in the nursery when we were babies). The fire in the Hall was only lit if there were guests.

We each shared our bed with a heavy stone hot water bottle, which made the mattress sag in the middle. The trick was to learn to sleep on the hill of the mattress on one side, and not to rap your kneecaps if you really had to turn over. These stone bottles were used until the early 1960s, but we were never allowed to fill them ourselves.

When we were still young, we dutifully kissed parents good morning on our way down the ninety-eight backstairs to a separate schoolroom for breakfast at 8.30 a.m. (in the little panelled corner room opposite the pantry).

Mother was always sitting up, having breakfast in her big bed[30] with a high-legged wicker tray, and Father was getting dressed to go down for his 9 a.m. breakfast with Uncle Ted and guests. He slept in the adjoining dressing room, where he reputedly slept on his back, and was allowed to snore as much as he liked.

During the wintertime, we were fascinated by our father's large wool combinations,[31] which we got a good look at while he was wandering around trying to locate his disobedient clothes.

Both of the bedrooms were kept tidy by the maids, however, Mother's big dressing table between the windows was covered in goodies which we loved to finger through. She had a lot of minor jewels in a silver casket, and silver-backed brushes, combs, and mirror with 'S.C.' on them. There was a sofa at the end of her bed, where she kept her warm red silk and wool dressing gown. This was also where her maid laid out the next day's clothes. She had a black Bakelite telephone and a bedside light. On her wall hung four pastel paintings of us children, aged from four to ten years old (these are illustrated on pages 205-11).

At Christmas, there would be a 20ft tree in the hall, on the far left-hand side, nearly underneath the balcony, with presents for every one of the estate children (from Mother's long fragile present list). There would be nearly 200 gifts carefully wrapped up and labelled with each name. Their parents were given money, a joint of beef, and extra milk and butter.

As they grew up, the children never forgot the wonderful meal afterwards with their parents downstairs in the servants' hall.

There was also a parish sports day on the front lawn in the summer each year, which are still remembered by our neighbouring families and us; they are treasured memories.

After the front lawn was mown on a dry day, with a horse and cutter, we used to try to practise the long bamboo-pole high jump, for we tended to refuse the fence on our feet when it got a bit high. Diana was disgusted with herself, 'I'm a bad stopper!' she mumbled in frustration. We berated ourselves for not being as brave as our ponies! There were no mats or sand pits in those days, which meant we were attempting to jump the bar straight on, somewhat like a high hurdle, and landing on the rough lawn. But in the heat of battle during the proper competition, we got a bit higher.

The older children took it all very seriously. There was the sack race, the egg and spoon, three-legged races, the high jump, the long jump, flower-pot walking, and different aged and distance running races. The younger ones had Grandmother's Footsteps, with a whole lot of laughter and skulduggery as the parents aided and abetted the little ones. Somehow, the smallest was usually allowed to win the parcel.

They were happy days, when every child went home with an armful of prizes of some sort. We were invited to other friends' houses for their sports parties as well, when they had running races and cricket on their front lawns.

The front of Castletown. (OPW)

The Red Drawing Room, with rich red silk walls and the Aubusson carpet. The Green and Red Drawing Rooms were the main entertaining rooms at Castletown and are where the young Arthur Wellesley (later Duke of Wellington) secretly wooed his future bride, Kitty Packenham, a Conolly niece and frequent visitor. (Courtesy of *County Life*)

The Green Drawing Room in 1964, showing the family portrait of Thomas Wentworth, 1st Earl of Strafford (1593-1641) and his secretary. He was a friend and chief advisor to King Charles I and was subsequently executed under the reluctant order of the king. His family heirlooms (including the Christopher Columbus Chest) came to Castletown with his co-heir Lady Anne Wentworth, who married William Conolly, Speaker Conolly's nephew. (Courtesy of Hugh Doran, Irish Architectural Archives)

The Long Gallery, which runs nearly the full length of the house, in 1964, showing the central desk, with the spinet piano on the left. (Courtesy of Hugh Doran, Irish Architectural Archives)

Christopher Colombus' Chest. A sea chest (fitted out with drawers inside), with 'Christof Colomb' carved into the top of the lid. This was a much-prized family heirloom, passed down to Lady Anne Wentworth, who married Speaker Conolly's nephew, from her ancestor William Wentworth, the ill-fated 1st Earl of Strafford. The chest was taken off a ship of the Spanish Armada when it was wrecked off the west coast of Ireland. Stafford's armour and swords lived on the top of this chest, which stood at the top of the front staircase, on the landing. (Courtesy of Victoria Browne)

Diana, aged eighteen, on the front page as 'The Youngest master of Hounds in the World', taken with her hunter Simon. She taught him remarkable tricks whilst out hunting. (Courtesy of the *Evening Herald*)

Patrick and Tawny Port at Badminton Horse Trials, 1973.

Diana and Barrymore jumping at the Mexico Olympic Games.

1992 Barcelona Olympic Games medal ceremony, showing Patrick (far right, red jacket) as president of the Ground Jury (Chief Judge), with Princess Anne. (Courtesy of B.P. Wilkinson)

Princess Diana, the Princess of Wales, talking to Patrick at Badminton Horse Trials.

Virginia McGrath (Conolly-Carew) on the Yellow Earl in the water jump at the Sydney Olympic Games, 2000.

Virginia Conolly-Carew (McGrath) and Ballywhatsit in the Junior European Championships. Ballywhatsit was home-bred, out of Ballyhoo.

Bunny, as Lord Lieutenant, with HM the Queen and the Duke of Edinburgh in 2009 having just planted a tree at Thirlestane Castle.

Bunny and Rossie Maitland-Carew with Prince Philip and his secretary Sir Brian McGrath in the conservatory at Thirlestane Castle; taken during the prince's yearly private visit, which he has taken for a few days for the last several years.

The top floor (farmyard end) of Castletown was taken up by bedrooms for a pony girl, the housekeeper, two housemaids and two kitchen maids; these were opposite our schoolroom and a large open play area. The four children, our nursery, the nursery maid, Miss Colls, and a nanny, were accommodated in the stable yard half of the top floor.

Our open play area had a ping-pong table, and the giant stuffed brown bear that had belonged to Squire Conolly, Lady Louisa's husband. It bore witness to our sillier games, like Murder in the Dark.

All along the top landing were huge glass cases depicting woodland scenes, with stuffed long-legged birds, weasels, rabbits, and glass ponds ... very Victorian. They looked dusty inside (how did dust get in there?), and tired somehow. But they were like everything else in the house, all trophies of a particular era.

Along the ground floor corridor were Zulu-type spears, shields, and great steel swords with filigree hilts, and walls of redundant weapons. I suppose, as young children, we took it for granted that everyone else had spears outside their loo too.

Squire Conolly's bear, which he kept beside his Hunt Kennels in the mid-1700s (in the area behind the church). He had the bear stuffed when it died, and put it on the top floor of Castletown, where the bear kept his furry body and glassy eyes on our open (pillared) play area (above the double-height entrance hall), which contained our table-tennis table. This top corridor had the nursery and the schoolroom, with bedrooms for the children, a nanny, a nursemaid, and young housemaids. (OPW)

The whole feeling of inanimate objects having a past life came onto focus for us with Christopher Columbus's chest, at the top of the main staircase. This seemed specially designed as a roller-coaster ride for our imaginations. As soon as Miss Colls told us of the adventures he and the chest had been on, sailing to the edge of the world, and capturing cannibals. We learnt of his involvement in blood-thirsty war dances (right up our street), and the 'birth' of America (a difficult concept for a six year old). The chest was not very big, luckily, because we could well imagine lugging it by its handles, up the sandy beaches of the Caribbean. We paid great doubloon coins to rescue the dusky maidens in grass skirts, and collected treasure from 'the baddies'. We stoically refused to contemplate the possibility that it might have once carried severed heads.

To fend off the natives, we valiantly attempted (and failed) to wield the hugely heavy weapons on display on the top of Christopher Columbus' chest; not realising that it was in fact the armour, helmet, and swords of one of our ancestors, the executed Earl of Strafford.[34]

The oldest treasure in the house was the tall statue of Diana, Goddess of Hunting, which had been excavated from Pompeii by Lady Louisa's husband Thomas Conolly, in the mid-1700s. He reputedly hid it in a coffin, and escorted it back to Castletown, where a niche was created for it in the Long Gallery. It looked so delicate and perfect; one could not imagine it being buried since the Roman times.

The other curiosity, which brought experts from all over the world, was the Castletown 'Mona Lisa'. This was a rare contemporary copy of Leonardo de Vinci's painting in the Louvre in Paris, painted by Luini. The Castletown copy did manage to recreate her allusive smile, and hung in the dining room. Of all the fabulous items in the house, Father's pet project was to research and to prove its history. He found out that it was originally owned by successions of Kings of France (like the Leonardo painting), and fantastically, was won as a wager by the swashbuckling Tom Conolly of Castletown during the Great Paris Exhibition of 1861, from his friend Emperor Napoleon III of France (nephew of Napoleon Bonaparte).

This was a wager between the two men, and entailed Tom's magnificent private carriage and four horses travelling to Paris, where they joined the French ruler and many other entries trotting their splendid carriages up and down the *Bois de Boulogne* to be judged for magnificence. This was a competition the Emperor expected to win. However, Tom won the bet, because his horses were shod in silver. The prize was the 'Mona Lisa'!

The Castletown Mona Lisa, by Luini, previously owned by the Kings of France (like the Louvre Mona Lisa), and won in a private wager with Louis Napoleon III by Tom Conolly of Castletown. (DG/SM)

Presumably, Tom Conolly had already told Napoleon III about Castletown originally being an old Geraldine Castle (FitzGerald) ... since the sitter for the Mona Lisa was a very distant relation; a Geraldine from Florence.

This painting was reputedly to have been lent to the Louvre, ready to stand in for the original the first time the Leonardo version was damaged. We do not believe it was used in the end.

Other prizes that day of the wager were Napoleon Bonaparte busts, which took up sentry duty underneath Speaker Conolly's portrait in the Hall.

8

UPSTAIRS/DOWNSTAIRS

We didn't know it at the time, but we lived in the last generation of the 'Upstairs/Downstairs' life, with a full compliment of staff to look after both the house and us.

They all lived in the servants' wing, which was their hallowed ground, their own private house. It was out of bounds for the Conolly-Carew children, who were taught to respect their privacy out of working hours.[37] In fact, despite the mischief that went on, we grew up with old-fashioned manners and deference to our elders.

There was a hierarchy in the servants' wing, every bit as strict as in the main house, where everyone had somebody else to defer to. Lord and Lady Carew, and Major Conolly (Uncle Ted) were at the top of the pile on the family side; just as Mr and Mrs Murphy (the butler and his wife, the cook) and Mary Smith the housekeeper were the law-makers in the servants' wing.

We would hear chastisements from the kitchen (the newer kitchen in the basement), and an unfortunate scullery maid would come tearing out towards the store of coal, in order to remedy a too floppy lettuce, or some such culinary disaster. (In those days you soaked the lettuce with a lump of coal to revive it.)

Murphy became the Butler in 1938, and moved into Castletown with his wife and two young children, James and Margaret.

When Millicent, the resident head cook left in the 1940s to marry Charles Beatty, a local farmer, Mrs Murphy took her place, having worked previously for Count John McCormack.

Millicent, the new Mrs Beatty, was very pleased to tell her old compatriots that she had thirty rooms in her farmhouse. She was as proud as punch because her husband owned the first combine-harvester in the area, and he hired it out to others at harvest time, including Castletown.

Some years later, Charles died, and their four children grew up and left home. Poor Millicent met a tragic death, when the house she was so proud of, caught fire.

Over the following eighteen years, Mrs Murphy oversaw the cooking and the provisions for the kitchen, checking the menus with Mother each week.

Diana describes one of her cherished memories:

I am left with a never-to-be-forgotten vision of Mrs Murphy bringing the white ducks in from the pond behind the farmyard each evening. They treated her as their surrogate mother, as she returned along the narrow path beside the pond, with the ducks solemnly in perfect formation, waddling in step, single file – left – right – behind her.

Vegetables for the house were brought in from the garden each day; meat and fish were temporally stored in the cool, tile-lined larder. Game was kept in a two-storey building, opposite the back door, where it was hung on the second floor.

She oversaw the preparation of onions tied in bunches, the apples stacked in racks, carrots and potatoes in sacks, eggs in water-glass, and fruit in large airtight bottles.

Turnips had to be cleaned up and the faults removed, and some poor kitchen maid had to hand-turn the cream in a wooden churn until her arm nearly dropped off.

Meals were prepared for the dining room, the school room, and the servants' hall. In the early 1950s, there would be between twenty-five and thirty people to feed each day.

Just as Mrs Murphy ruled the kitchen staff, and lived with her family in a spacious seven-room apartment in the servants' wing, the housekeeper, Mary Smith, also had her own rooms.

She had charge of the young housemaids, who did the general cleaning and the laundry, and who were mostly live-in local girls fitting in time between school and marriage. They came and went fairly frequently. This situation meant she was always training someone. They went around as a team, chattering like starlings. If they saw you, they'd say 'Morning, Miss' in perfect unison, as if someone had said, '1, 2, 3, go ...'

One of their endless tasks was to clean the windows. The story went around ... there were 365 windows to do ... (not quite true) ... but to keep them in line, they were told to shut up two windows, so that Castletown would not rival Buckingham Palace! We had no idea which two windows were left shut. Every morning they cleaned out the grates, and re-lit the fires in the nursery and the sitting room. They kept their brooms, dusters, and two or three Ewbank sweepers in a cupboard halfway up the stairs on the stable side (between the ground and the first floor).Frequently, they preferred to brush the carpets with their brooms, working together in a line of industry.

When the housekeeper retired, unfortunately her replacement did not last very long. She appeared to have somewhat furtive tendencies, and was suspected of drinking on duty. When the parents left the dining room one lunch time, Mama quietly went back in, peered around the screen, and caught her red-handed. She proved to be the last housekeeper. After that, the laundry was regularly collected and delivered in White Heather Laundry vans from Dublin.

The maids had one day off a week to do their courting in the village. But it was impossible for a young maid if she fancied one of the footmen. They lived in too close proximity for their romance to go undetected for long. The girl was packed off to her family.

The smooth running of the house, and the separation of the sexes, depended on the iron rule of the butler, the cook, and the housekeeper.

All the outside doors were locked at night, and the sexes hardly met while on duty, except for the meals they all took together in the kitchen.

The footmen and pantry boy looked after the dining room and the pantry behind. Firstly, they took the prepared food out of the small pulley service lift in the pantry, which came up from the kitchen below. They then brought the food onto a serving table inside the dining room, which was hidden from the guests, behind a screen. From there, they took the plates to wait at table, serving the ladies first, from the left-hand side. (In later years, when the footmen had gone, the older maids would serve at table.) They cleaned the silver, and looked after the downstairs fireplaces, and did the washing up in a big sink in the pantry.[38]

One enterprising red-headed pantry boy was a good footballer on his days off, and keen on the village girls ... but he drank too much in Celbridge.

He was an excellent and popular worker in the house, and particularly liked serving at the table alongside the butler. However, he got bored with his more menial daily tasks, and decided he had definitely had enough of cleaning the seemingly endless supply of silver cutlery. Instead of constantly polishing the knives, forks, and spoons of every size and shape, he started to chuck the dirty cutlery into the ha-ha outside the window. That would save cleaning it!

This went on for days, and the dining room staff were unwittingly getting closer and closer to having nothing for the guests to eat with. Eventually, one fateful evening, he staggered back from Celbridge just before the back door was locked-up at midnight. Befuddled with drink, he wandered down the long dark passage towards his bedroom, which was almost opposite the kitchen.

'Give up the drink,' he heard a terrible voice out of the dark. Whereupon he took off down the passageway in fear of his life. 'Give up the drink,' he heard again. He reached his bedroom at last, and locked his door. He fled Castletown the next morning, and never returned. There was a hue and cry when both the boy and the cutlery were found to be missing. Luckily, the mystery was solved before they ran out of knives and forks. The dirty silver was unearthed, hidden in the long grass at the bottom of the basement ditch just below the pantry window.

The overall ruler of the domestic household was Michael Murphy, our butler. He was our true link to the earlier age of carriages and horses.

Born in 1879, he was brought up on a smallholding in Bliary, Athlone, South Westmeath, and went as a teenager to work at the famous house Lissadell, in County Sligo, home of the Gore-Booth family.

Countess Markiewicz was a married daughter, who became an infamous IRA rebel in The Troubles, and later a member of the Government.

Many famous literary people, artists and poets, stayed or lived there, including her Gore-Booth sister, and the greatest of Irish poets, W.B. Yeats.

Murphy was there for the census of 1911, as a liveried footman/postillion, who rode on the back of the family coach in his uniform, opened the door of the carriage, and put down the steps.

Murphy then went as valet to the world famous singer, Count John McCormack (a Papal Count), who had rented Moore Abbey, in Monasterevan, Co. Kildare. He accompanied McCormack on his singing tours all over the world until the Second World War started.

Murphy married the young cook from Moore Abbey, whose home was in Newtownforbes, Co. Longford. She was nearly thirty years younger, and they came to Castletown together in 1938.

He told wonderful stories of his time at Moore Abbey; how the great tenor walked through his woods singing at full volume; how the singer spent one fortune doing it up; and another on racehorses trained for him by More O'Farrell at Kildangan; how Lord Clonmel came to stay with an extremely heavy suitcase, which had to be carted up many stairs and when the maid went to unpack it, found it to be full of coal. 'I was told it was very cold here, and I needed to bring my own fuel.'

At Castletown, Mr Murphy and Mary Smith, the housekeeper, sat at either end of the long table in the servant's hall, next to the kitchen. Mrs Murphy ate with her children in their apartment. She always wore a white pinny, and changed into a clean one several times a day.

Generally, in the downstairs life of the female maids and kitchen staff, Mrs Murphy and Mary Smith provided the eagle eyes for bad manners amongst the servants – much as we were watched over, upstairs. And Mr Murphy controlled the footmen and pantry boys with a rod of iron.

A succession of butlers and footmen had served in the house since it was built. Guinness was one of the first, serving Speaker Conolly's widow. He brewed his beer in the cellars for the servants to drink (upstairs they drank wine). We can still see where he rolled his firkin barrels down the window ledges on the lower floor. This was in the days before the Dublin Guinness brewery was purchased.

Mr Murphy also was responsible for the strongroom, which had a large solid door hidden behind a curtain in the inner pantry, where spare silver from every generation was kept. There was cutlery, candelabras, trophies, old serving dishes, silver salt and pepper sets, along with glass of every sort. By tradition, the master of the house kept the key.

Murphy was not a typical butler; he was neither aloof nor stiff. He was a smallish, dignified, and an extremely kind friend to us all, with manners that made us two Conolly-Carew girls feel ashamed of one of our escapades.

Up to mischief, we cut up pieces of soap and wrapped them in our sweetie papers; selecting the most likely candidate to accept them. So, with friendly little hands outstretched, we offered the 'sweets' to Mr Murphy. Not showing the slightest surprise at this great honour, as if he was accepting a medal, he leant down to our level, thanked us, and carefully selected a sweet from each of us. He hesitated. 'But you must eat it ... now!' we insisted.

'Very well, Miss,' he said politely as he unwrapped them. He must have realised they looked nothing like a sweet inside, but to our shock, horror, he did pop them in – before he started frothing at the mouth, we scarpered.

We were on tender-hooks for days, but he never said a word; he was ever our ally. If we dropped something at table, or secretly discarded a piece of inedible gristle, he would manage to scoop it up without anyone noticing. Table manners were fierce, elbows in, fork held correctly, sit up, don't talk with your mouth full, in fact don't talk at all (unless you're spoken to), and eat up everything on your plate.[39] What fun it was, unlearning all those manners later!

One of Murphy's other duties was to close the big shutters with the pantry boy each evening in the winter. In summer, Father closed the dining room shutters when he was the last person out of the room after dinner.

When Patrick, aged eight, was off to boarding school, and rather miserably packed up to go, he would shake hands with his father in his study, and receive a lecture on good behaviour. He would give his mother a peck on the cheek; but it was Murphy who stood at the front door pressing an extremely generous 10 shillings into his hand (a term's worth of tuck).

Only years later, Patrick learnt that, at the end of the week, Murphy would give Father a bill for 'miscellaneous items', in which was listed '10 shillings for Master Patrick'.

Murphy retired in late 1957, and remained living in the Castletown Wing. Mrs Murphy continued to cook full time for us for another three years.

In 1960, they bought a fairly new house in St Patrick's Park, on the Maynooth Road in Celbridge, for which he paid £100.[40] Mrs Murphy then retired, and we used to stop and see them frequently as we rode past on our horses. Sadly, Murphy died of a heart attack, aged eighty-one, one year later. Mrs Murphy came back occasionally to cook for parties, dances, the Dublin Horse Show weeks, and the odd weekend.

Castletown's telephone number was Celbridge 17. On the landing outside the pantry on the ground floor, there was a telephone exchange, with rows of disks that popped open when a call came through, and set off a noisy rattle. In order to make an outgoing call, you had to wind up the handle on the side of the exchange board with considerable vigour. Murphy liked to be the one to handle it; he reckoned he had the right touch.

It looked impressive, as if it should belong to a hotel. It had an earpiece hung on a hook, with twenty lines available. In fact we only used three; the exchange; in Father's study (near the front stairs); and in Mother's bedroom.

Any telephone call, whether incoming or outgoing, was a fairly public affair, being routed via Celbridge Post Office, where the post-mistress connected them onwards. Part of the perks of her monotonous job was to listen in for any snippets of scandal, so anything personal had to be in code-breaking mode. (It must have been annoying to her when another call came in too soon for her to hear the latest news.) So she listened in; Murphy, the butler answered the telephone exchange at Castletown, he pressed the appropriate button for the study, and he listened in. Everyone shouted down the telephone, for the line was not always good – so the whole house either listened in, or passed the message on. It was very handy; everyone knew the news in no time at all.

After Murphy retired, the next butler, Carroll, was a bit 'gone in the wind'. He would give himself away by huffing and puffing down the telephone, and could be heard quite clearly.

'Excuse me,' we would say, pretending we didn't know whose puffing it was. Disappointed, he would have to hang up at his end, and the phone would click.

But Murphy's story in this book does not end with his death. His son James describes his own childhood at Castletown ...

He never rode, but was unwisely put up on a pony, while it was being led to the field, without bridle or saddle. It got away, and he fell into a hole being dug to make the tennis court. He never tried again.

In the term-time, he went on the Number 17 green double-decker CIE bus to Dublin, each morning at 7.30 a.m., on his way to secondary school. The buses parked along the Liffey, near O'Connell Bridge. He remembers all the children running and playing on the ice on the back pond (behind the farmyard) in the very hard winter of 1947. But most of all James was gripped with the constant fear of his personal Castletown ghosts.

He was walking up the avenue in the dark, when a white small figure floated in front of him a few times. He started to walk faster, more terrified. He let out a big kick, and felt he had connected with something – then it disappeared! He shot into the house, shaking.

A few days later, the herd in charge of the animals said to James' father, Murphy: 'Very odd ye know. There was a big old lamb dead on the avenue the other day!' At least that one was explained. But it does show how frightened the children were of the avenue in the dark.

Another time, James was bicycling home in the winter on a dark night, with the big trees creaking. More than halfway up the avenue towards the house, he heard a rattle of a chain. He pedalled faster and faster, and flew into the house, still hearing it behind him. It was chasing him!

The next morning, he had to bicycle back down the avenue before 7.30 to catch his bus, and it was still dark! Horror upon horror, the rattle was still there! He still talks about 'his ghost', but we subsequently worked out that it must have been the bull's chain in the nearby field.

As he grew up, Father offered to sponsor James to train as a gardener, but his talents lay as an electrician, and he became a top technician for the ESB. He tells the story of how, years later, he brought his new fiancée to the last Hunt Ball at Castletown, to dance the night away in the house he remembered to well. He could not persuade her to enter the Night Club, in the basement, which had been eerily lit up with red lights, to show specially painted scenes of foxes sitting at table, dressed as members of the hunt. There was a head in the middle of the table being carved and enjoyed by the foxes; this was clearly the head of the Master of the Kildare Hounds with his hunting cap on, and adorned with an apple in his mouth.[41]

In later years, the house was full of volunteer students when the Irish Georgian Society was renovating it. James Murphy's daughter, Sharon, met Prince Caspian Guirey, a Russian Prince, at Castletown, when they were amongst other students who lived on the top floor, in the old children's rooms. Sharon married her prince, and became a princess.

There were two other, outside-based helpers; the first was Bob McGuire, who had been an orphan, and who worked at Castletown from his early teenager years. He fetched and carried water from a well in the front of the house, as well as collecting coal, cutting the wood in the kitchen yard, and cleaning the shoes for Uncle Ted Conolly in the earlier lean years.

In our day, he humped buckets of hot water all the way up from the kitchen in the basement to the top floor, for the children's hip bath every evening, in front of a roaring fire. He stoked the boiler just twice a week for baths, (once a week during the war).[42] He carried the coals and wood for every fireplace in the house, including in the servants quarters.

We knew to pass him carefully on the stairs, for he prided himself to never spill a drop. Bob was also in charge of the sewerage clearance. There had been a ram in the stable yard, since the 1800s, which dealt with the water; when it occasionally became blocked, a pump in the stable yard was used to bring up river water. It took four men to turn the big wheel to pump the water.

In 1784, the Hearth Tax for Castletown listed ninety-four fireplaces! (Perhaps that included the cottages on the estate as well.) There were certainly forty fireplaces in the main block of the house alone, though they were not all in use at one time (with probably thirty to forty more in the two wings). There are two vast chimneys on top of the central part of the house; each chimney has twenty tunnels; which made the occupation of chimney sweep a somewhat hazardous one. How do you identify the right tunnel to clean? Presumably, they poked a thin tree up from the bottom? Or, perhaps, an unfortunate boy?

The other vital helper was the multi-talented Bob Smith. He was much loved, and he gave over fifty years of his life to the family, both at Castletown, and subsequently at their new home, Mount Armstrong, Donadea, when we moved.

Bob came to Celbridge with Canon Sinclair, who taught him most of his expertise as a master carpenter and joiner, as well as every other building skill you could name. Without Bob, much of Castletown would have given way long before. He patched, replaced, or rebuilt everything outside the house as necessary. He built a superb new sawmill, four new stables on the far side of the stable yard, as well as more stables and barns in the fields.[43] He constructed and painted show jumps for us, so we could practice over a railway gate, or maybe a wooden wall. He was out in all weathers altering and building the cross-country course for the Castletown All-Ireland Championship Horse Trials and Hunter Trials every year and it was Bob who solved the problem of the back-breaking task of taking a great number of sacks of oats up to the big room above the stables.

Previously they had been carried up and down the rickety winding iron stairs from the yard, until Bob enlarged the window overlooking the yard entrance, and installed a pulley system to raise the sacks from the back of a tractor and trailer. The pulley system can still be seen on the outside wall.

Bob was a very rare man, unfailingly dignified and polite. He lived in his own fine house on the other side of the road from the front gates.

Over the years, Bob saved and worked, and bought several run-down houses in the village. He and Johnny O'Neill worked at night to restore them, often by candlelight; he sold them again, and made his family independently comfortable. His wife played the organ in church for many years.

To visit Bob's garden, in a large area behind his house, was a treat we never forgot (he gave Diana her love of growing her own fruit and vegetable in later life). The precision with which he planted, separated, tended and harvested his profusion of vegetables and flowers, was more than worthy of the Chelsea Flower Show. Every bed was exactly two-and-a-half feet from its neighbour, and the earth lay tall and pliable with its manure mixture (a weed wouldn't dare!). His workload bore witness to toil both night and day.

After Castletown was sold, Bob went to work for the family at Mount Armstrong, near Naas, when they moved. He was travelling backwards and forwards each day by car; and then later helped with a further move to Diana's house at Oakville nearby.

For years into his old age, he lovingly tended the graves of our parents in the churchyard opposite his house.

He died some years ago, but Mrs Smith and their daughter, Audrey, still live there. The family owe him a very great debt.

COSTS AND WAGES IN THE 1950S (PER YEAR)

Schooling	Patrick at Harrow	£200
Governess	Miss Colls	£72
Butler	Mr Murphy	£72
Cook	Mrs Murphy	£52
Odd Job Man	Bob McGuir	£30
Groom		£39
Hallboy/Footman		£36
Electricity		£200
Subscriptions		£60
Wines		£100
Smokes		£80
Car		£50

9

PONIES AND A SCOTTISH INVASION

There were several other people living with us in the main house, including the head groom and his family, who had a flat in the basement at the stable end; and April French-Mullen (later Countess Mervelt), who lived as a member of the family. She taught us to ride, and hunt, and helped Mother buy suitable ponies, and also trained them.

April had been in the British Army at the end of the Second World War, when all military personnel were offered a free training course in England. She had applied for permission to take a course in horsemastership in Ireland instead. Her application happened to arrive on Father's desk, who that time was working for the British Legion in Ireland, dealing with the problems of returning ex-servicemen looking for training, housing, and a job. He approved April's application in 1948, and assigned her to Col. Joe Dudgeon's Riding and Training School at Stillorgan, Dublin, for one year – Col. Dudgeon was training the British Jumping Team at that time.

April found herself in the first ever intake of Irish taking a British Horse Society Preliminary examination. Amongst her many courses, was a one day's intensive instruction in riding and jumping side-saddle. One of her most memorable duties was riding Col. Dudgeon's hunters through the centre of Dublin, with about six others. (Col. Joe was a Master of the North Kildare Harriers with Father.) The riders' route took them from Melville, Stillorgan, through the thick of the traffic via Palmerstown, passing pigs in gardens, and trotting along beside the main A1 trunk road. Their destination was Mrs Nancy Connell's house, St Catherine's in Leixlip, where the horses were to be stabled for the hunting season. Mrs Connell was also a joint master.

April was kind and very firm; a whirlwind of action – everything had to be exactly correct.

If the family had Olympic and international success in later years, it was largely due to April, and we have passed many of her methods down to our own children.

One story she tells of those years: She had missed an important day's hunting. 'How was the opening meet?' she asked.

'T'was grand, Miss, there were horses' heads popping out of every ditch!'

Through the years we had several pony girls, among them were Patricia McCormack,[44] Ann Joyce, and Christine Middleton. They usually had one or two girl apprentices to help, who were frequently working towards their BHS exams, to train as qualified grooms. Some had trouble with the men; one was suspected of somewhat enlivening the life of the new butler, Carroll, which only went to hasten his rather prompt demise!

In the stables, there was also a series of male head grooms.

Stone (who had a baby daughter born at Castletown), Walsh, O'Flaherty, and Sloan were the early ones. Sloan was tall and thin, and several of his family were also employed. His son, Charlie, helped him in the stables; another son, John, was a farmhand; and Sloan was also the father of our nanny, Maura.

O'Flaherty told the story of Mother selling a small lame pony to Ned Cash, our local horse dealer from Clane, declaring it unsuitable for her children.

A few weeks later, Ned Cash sent a replacement pony on trial. It was very smartly turned out, and very sound. 'Look!' said O'Flaherty, who was immediately suspicious. He shut the yard gate, clapped the animal on its backside, and let it loose in the yard ... in it went, straight to its old stable. 'Same pony!' said the wise groom.

King and Tynan, as we will see later, were both artists in training young horses to drive in long reins. They were responsible for the welfare and feeding of approximately thirty horses and ponies, from brood mares and foals, to jumpers and hunters; and they trained the young horses ('broke them in'). But it was April who taught us children to ride.

In 1943, during the war, the Connemara Pony Society gave its official permission for a grey thoroughbred stallion called Winter, to cover registered Connemara mares. This was done to improve the breed; however, he only lasted one season before he died. He was the sire of the first twins recorded in the Connemara Stud Book, when Clare Girl gave birth to twin filly foals in 1944. Twins are still very rare in the breed.

Mother bought the twins as two-year-olds in 1946, along with two other pure-breds, and one or two other part-breeds. These youngsters ran as a mini-herd in the front field. They were 'broken-in' and trained the following year, and were all sold except for one of the twins she called Twinnie, which Diana rode as a show pony with success at Dublin. She then bred three lovely foals, and was sold as a successful mare.

Mother became known as having a good eye for a pony, and received requests for good mares for English clients, who also wished to breed Connemaras. Sometimes these became British Connemara Champions, the most beautiful being a palomino called Golden Wonder.

Later, Diana rode Twinnie's daughter, Lovely Lady, to be Champion at Dublin. She was by a famous Arab Stallion called Naseel, who was the sire of the greatest show ponies ever bred in Ireland.

Mother became President of the Connemara Pony Association, and an expert on the breed.

When Diana first started jumping, she rode her first beloved pony called Little Star, which was a bit too big for her, as her legs did not reach below the saddle flaps. Diana earned herself the nickname 'I's-Bounces' by our parents, because she got flung into the air as her little legs were too short to grip on. No doubt all the balancing exercises April put us through, ensured she landed back down in the saddle each time. With her fair curly hair spilling out underneath her hard hat (always a hard hat), she shot high above the pony over the jumps.

She started to grow, and the whole affair began to look more comfortable. Alas her best and only pony friend in the world suddenly became ill one night, and died of colic. 'I'll never ride again,' Diana vowed, completely heartbroken. However, she was firmly plonked on top of brother Patrick's outgrown Mick Be Nimble, and Diana soon discovered she had found another pony to love and an extraordinary partnership was born.

Mick came from a great friend of Mother's in Co. Sligo, and was bought as a pony for Patrick. He was a dark/liver chestnut, 12 hands 3in high. He was only three years old, and was already a seasoned hunter. He was trained to follow behind a designated grown-up, whose job it was to look after the small family jockey.

It was his white face and socks that gave the pony character. All the front of his face was white, a very unusual marking. (Usually there is a star or a blaze like an exclamation mark.)

His other feature was his ability to jump. He appeared to have springs on his feet, and simply flew into the air over a pole. Mother brought him home, and called him 'Mick Be Nimble'.

Mick and Patrick learnt to jump proper fences together. He belied his age, and was sensible, kind, and a brave little lion. Hunting over vast ditches were no problem to such a 'nimble' pony; he could creep down the bank, hurl himself over the ditch at the bottom, and scramble up the other side. He sometimes went where the larger horses could not go.

Jumping competitions had just started after the war, when petrol became more readily available, and Patrick and Mick used to enter the children's classes, though Mick was always the smallest pony because at 12 hands 3in (12.3) he was competing in classes for 13:2 ponies

By the time Mick was passed on to Diana she had longer legs, and was 'bouncing' no more. She was developing a 'sticky seat' (would seldom fall off), a very correct position in the saddle, and 'giving' hands over the fences, thanks to April's teachings.

Now she felt the first challenge and thrill of larger fences and got the jumping bug. They developed together, and Mick soon became a serious jumping pony, with the spring of a little lion ... and his little rider loved it! She did not bounce any more, for she found that growing longer legs and hunting helped her balance.

She describes the early days of clinging on tight to a hunk of Mick's mane, kicking like mad, shutting her eyes if the hunting ditch was huge, horrible and deep, and shouting 'Hup!' He always got his little rider to the other side safely, and they came to an understanding – they could jump anything together, and he would look after her.

In the giant, gracious arena at the RDS, for both the Dublin Spring and Horse Show, Diana and Mick looked very small from the stands. They were always competing against much larger ponies, for there was no class for his size. Time after time, they won their class.

Their one ambition was to qualify for the Champion Jumper on the final day (this competition is no longer allowed in pony jumping). There was no thought that the fences would be too big; tiny Mick and his fearless, curly-haired rider would tackle fences that were higher and wider than they were. They found themselves jumping against other ponies that looked more like small horses in size.

The greatest danger to both of them, were the large round poles that were used for the fences in those days and which were far heavier than the modern ones. Mick was a sensible fellow, a hunting pony, and he was going to look after both himself and his little rider. When they were faced with something enormous,

'Hup!' she yelled, and he knew to respond. He could jump the height alright – 4ft 11in was his highest fence (which equates to a full-sized horse jumping well over 6ft), but, for the championship, the fence builder always pulled the back pole of a wide fence, way out beyond the stretch of a tiny pony.

Mick circumnavigated the problem in his own fashion. He taught himself the art of lightly 'touching down' directly on the back pole (landing with his front, and then his back feet, and took off again in a flash) and arrived safely on the grass on the far side, never disturbing the pole. This interrupted jump must have felt uncomfortable for Diana on top, but they were a team, and they always landed in one piece.

They never won the Championship, but were twice 3rd against 14.2 ponies that towered over him. Though she was not to know it, this was the start of Diana's great success jumping, which was to last from 1951 to 1973.

Mick's reputation was well known around the country. One day, after a Dublin win, an advertisement appeared in an Irish horsey newspaper:

FOR SALE
Grand Jumping pony
Related to Mick Be Nimble

Mother telephoned the number given: 'What is the breeding of the pony you are selling?' she asked. There was a short silence on the other end of the line. 'I only ask because we have never known what Mick Be Nimble's breeding was, perhaps you could tell us?' There followed the unmistakeable sound of the telephone handset being quietly replaced at the other end.

We were none the wiser.

When Bunny first went to his boarding prep school, aged eight, he had taken over the ride on Mick from Diana. They were already best friends.

At the end of one Christmas holidays, Bunny and Mick went to a children's meet at Furness, near Kill. Sandwiches and orange drink was dispensed to the excited riders; and the large-sized master, Major Beaumont, gave them a talk on behaviour in the hunting field. He orchestrated the day, accompanied by a few other grown-ups to help. The covert at Furness was usually a safe bet for young children, as it seldom provided a good run. The children usually found themselves riding along the paths from wood to wood, with the odd canter across the field.

However, that day there was obviously a travelling fox passing through. It was early January, the time when some foxes covered great distances to find an unrelated mate.

Away went 'Mr Fox', running straight towards his own home, the not too distant Wicklow Hills. After several miles, the Major found himself with about eight well-mounted children, and no other grown-ups to help. They came to a bog. It could have been a bottomless pit. Over went everyone, except Bunny and Mick, much the smallest pony. Bunny was terrified his precious pony would sink, and flatly refused to cross. The Major was in a pickle – he could not leave one child behind on his own.

'Boy!' he roared across the bogey bog, 'if my big horse can cross with me, you won't sink!'

All the other children yelled: 'Come on Bunny', and over shot the dainty Mick with his precious cargo intact.

On they went a little further until the hounds finally lost the scent of the clever Mr Reynard; and the Major thankfully delivered his young charges safely back to their parents.

At the beginning of one holidays, Bunny had a trick played on him. His friend Mick was housed in the first stable on the right (the stable of honour). For a laugh, a rocking horse was stripped of its bridle and saddle, and settled deep in the straw beside a rather suspicious Mick. 'Mick's had a foal! Mick's had a foal!' we all danced with excitement when Bunny arrived home from school. Not stopping for anyone, Bunny dashed to the stables, quite forgetting that his best pony friend was a boy! Everyone was following on behind to see what would happen.

Lifting him up to look over the door, King, the tall, dignified head groom, showed him the new arrival nestling in the straw. A doubtful look crossed Bunny's brow, and crossly said, 'Don't be so silly ... Mick can no more have a foal, than you can have a baby!'

Everyone collapsed with laughter

'Oh my!' said King. 'The size of him to say that!'

Mick was the only pony that we all rode in turn. By 1957, I had just outgrown him, and found it totally incomprehensible not to retire him at home, happily in a field. But he was only fourteen, and might well have got laminitis (a crippling disease of the hoof from too rich grass) if he was turned out into the fields full time. In truth, he had many active years ahead of him. So, we lost our little companion to lovely family friends near Thirlestane, in Scotland.

But there was a proviso; Mick would be sold cheaply, and not lent (Mother believed that a trusted family must have the right to do what they wished with a pony. She said she would never lend one.) He was not to have to jump the biggest fences any more. He was in semi-retirement, but he still hunted, and did smaller Pony Club activities.[45]

I could never imagine Mick being happy anywhere but with me, but of course he was. In reality it was me who would be unhappy without him.

The start given to the Conolly-Carews both by our teacher April French-Mullen, and by Mick, was surely the basis of any future successes.

In July, every year, Grandmother Lauderdale came over to fish in the West of Ireland, and stayed for the Dublin Horse Show. She brought her butler, Lawrence, lame with a wooden leg; her eccentric cook, Nan; and her personal ladies maid, called Nanny Marsh, so called because she had previously been Mother's nanny.

Every year she hired a car, 'Any colour but green,' she insisted. One year, proudly on the quayside stood a green car. 'Won't use it', she said, and went on strike until another colour was produced.

After the Dublin Show in early August each year, the whole family, with Nanny Maura, the girl groom April, and about four ponies, travelled on the overnight cattle boat from Dublin to Scotland, on their way to Thirlestane Castle for a seven week summer holiday.

While they were away, the remaining mares and one or two horses that had not been sold at Dublin were turned out into the fields, the stables swept out and disinfected, and the walls white-washed. Oats were harvested and stored above the stables, and the muck-heap was completely removed.

The farmhands finished the bringing-in of the harvest; and the indoor staff were kept busy clearing out clutter, cleaning endless silver and brasses, and giving the house its yearly polish. In the kitchen a whole industry was put into gear to tackle every cupboard, every dish, and to preserve the eggs in water-glass, while the gardeners delivered enough of their wares to make jams and bottled fruits to last the coming year.

Eventually, Mr and Mrs Murphy, their children, and some of the other servants, went to Butlins Holiday Camp for two weeks, and had the time of their lives. The housekeeper would be left in charge at home.

The journey by ship was an adventure to us, with ponies, their kit, our luggage, and all but the kitchen sink. It took two cars towing two trailers, and a lorry to carry it all to the boat. On one or two occasions, the whole convoy ran over the odd case when it fell out of a car boot.

Someone was unlucky, with clothes all over the Dublin docks, which inevitably landed up in the River Liffey.

The fare for the horses was £5, and they walked onto the boat via a high-sided gangway after all the cattle had been loaded. They were put below in separate stalls, with the cattle beside them in pens of ten. We would go below to feed our ponies, threading our way carefully among the cattle, several cars, and many other horses on their way to Scotland after the Horse Show.

Ever resourceful, Granny Lauderdale always managed to commandeer one of the two VIP cabins; a great luxury, she had her own toilet. The ship was always full of passengers, many dozing on chairs. There was a restaurant and a bar on board, and the ship usually rolled menacingly on its way across the Irish Sea. We could hear people being sick in the passages outside our four-berth cabin. Even the horses went off their hay and feed on some crossings. (A horse cannot be sick, so they get ill very quickly.)

We were fascinated by the view on each side, as we sailed up the River Clyde the next morning. We were on our way further upriver, into Greenock Harbour, passing the slipways full of ships in all stages of construction, with workers all over the growing carcasses, with welding sparks lighting up the early morning. The long cranes bent and swung. The industry of it all was a wonder to us.

The whole process would be reversed when we returned to Dublin at the beginning of October. The Dockers were obviously fed up with the shouted instructions, and with the amount of our stuff they had to carry to all different parts of the boat (including smuggled bags of Dutch bulbs on one occasion, masquerading as a sack of pony nuts!).

One year, there was a Lauderdale car, four ponies, and fifty-two pieces of luggage to be transported into the ship; with twelve adults in our group, telling them what to do.

'That Lady Carew comes over once a year, causes a strike, and is gone!' grumbled one docker to a bunch of onlookers.

'You're talking to her daughter!' said someone else.

Mother's old home stood up to this friendly invasion each year, with a get together of no less than eleven cousins. Tragically, Mother's brother, Ivor, had been killed in North Africa, towards the end of the Second World War. His three daughters, Mary (later Lady Mary Biddulph), Anne (later Lady Anne Eyston), and Lady Elizabeth Maitland, were accompanied from London by their mother Lady Helena Maitland (nee Perrot), and their indomitable Nanny Boon. Our other Maitland cousins, also from London, added to this soup of relations,

Their branch of the Maitland-line was now the next Earls of Lauderdale. The Reverend Uncle Alfred was due to become the 16th Earl, after our grandfather died. He and his wife, Cousin Irene, were a quiet couple who brought their bikes for a few days holiday. He was a Canasta (card game) enthusiast, which we children had learnt from Grandpa Lauderdale, and which we played in preference to the dreaded Bridge.

One of Grandpa Lauderdale's porky-pie stories backfired one day. He told Patrick and Diana that Cousin Irene had a whopping gap in her front teeth. Hadn't they seen it? The children hid under the table in the small front hall, to observe her the better, and got caught peering up her skirts. 'Yes, Grandpa,' they reported, 'you are quite right!'

These cousins were Ian (the current 18ᵗʰ Earl of Lauderdale); Olga (later Lady Olga Hay (Maitland); Lady Caroline Melitsa Maitland; and Sidney (later Revd, The Hon Sydney Maitland). Their parents were Patrick Maitland MP, the Master of Lauderdale, (later the 17ᵗʰ Earl) and Stanka (nee Losanitch), from Belgrade, whose mother had been a lady-in-waiting to the Royal Family of Yugoslavia.

During the Second World War, Cousin Patrick found himself in Albania, where he reputedly escaped assassination three times in one week, once by hiding in a harem.

In later years, he became a larger-than-life figure, often travelling around in a large Inverness cloak. On a railway station one day, he was enchanted to be accosted by someone believing him to be Charles Dickens' 'Mr Pickwick'.

The three nannies tried to look dignified while they desperately attempted to keep tabs on eleven children. The older children, Patrick Conolly-Carew, Ian Maitland, and Mary Maitland, formed an officer corps, who took it upon themselves to issue commands to the unruly younger troops. Elizabeth and I (Sydney was a baby) were the youngest, and they were ordered about all day long, it seemed. Patrick Maitland (Lauderdale) and Father built a wonderful wooden, two-storey playhouse, which was used constantly, and fairly frequently as our courthouse. Mock trials were held if there was an infringement, like not bowing low enough to your 'betters'. Heinous sentences were handed down, like staying by a hole till a rabbit came hopping by, which you faithfully did for hours, until a harassed Nanny-on-her-white-charger came to rescue you.

So, what with 'torture' (not too bad), and wild children's games, the freedom of Thirlestane was magical.

The children and nannies were divided up into families. We occupied the second from top floor, which was a long corridor called High Street. (The castle had ninety-eight rooms in all, and during the war years a school of 100 girls occupied High Street and Upper High Street above it, without coming anywhere near where the family lived). Patrick Maitland's family were in a flat half way up the turret staircase, and Mary, Anne, and Elizabeth slept in the main family wing.

Many of the fourteen staircases were turrets, and there were so many turrets and towers, it was difficult to remember which led where. One of these had a secret door, where you could sneak down and listen to unsuspecting adult conversation, all the while desperately hanging on to a flickering candle (if it went out, you would get spooked).

There was definitely a ghost, somewhere ... children's imaginations run wild ... but the chief protagonist was a spectre seen strutting her stuff in one particular Upper High Street bedroom. This eerie lady floated about causing family mischief by appearing in ethereal long dresses in the middle of the night, and banging on the furniture. Several elderly relatives declared she wafted in their faces in an extremely upsetting manner; enough to put you off a jolly good breakfast the next morning, they said.

To our disappointment, this lady was kept firmly locked in her bedroom for her ghostly indiscretions, and still is today (at least she didn't float through the solid old walls).

Another turret had a hole in the top floor, where unfortunate prisoners were pushed 100 feet down onto a dead smelly prisoner heap at the bottom, with a goodly, wicked-looking iron spike at the bottom. 'A great way to deal with the baddies,' the elder children pronounced bravely. Us younger ones tried not to dream about it.

In the 1500s, this was usual practice to the enemies who dared to lay siege to your castle. You sent out raiding parties at night, captured them alive, and threw them through the hole at the top of the Oubliet Tower, which was one of the few in the UK where prisoners were thrown to their certain deaths, with no apparent way of escape. Some prisoners managed to dig their way out from the base of the tower, to surface half a mile away near the local village of Lauder. (The exit hole of the tunnel is still there.)

Bloodthirsty stories tickled the imagination around every corner. No wonder the nannies tore their grey hairs out. Where the devil were they to find us?

The domestic side of Thirlestane was run by Lawrence the butler, a tall, courtly man, with a gammy false left leg (at Castletown, some years later, we had a red-haired butler called Carroll, who was dreadfully lame on his right leg. When Lawrence travelled over from Scotland with the Lauderdales, the two butlers would hobble opposite ways around the dining room table, making you cross-eyed with certainty they would spill something).

The other vital character at Thirlestane was Nan, the cook, who was, quite definitely, very odd. She had been there since coming from the Highlands and Outer Islands of Scotland as a young girl. Now she was of indeterminate age (possibly mid-fifties), and terrified the life out of us. The whole family knew she prowled the ground floor/basement area at night with a candle, loudly calling on the spirits to, 'Keep Aweee!' She was thin, and would have been tall if she had ever stood up. Always stooping, she wore small wire-rimmed glasses half way down her nose, and muttered angrily wherever she went.

Unfortunately, Nan gradually developed an urgent frenzy to scrub the kitchen and scullery within an inch of its life every night. This inevitably meant she was unable to get up in time to make the family breakfast.

Granny Lauderdale devised a cunning plan. She installed two buttons (like pedals) on the floor, hidden near her feet in the dining room. Very practically, the first button rang in the pantry to warn the servants whenever the next course was needed. But, after the last course had been sent up from the kitchen (in a small hand-wound lift), Grandmother trod on the second button; this one turned off all electric lights in Nan's kitchen area below.Nan was reduced to candlelight so she retreated to bed. (Though sometimes she walked the cellars with her candle first). In the morning, the lights would be turned on again, and lo! – breakfast would arrive!

Nan's cooking was somewhat 'hit or miss', but she did make the most divine scones ... all day ... every day. Despite Grandmother's pleas to control herself she churned out the hot scones until every available space was full. It was an obsession that we adored, for when we were ravenous we became brave, and appeared at the kitchen window to receive a hot steaming scone and jam.

The only comprehensible thing she ever said to us was, 'Chilly for June'. A conversation was impossible because you often couldn't understand a word. All that mattered was that Ivy Lauderdale understood her.

Years later, Grandmother and Nan were to travel on a bus, somewhere in Berkshire, in England. At least, they were *meant* to get on the bus. But Nan stood in the way, and blankly refused to let her employer on. The bus departed, and Grandmother was furious; but in her weird and strange way, Nan was protecting her employer. That bus had a serious accident some minutes later, and a lot of the passengers were badly hurt.

Another time, Diana was travelling in the car going to the Scottish Royal Highland Show, held in Edinburgh, and Nan was also a passenger. Diana was the picture of elegance in her show jumping outfit, proudly wearing her Irish green show-jumping coat, with the Irish flag sewn onto the pocket (given if you represent your country), white breeches, a stock (like a cravat), black boots with brown tops and riding hat.[46] Nan had never seen Diana dressed to compete. She kept casting furtive glances at her in the car. 'My, you look like a fairy! said Nan. Some fairy![47]

Grandpa Lauderdale once told us a story that one day, there was an old woman who had been persuaded to come to church. She had on her very best starched pinny, but it *was* a bit old. All went well until the congregation started saying, 'Holy, Holy, Holy,' she leapt to her feet, and furiously replied, 'It may be holy, but it's clean!' (We always fancied it was Nan.) I bet he made it up!

The Conolly-Carew ponies were installed in the stables on a steep hill, half a mile to three-quarters of a mile away, near the entrance. The Castletown children suffered most from Grandmother's two golden rules: never to be late for lunch, and always to be tidy and clean.

We trudged from one steep hill (where the castle was) to the other (where the ponies were) each day to ride. But we were always running late for lunch.

At five minutes to one, the four of us hared down the stable hill and accosted the unfortunate retired pony (from the pony and trap days) in a field at the bottom. We all piled onto its fat back (and along its wide rump), and it made a valiant effort to carry us at the gallop up the steep hill to our destination.

Well, you can imagine what happened. The smallest at the back fell off (legs too short, rump too fat). The two at the front got to lunch just in time; the youngest ones, glad they hadn't landed in a cow-pat, ran like hell, and stuffed their riding hats and gloves, sticks and what-nots, into the loop of Grandmother's curtains along the corridor outside the dining room. With no time to put them away tidily, and wash the hands, we usually managed to creep in at the end of the long line of eager eaters.

After lunch, if Grandmother Lauderdale was in a bad mood, she trailed us all behind her as she walked along the corridor tipping out all the contents of the curtains. She charged us 3 pennies for every article; which was interesting since we were lucky to get one penny every blue moon for pocket money, and I don't remember ever having 3 pennies in my pocket. If we did not pay up, she confiscated the offending articles. If you did not have a hat, you could not ride, so we had to be good for days to get it back.

In 1953, while in Scotland for the summer, the three eldest Conolly-Carew children, Patrick, Diana and Bunny, asked permission to be able to enter the Scottish Pony Club One-Day Event Championships, as an entry from the Kildare Pony Club. This was a qualifying competition for the UK Championships held in England (Ireland had no equivalent event of its own).

Thinking nothing of it, they were allowed to compete, and caused a furore when they won. This competition consists of Dressage, Cross Country, and Show Jumping. The scores of the best three were counted, in each team of four. There were only three of them. Patrick was on Polly, with her soup-plate feet, Diana on the chestnut Copper Top, and Bunny was on wee Mick.

The youngest were Bunny and Mick Be Nimble, and they manfully climbed the fences to become the Boys Champions of Scotland, while Diana became the Under 16 Champion on the lovely half-arab all-rounder, Copper Top.

Col. Guy Cubitt, chairman of British Pony Club, and incidentally Patrick's future father-in-law, kindly allowed the team to represent Scotland, and poor little Mick had to bank a few more solid fences. He must be the smallest pony ever to have completed there. (Nowadays, most of the competitors have horses.) They came sixth, out of many teams. The course was so difficult, only six teams managed to finish.

They did much the worst in the Dressage phase; and were in difficulties in the Cross Country, because Mick and Bunny had already had two stops earlier in the course, as they arrived at the last fence. (If you have three stops you eliminate your team.) Diana was standing there watching, as Mick slipped on the muddy ground in front of it, and seemed to have no hope of jumping the fence. She knew him so well. 'Hup Mick!' she yelled (as she had taught him), and the sweet pony responded to her voice and scrambled over somehow, with his rider still attached. They were safely home!

The Irish radio station came to interview Diana, who was left to explain to a confused audience how an Irish team came to be representing Scotland!

The following year, Ireland was granted her own Pony Club qualifying competition for the UK Championships.

Diana and Mick Be Nimble at the Dublin Horse Show, where the fences were bigger than them. Mick was the only pony we all rode.

The first ever Pony Club Championship in Ireland was held at Castletown. The family team won again, this time with a vital fourth member, Gillian Moore on her skewbald pony. The team were seventh in the English final, with Diana still on Copper Top, Patrick on her hunter Simon, and Bunny on pure white Dazzle. And so the Irish Pony Club has continued to hold their own Championships ever since!

10

WALKS AND RIDES, YOUNG FRIENDS AND HORSE TRIALS

In 1953, our practical joker grandfather Lauderdale died of a heart attack while on a cruise with Ivy, and was buried at sea. His tombstone was erected in Jamaica. We would miss having our legs pulled all day long.

There is a Conolly-Carew nonsense rhyme, which is used as a sort of right of passage within the family. This ditty is still religiously taught to all the young in our extended family (including ten children and twenty-one grandchildren). They all know they will be thoroughly tested on every family occasion and so on holidays, at weddings and christenings, the children get into a huddle and begin the joint incantation. With the noise level of an unstoppable express train, their voices get louder, as the excitement level rises towards the middle of the verse ... there is a pause for a giggle ... and they progress in unison to the climax, and then fling themselves about the floor in glee.

If you ever heard it, it starts like this: 'Chick-en-ack-a-chou-chou', and has something to do with 'Hit him on the boco' in the middle, and seems to end up with the poor fellow being quite unable to waddle along.

No – I can't teach it to you! (Your grandchildren will have to marry ours in order to learn all the verses!)

Who started it? Why, the family mischief-maker, Grandfather Ian Lauderdale of course!

Just before Miss Colls, our governess, retired we were all keen to go to dances; parties for mixed ages, from nine to ninety.

There were plenty of 'Paul Jones' for the shy ones, where the girls circled around one way, and the boys the other until the music stopped. It was potluck who was opposite you when you came to a halt, and you had to dance with them. They were enormous fun, as long as you could somehow avoid several of the elder men with red noses, who would clasp you in a canter. Our favourites were the eight-some and four-some reels, and Split the Willow.

Diana was nearly five years older than me; she seemed very grown up, and had her first boyfriend. Often stuck for a playmate at home, I would call out to the groom's children, 'Can you come out to play?'

We used to climb along the outside ledge of the stable block, and leap from pillar to pillar in the colonnades, receiving constant grazed knees for our trouble.

When the boys were home, we sometimes all piled on one bike, and sped down the steep back slope, outside the back door. With a gravelly path at the bottom, we knew there would be endless grazes and cuts when we all fell off. We seemed to carry our wounds around all the time.

While Patrick was at Harrow, his best school-friend was Robin Butler, who spent many happy holidays at Castletown. They were the same age. Robin was very tall, fair-haired, strongly built; yet he had something of 'gentle-giant' spirit about him. We teased him, for he had the most enormous head. He obviously had far too many brains! We were unable to find a riding hat big enough for him. When we insisted on taking him riding, the closest fitting hat was perched comically on the back of his head. We were very aware we must not let him fall off onto his head, for he definitely had an altogether better set of tools in there than us. One of his escapades was to threaten to climb the wonderful barn, near Castletown, in the days when it was no longer safe. We begged him not to.

At school he was a scholar and a wonderful athlete. He was in the Harrow 1st 11 for cricket, the rugby 1st 15, and the Harrow football team; much of his cricket career at Harrow he opened the bowling with Patrick.

He spent twelve consecutive years staying at Castletown for the first half of the Easter holidays; and for the second half, Patrick went to stay with him at his home at Harrow on the Hill. Each day they were coached at Alf Grover's famous cricket school in Putney.

Later, he entered University College, Oxford, where he got a double first, and two rugby blues. He chose a career in the Civil Service, and our father introduced Robin to one of *his* greatest friends, Sir Edmund Compton. This was where Robin spent all his working life, from 1961-1998, starting off in the Treasury. He went on to serve as Private Secretary to five Prime Ministers (Heath, Wilson, Margaret Thatcher, John Major, and Tony Blair). He became the Secretary of the Cabinet, and the Head of the Home Civil Service (1988-1998).

Early in his career, he was occasionally confused with his rather rotund namesake Rab Butler. Somehow Robin still had time to play first-class rugby during these early years in the Civil Service. One day he received a letter which read: 'You have been selected for the Harlequins 1st XV on Saturday. Please be at Twickenham by 2 p.m.'

Underneath, in Rab's distinctive handwriting, was the message: 'Dear Robin, I am not free on Saturday. Please could you deputise for me? Signed: Rab.'

Robin was honoured by the Queen on his retirement, became a Knight of the Garter, and Master of his old college at Oxford, and is now known as Lord Butler of Brockwell. How glad we are that he never fell on his head!

My best and lifelong friend was Deirdre Guinness (now Mrs Egerton Skipwith), from Lodge Park, 5 miles away in Straffan. Deirdre was not an everyday rider, but her house offered other adventures. There was a tree house high up out of the reach of nannies, a switch-back truck run, with hills and troughs, and all things bumpy and fun. There was a rowing boat on the river (Liffey), a whole wing full of precious model trains, and, to cap the lot, her mother Esme (who treated me as one of her own) produced teas like I never saw anywhere else. There were cakes of every colour, scones, hot toast, butter, cream and jams. Heaven!

Deirdre had a governess, Maury, and older sisters Meryl (Mrs Christopher Gaisford St Lawrence), Shaunagh (the late Mrs Tony Aylmer), and brother Robert, who had all left home or gone away to school.

Deirdre remembers:

When I was about six, my mother used to drive me over to Castletown to play with Sally, who was four months younger than me. The Conolly-Carews were always terribly busy with horses, and then there were lessons at home in the mornings with our respective governesses, Miss Morrison and Miss Colls, so my visits had to be fitted around these activities. Generally, my mother and I went to tea and then she and Lady Carew had a chat while we played. Tea, which took place at one end of the dining room on a long table covered with a white tablecloth, was a rather alarming experience as all the grown-ups were there, including Sally's Uncle Ted who, to me, seemed very old. He put me firmly in my place one day, by saying, 'Do have some more scone with your jam,' when I had taken far too much.

When we drove up to the Castletown gates, they were always shut, so we had to stop and hoot three times for Mrs Mooney to hurry out of the lodge and open them. My mother would drop me off at the 'shute', which was a covered wooden staircase straight down to the stable yard – 'So the Carews could get to their horses quicker,' my family used to say. Then I had the problem of trying to find Sally on my own. Great joy if she was in the stables, that was easy, otherwise I had to go up the 'shute' on my own and try to find her.

The 'shute' brought you out on the ground floor of the house, and there was a night-watchman's chair right there, which I used to walk nervously past, as one day Sally had hidden in it and scared the living daylights out of me as I came past. Then I went on up the winding staircase on the stable end of the house – eighty-four steps. I used to count them – turn left, past the lift-well door, very firmly locked as there was no lift, and then the next left was the nursery, a lovely big friendly room with two windows looking over the front of the house.

Sally was always full of tall stories, which I explicitly believed. One of these was responsible for my great fear of the spears hanging along the walls of the downstairs corridor. 'Don't touch those,' she warned, 'they are all poisoned.' Another time I asked her what happened on the other side of the dining room where Murphy's pantry was. 'Don't go in, Murphy keeps a wolf there,' she solemnly told me.

We used to be sent for when my mother was ready to leave, and then we would go to the boudoir on the first floor to say our thank you's. Lady Carew was a stickler for good manners. But I so loved going to Castletown.

Sally and I played ping-pong incessantly. There was a table further along the top passage in what must have been an open hall, but then had odd bits of discarded furniture. Another game we played in the summer was to see how far you could climb along the front of the stable block without touching the ground. This was extremely difficult and I never got very far, but I seem to remember Diana was very good at it.

Diana was always good fun but quite bossy, and I remember one morning she received a postcard with a rhyme on it that is etched on my memory. She told Sally and me that we could not go and play until we had learnt it. She put it on the wall above her bed, it read: 'The little lanes of Ireland …'[48]

We used to play a lot in the hay until Lady Carew found out, 'How would you like me to jump about on your dinner?' she said.

I only stayed at Castletown once, when I was about nine. I shared a room with Sally, who refused to open the window, and I thought we might die in the night

*through lack of air, but there wasn't much chance of that – I remember it was very
cold.*

*I must have been about seven, when my mother (amazingly) managed to
persuade Lady Carew to allow me to ride with Sally. I was terrified, they were all
incredibly good and I was hopeless. The slightest bump or undulation sent me into
paroxysms of fear. My mother refused to believe that I would never make a rider.*

*Lady Carew and my mother were leaning over the fence of the field in front of
the house – Lady Carew in that lovely furry bonnet that she always wore. A whole
group of us came out into the huge field led by Diana. She started to canter and I
was terrified that this would turn into a mad gallop, so I quickly threw myself off
the pony right in front of them. That ended my riding days at Castletown, until one
morning when I was about eighteen, and Sally said she had something 'terribly quiet'
that I could sit on and exercise. We set off and the first thing we encountered was a
haystack that was covered in plastic and flapping in the wind. Well. I just managed
to get past that one, and then went into a field. It was very foggy, I remember, and
Sally explained to me she was going to make a circle and that I should do the same.
When I protested that I was quite sure my horse would want to join hers, she said
'You have to make it do what you want it to do' – which, of course, I agreed with, but
was not sure I could carry it out. So, we went to our separate corners of the field and
Sally says the next thing she remembers is 'Seeing a rider-less horse with stirrups
flapping careering out of the mist towards her.'*

Talking about our early innocent childhood years – how incredibly lucky we were
to grow up where we did! We explored and adored every nook and cranny of
Castletown, and except where we were forbidden (mostly in the servants' wing),
we found fascination and amusement in every part of it; unknowingly treading
in the steps of six generations of curious children before us.

The fact that we lived in a very cold house with such lovely contents, was taken
for granted; not for prideful reasons, but because all smaller children take their
upbringing for granted, wherever they live. Certainly, it was not until our teenage
years that we were fully aware of how amazingly lucky we were to be surrounded
by history, treasures, and so much space and light; to say nothing of our dozens
of helpers and servants.

The outside of the house seemed to embrace us children, with trees to climb,
and a multitude of terrific hiding places. You could stay hidden for as long as you
liked, if you had a mind to ... but a worried nanny soon wheedled you out of your
sulks.

We loved the changing seasons, especially the young growth of trees and
flowers in spring, everywhere the green grass, and the variety of animals in the
fields. Out of the window, at a safe distance, we watched the fierce swans' annual

fights for the coveted nest on the small island in the middle of the front lake. We watched the lambs playing tag and woolly races.

We were assaulted by the aroma of the sweet-smelling lime avenue, which greeted us on every return home, yet we were secretly thrilled by the local night-time tales of fear and ghosts along its three-quarter-mile length. Of course, we children knew it was perfectly safe ... didn't we? Anyway, we were never allowed out at night to see for ourselves!

Looking back on our early years, we realise how regimented was our family life. Daily, we were completely organised, guarded, and secure.

Out hunting, and in competitions,[49] Patrick and Diana prided themselves there was nothing much they would not jump. Outside of their own front door stood the ultimate challenge – the front hedge at Castletown! It was at least 200 years old, over 5ft high, and wider than a motor car, with thick branches that looked as if it would only break if an elephant sat on it. They egged each other on, and waited until parents went to Scotland for a weekend's shooting and fishing. Selecting the bravest in the stables (not Mick, thank goodness, he was too small) they dared each other to jump it. Patrick went first. His horse looked aghast at the hedge, you couldn't see the other side, but obeyed his trusted rider and took off. Well, it simply was not possible! The poor horse fell slap in the middle, and could not move, wedged in by the thick branches. Diana's effort was cancelled as they tried to work out a way to extricate the horse. Unbelievably, the horse had no terrible stake wounds, just scrapes and bruises, and a fear of hedges forever after.

All weekend the children worried themselves sick how they were going to explain the hole in the hedge to parents when they got back. That hole still has not completely grown back, some fifty years later!

So much for daredevils!

With the help and encouragement of Uncle Ted Conolly, Father, Lord Harrington, and Col. Joe Dudgeon (a man who was everybody's font of knowledge on all things to do with horses), Castletown was suggested as the ideal venue for the first All-Ireland One-Day Event for Adults; as well as the first Hunter Trial Championships (for hunt teams of three or four) from all around the country.

These were new concepts on our shores, and were the founding of all Irish competitions going cross country. It was the start of the Irish Olympic Horse Trials, held from 1953-65 at Castletown, with Father as president. (It was also held there later in 1993-95, run by his granddaughter, Virginia McGrath)

The Hunter Trials were a natural progression from the hunting field. The biggest problem was that a normal horse, hunting with the Kildare Hunt, for instance, usually jumped only ditches.

For the first Hunter Trial Championships, each team of three had to jump bushes, hedges, gates, poles (3 miles of solid fences), ditches, and horror upon horror ... a water jump, which they were required to jump into, and out of. This obstacle gave the willies to most of the intrepid competitors the night before, after they had seen the course. The jump was placed in the main stream flowing down to the Liffey, below the Temple, in the middle of the ancient road to Dublin (which runs beside the bank),

Copious 'dutch courage' was required the next morning, as a lot of pale, brave hunting folk tried their luck.

The crowd was huge that day, every hunt had its supporters, and spectators came from every corner of the land. Many congregated by the water jump, for amusement there was endless. The stream had been widened, and given a safe gravel bottom, and the water was about a foot deep. But the horses didn't know that. It looked dangerous. They had been taught to jump over water, not into it. Chaos ensued as team after team arrived at the jump to add their numbers to those who were cursing and swearing, and generally encouraging their horses to go in. As a spectator sport, it was rib-tickling, rather like a good variety show! Many riders stayed there until either they or their horses got too tired to argue the toss. A few managed to get their horses to jump in; and those that did, found it difficult to get out. Some horses stopped for a drink in the middle, or started to paw the water, threatening to lie down. The really popular ones fell off! The water jump judge had a very hard time.

In the middle of this came the revelation that Father had pre-planned a publicity coup for his new jump. Pat Taaffe had recently won the Aintree Grand National, and had been asked by our father to purposely fall off in the middle of the water, for which he would be rewarded with £50. The next day, the photograph was on the front page of the *Irish Times* – mission accomplished! So, everyone went home and built their own water jump and I learnt more swear words that day than ever before!

The winners were the Galway Hunt, who were well trained over stone walls. After that first year, the fences were made knockable for safety.

The family never won anything. The only time there was a home team, Patrick, Diana and Celia had the memorable score of 999 faults – actually they had more, but the scoreboard couldn't hold any more numbers!

The One-Day Event was an entirely different competition. The horses were meant to be specially trained to perform an obedience test in a dressage arena; to jump

any solid obstacle put in front of them cross country, and then to complete a show jumping over coloured fences you could knock down.

Even staying inside the dressage arena was difficult enough for the first-timers; they were instantly disqualified if they couldn't. Dressage was meant to be a series of balletic movements performed by the horse. The effect was not always very balletic, as the riders struggled to remember where they should canter, or rein-back, or where to stop, all the time mumbling instructions to themselves and their mount. One or two riders and horses had competed in England, and knew the ropes.

One such was Penny Morton, from Col. Dudgeon's stable, riding a horse called Copper Coin. Their balletic movements were a joy to watch; he danced around the dressage arena; he flew around the cross country course, which included one jump that required horse and rider to land at the bottom of a very deep quarry in one piece (near the front drive); and they cleared the show jumps.

Later, Copper Coin was sold to America, renamed Grasshopper, and won an Olympic Gold Medal. Penny Morton went on to represent Ireland on a number of other horses.

The more informal sport of Hunter Trialling (with teams of three horses, the winners being the fastest team) soon became the clever art of knowing whose horse was the bravest and liked to go in front, or whose was the slowest.

Desmond Guinness and Diana worked as a team, even when they were competing in individual hunter trials. The key to Desmond's success was the fact that their two horses were best friends.

Diana's horse was my 'Little Donkey', who never made a mistake, but was quite slow. Desmond's horse was beautiful, black, and very fast, but did not like jumping alone. In the individual events, the riders set off on their own at three minute intervals. Off first went Diana; and Desmond's horse was so annoyed his 'donkey' friend had gone on ahead without him, followed his pal like the wind ... and, galloping to catch up, he won with the fastest round of the day!

In 1955, Diana was fifteen, and had Copper Top, the chestnut half-arab pony, which showed, evented, and jumped for the three youngest children in turn. He came second in the Pony Club Eventing Championships in England, and later qualified for the Irish team for the Junior Show Jumping Championships with me, but was considered too small, and we did not compete.

Mainly due to Mother's amazing eye at buying a good-looking horse or pony as it stood muddy and woolly in a field, we both rode show ponies as well, with

Diana winning the Show Pony Championship at Dublin, and I came Reserve Champion another year.

Mother believed you never knew if the next pony you bought might turn out to be a true champion, and she loved the challenge. One of our most successful was a little 12.2 bay pony called Moonbeam, which was bought for me to ride. The newspapers carried the story of the Dublin Show: 'The Pony from the Bogs beats the Blue-Blooded Aristocrats.'

Moonbeam had been bought for £60, and showed such promise that a smaller rider was found. Jessica Fowler (now Jessica Harrington, the famous Olympic rider and racing trainer) completed the perfect picture on Moonbeam, and, despite his miniature size, became the smallest Supreme Champion Pony at the Dublin Horse Show. I was furious having been 'jocked-off' for being too tall and gangly.

Bunny and Dazzle at the Pony Club Championships. He always liked going fast.

When I was aged about twelve, I was asked to ride Col. Joe Dudgeon's famous pony jumper, Sea Rover, who had been ridden to great success by Jan White from England. Sea Rover fancied coming out of retirement, and Col. Dudgeon wanted a light rider, for he had tender old legs. Unfortunately, Sea Rover's legs only lasted for a few shows.

We took the same walks and the same rides that Lady Louisa had taken, and where Uncle Ted's mother, old Mrs Conolly (Sarah Eliza Shaw) used to drive her pony and cart within living memory of the O'Neill family. But before we went riding anywhere, we had to stick to the rules: *Never* jump alone; (and the hard and fast rule) *always* wear a hard hat.

From the front of the house, opposite the old castle, you turned down on the far side of the lake, and followed that narrow field down towards the Temple and the river. Turning left alongside the river (on the original Dublin Road), past the ruined Bathing House, past the perfect trout pool where Uncle Ted used to fish, past the Ice House (where ice collected from the river in winter was stored and used to preserve food in days gone by; and where everyone had lent a hand to extricate some trapped cattle in our day), jumping the small Ice House draining-ditches as you went, and on towards Batty Langley Lodge, the gothic gate house (which we called Greene's Lodge, after three generations of the Greene family who lived there).[50]

In the 1940s, Johnny Greene's grandfather came from Wexford as a skilled ploughman, with nine children to support, they, in their turn, looked after the domain gates beside them.

This lodge had been one of Lady Louisa Conolly's projects; she had planted an enchanting bluebell wood, some 300yds long by 100yds wide, leading down to the river below.(Beside the river there, the remains of a tunnel has recently been discovered; it was reputed to have run underneath the river Liffey, and emerged in the grounds of St Wolstan's on the other side. It is said that the IRA used the tunnel to hide their weapons and stores, but nowadays it provides shelter beside a favourite fishing spot.)[51]

We often rode through these gates (leading to Leixlip), and were reminded that this was the most used gateway in past generations, as it was the most direct route for horses and carriages to Dublin.

We passed the remains of a row of worker's cottages along the estate wall, and on to New Bridge, which we often crossed towards St Wolstans.

Years ago, this had been the last stop on the horse and carriage Stage Coach route from Dublin, via the Strawberry Beds near Lucan.

In our day, the cars that passed us on the open road had to be doubly careful; for they had to keep a sharp eye out for straying animals, like cattle, which had the

Castletown back entrance to Leixlip, showing the Batty Langley Lodge, built in the fashionable Gothic style by Lady Louis Conolly. This was most used in the days of carriages and horses, when it was the fastest route to Dublin. (DG/SM)

right of way on Irish road up until a few years ago. They caused many accidents.

If we did not want to go out of the estate, we would often jump in and out of the Long Wood beside Batty Langley's Gate Lodge; cross the field ahead and, turn left up the Kilmacradock Drive (the present entrance), beneath the line of huge trees, and back home.

From the back of the house, we rode along the garden path for half a mile or so, passing the dog cemetery on the right, and turning right after the bridge into the Great Wood, where there was a multitude of ditches (if we felt like jumping). There were banks of primroses and cowslips in season beside every path, with carpets of bluebells in the spring, and wild strawberries along the banks in the summer. On reaching the clearing, which was the vista from Castletown to Conolly's Folly, we turned left up the View, and reached the Gamekeeper's

Cottage. Turning left again, we rode our 'discovery' ride, where we would push through into the laurels and find old temples overgrown with old arbours and the remains of old seats. These were once clearings and secret meeting places. Although it was sad to see them neglected and forgotten, our imaginations often took flight with lover's bowers and hidden romances; we then rode home, via the garden, through its old double gates,[52] past the Garden House (now a nursery school) and the old vines, and always raided the line of raspberry canes, which stretched more than half the length of the garden near the far wall. There was an acre of outside strawberries as well, but they required you to dismount. Diana, always teaching her ponies tricks, taught Copper Top to eat the grass surrounds and wait for her, while she got down to the serious business of helping herself to the juiciest fruits! I could only raid the nearest strawberries, for without the gift of tricks, I had to hang onto my pony's reins. The ponies always lived indoors in the stables, so to eat the grass was a treat for them too. We then turned back through the Garden Lodge Gate, and rode straight home via the farmyard.

Before the 3-mile cross country track was rebuilt for the following year, we were allowed to follow the line of the old course, and jump occasionally if we wished.

We often rode for miles along the quiet roads, and through the village, passing the old cinema which overhung the footpath, and generally called 'The Flea Pit'. Even then, Celbridge was busy with many shops.

We passed Mary Norris the hairdresser, and sometimes collected our sweets from Bridgman's sweets and cobbler shop, and stopped at Walshe's chemist or Kiernan's post office. We passed Broe's grocer, Ahern's butcher, Kiernan's grocer and fish shop, Murray's grocer wine and spirit merchant, McKenna's biscuits and grocer, Muldoon's grocer, Gogarty's hardware, Young's butchers shop, Reiddy's Pub, and Dun's paper shop. We passed where Guinness was first brewed, and where we took our bikes to be repaired at Mahon's on the old Mill premises.

Diana remembers rows of cart horses tied up outside, with their heads down dozing, or eating from their big leather nosebags, while their drivers partook in a drink across the road. The carts were laden with turf (peat) or hay, en route to the Dublin markets. After stopping in Celbridge, they would cross the Liffey, and continue the 12 miles to Dublin, walking, or at a slow jog. Sometimes, they would be required to take their loads to Phoenix Park, and add them to the long neat stacks of peat piled high beside the main road.

On their return journey, the drivers would be fast sleep on their carts, while the horses towed them home all on their own; they went along quietly and smoothly on the correct side of the road in single file.

On a bad, dark winter's night, local car drivers had to take care to watch out for the looming presence of a carthorse loyally plodding its way home with a sleeping driver, usually carrying no lantern on the back.

We used to roam through the Great Wood at the back of the house, and knew the secret places where the bluebells nodded to us in May time, and where the white and rare-coloured violets lived, the honeysuckle, the banks and ditches carpeted with primroses, and, of course, where the delicious wild strawberries hid themselves.

There was evidence of plants and decorative bushes at the top of the polo field (on the right of the new entrance drive), where lines of horses and carriages would have pulled up to watch the games over a century ago. We remember old stalls there for the polo ponies. Polo was quite the fashion in those days too!

Diana discovered a rare plant one day, and showed it to our neighbour Mrs Pym, who owned a flower shop in Dublin. She and Capt. Pym were great friends, and came to play Bridge with our parents fairly frequently. They were very kind to us children, and we loved playing hide and seek in the dark around their house outside the back gate. However, I once accidently stumbled upon Mrs Pym's Peke dog with new puppies, and got thoroughly bitten through the lip.

Vera Pym was in her flower shop one day, using her usual sharp knife to cut the stems, the knife slipped, and she cut her forefinger clean off. Her assistant came in, took one look and fainted. A customer came in, took one look and ended up alongside the assistant on the floor. And there she was, left to pick up the offending appendage, and drive herself to the hospital to have it sewn back on again.

CUT BACKS, THE FIRE AND THE IRA

In his eightieth year, our dear old (great) Uncle Ted suffered a stroke whilst being driven to Clonmel. His bedroom had to be moved downstairs to the ground floor state bedroom, our library.[53] He was nursed around the clock by two male nurses, who pushed his wheelchair out into the garden every day. Two years later, in 1956, he died aged eighty-two.

He was a kind, gentle man, who had given his own happiness up for the sake of the house.

At his funeral, in the church by the front gate, there was a huge turn out, because all the estate workers defied their own parish priest, and not only attended the Protestant service, but carried his coffin. They wished to pay homage to the man who gave them work through the bad times, after the war, when others were being laid-off, at a sacrifice to himself.

Happily, he had lived to see the rebirth of the good old days at Castletown, with children, servants, horses and ponies.

He is buried in the family plot beside the church.

Talking about coffins, one has to recognise it is not totally unusual to find an empty coffin in Ireland. There are, nowadays, several reasons, quite apart from the olden-day practice of grave robbing or body snatching.

Our father told a story about a funeral he once attended near Celbridge: A prominent member of the community, who was a friend, died and our father was invited to attend his funeral, at a time when it was not all that usual for a Protestant to attend a Catholic funeral.

Feeling honoured to be asked, he attended the church service, after which everyone was asked to follow the coffin to a very special burial place.

A hundred or more trooped along at a fair pace, behind the coffin, and they filed down the length of the village, before turning along a country lane for a mile or so. An iron gate was swung open, and lifted off its old hinges to let the coffin proceed into a large field. Notwithstanding the muddy entrance, or the docks and thistles, the nettles and the odd boulders, the badly shod mourners followed as best they could.

At the head of the procession, the coffin was borne with increasing difficulty and a great deal of tender care by a changing relay of sturdy supporters, trying desperately not to lurch this way and that.

Once the road was left behind, the accompanying Garda could stop regulating the traffic, remove their caps, and join in the procession. Eventually, the rag tag mourners (in their best suits, but now filthy and tired) toiled up to the top of a hill, and sat down at last. They were asked to surround the coffin, which was promptly unscrewed, and the lid lifted – to everyone's despair. Behold! It contained large bottles of Irish whiskey and the best Guinness, complete with glasses for all. The family said a few words: 'Our dearly departed brother has requested to be interred privately elsewhere, but his last request was that all his dear friends should enjoy themselves here on his beloved farm.'

You can be sure that everyone manfully did their duty.

Uncle Ted's funeral came two years after our Scottish Grandfather's unexpected death at sea, and the Conolly-Carew and Maitland families were caught in a double round of Death Duties and Inheritance Taxes. I wonder if he knew that after his death, the great estate would start crumbling around us? I pray not.

Almost immediately, even to us children, it became obvious that the woodland rides were no longer cut back and tidied every year, the numbers of farm workers were drastically reduced, and the numbers of servants in the house cut from twelve to six. But the stable-staff and the number of horses continued to grow, and they began to be a serious drain on the estate.

Mr and Mrs Murphy, the butler and cook stayed on for a little time, but there were no scullery maids, kitchen maids, under footmen or boot boys. The nursery maids left, and money started to get more difficult.

In the middle of this time of drastic cuts, an incident occurred which had a profound effect on everyone. We woke one morning to find the front door daubed with a message, written in large white letters on the old door:

Since the 1920s, the IRA had been known to hold drills and manoeuvres on the Curragh, Co. Kildare, but in the 1950s, they were not believed to be an active threat to peaceful existence.[54] We were told that it had been done by some pranksters, but we could tell that the grown-ups took it seriously and we dreamt of the IRA coming to 'get us' for a long time afterwards.

IRA message painted on the front door in the 1950s. The children were told it was 'just a prank'; but we could tell the grown-ups took it seriously.

During one winter, the stabled horses caught an infectious disease called 'strangles', where the glands in the horse's throat swells and can burst open. The brilliant vet said: 'Stop riding them, take off all their rugs and turn them right out into the fields. They must stay there for about two months, and only eat the grass.'

All of the horses and ponies were used to being stabled all the time, except for the brood mares and foals, and some newly bought youngsters. They were certainly not used to such rough treatment in the middle of a cold winter.

We felt sorry for them, but the large herd of horses were put into the church field, and left to their own devises. They had excellent shelter from the avenue trees, from the big quarry in the middle of their field, and they had the River Liffey to drink from.

As it turned out, these conditions were perfect for their recovery, and they all eventually returned to their stables, tack and fodder, which had been disinfected over and over again.

Nobody knew how the 'strangles' had started, but the cure worked.

During the whole of our parents' time at Castletown, they often had friends staying for a time, as 'paying guests' (PGs). It seemed an acceptable thing to do, to offer to share your house with a friend if they were in need, between houses, or just for the company. One of Mother's greatest friends, Lady Athlumney, was a 'paying guest' during the war, after her husband had died.

In 1950, the Barton family, who owned the large Barton & Guestier vineyards in France, joined us as PGs for several months.

Captain Derek, his wife Joan, and their two sons came after they sold their lovely Straffan House (now the K Club). Christopher and Anthony Barton rowed together for Cambridge in the Boat Race some years later; Christopher also stroked the GB Olympic Rowing Eight.

Julian and Carola Peck and their two young boys were other family friends who joined us in 1956. They took over our old schoolroom (in the main part of the house) and some of the adjoining bedrooms on the top floor. Their nanny had left their baby son, Colin's, clothes drying on a heater overnight, and Castletown caught fire.

To explain how the fire took hold, it is necessary to describe the interiors of the walls: Castletown's dividing walls were made up with large crossed timber beams, reaching from floor to ceiling, from corner to corner, and filled in with brick. Any small fire that started at a section of the wall where there happened to be a wooden beam, would run up the eighteenth-century timber like a matchstick. As this was the top floor, the fire would set light to the roof rafters as soon as it had burnt its way to the top of the wall. Should fire reach the roof, Castletown would be engulfed.

'Wake up! Wake up! The house is on fire!' We heard pounding on all the bedroom doors along the top floor. Miss Colls only heard part of it, as usual, 'What? What? Shall I get up?' she said, confused by all the noise.

Sleepy, standing in short drawers in our doorways, with heavy smoke billowing from the opposite end of the corridor, we got the message from a series of people running, laden with buckets of water, 'Go downstairs, quickly!' That was easier said than done!

Since both staircases on either end of the house were full of running men with buckets, the only escape route was out of the window, via a webbing harness and line, provided in every bedroom for just such an occasion.

For many years, we had looked with great suspicion (and not a little disbelief) on the neatly curled lines of webbing in our rooms. There was no pulley or play-out mechanism attached.

A fire drill had never been conducted! Were we meant to jump out willy-nilly, and slice ourselves in half when we reached the bottom? Had anyone ever bothered to measure the distance to the ground, it certainly wasn't 10ft; it was more like a hundred! It was not elastic in any way (even if it was, can you imagine bouncing back up past your bedroom again!)

This was long before the days of bungee jumping, and, although we prided ourselves in taking on any-sized jump, the idea of flinging ourselves out of the window on the top floor was unattractive, and surely beyond the call of duty. Besides ... what about our clothes? There seemed no point in us arriving on the ground below without something to put on.

The fire was discovered, sometime before 7 a.m., by our mother, whose bedroom was immediately below. She had been asleep, and, strangely, dreaming that the house was on fire. She woke up, and found that the wall behind her bed was creaking and roaring hot. There was obviously a fire above her. She dialled 999, and woke Father, who sprang into action and ordered the farm bell to be tolled and tolled, in order to summon the workmen.

Most of the heavy furniture and paintings were taken out which resulted in some strained backs the next day.

Having raised the alarm, Mother grabbed her jewellery first, and then her precious television! (It was the first ever television at Castletown, in the sitting room next door.)

Very miffed to recognise my own lack of bravado, I could get no useful response from the running buckets as to how urgent all this was. Still unwilling to be separated from my clothes, I stuffed the most important bits into two of the largest bottom drawers of my chest-of-drawers. Knickers, a warm vest, woolliest socks, shoes, and two sets of riding clothes. Added to this pot-puree, were precious knick-knacks, a packet of sweets, and Chunky, the ever-faithful cocker spaniel. (He ate the sweets.)

Firmly left behind without a second thought, were school-books, *Treasure Island*, and anything vaguely pink and pretty.

Pushing and tugging the first drawer out of the bedroom door to the top of the stairs took a lot of energy, and caused more curses from the passing buckets.

However, when I started backwards down the stairs, thumping the drawer down one step at a time behind me, there was now no room at all for the buckets bearers to pass, except by treading in the drawer on the way up (and down)...and Chunky jumped out.

To an eleven-year-old, the thought of living her life without some clothes was a nightmare. All was going well, until the bottom fell out of the drawer. By the time the running buckets had finished, and the size thirteen feet of dozens of firemen from Dublin and Naas had been up and down the stairs over the next few hours, there was nothing recognisable left of the clothes.

Somehow, a sensible person came to my aid and wrapped the contents of my second drawer into a large sheet, tied the corners, and flung the bundle out of the window; where it landed with a splash in the only large-sized puddle in the stable yard.

The old Castle Bell was tolling continuously while our father was in the middle of dense smoke, fighting the fire on his own, with the relays of buckets being passed to him.

The fire engines arrived, but had to send for more hose so they could reach the lake in the front field and pump the water up from there. (There had been a well in both the stable and the kitchen yards, but they had been filled in.)

Knowing what would happen if the rafters caught fire, Father worked for well over an hour, and ended up ruining his chest with the smoke. He was left with a chronic cough for the rest of his life.

Years later, it was interesting to see the old schoolroom wall (where the fire had started) stripped down during renovations; because the blackened timber braces witnessed that the fire had very nearly reached the top.

Major Michael Beaumont was a commanding figure as Master of the Kildare Foxhounds. He and his wife, Dodo, were the 'little and large' of the Irish hunting scene.

As children, we used to watch her walking beside him, and could only conjecture that she was more our size than his. Her petite shape seemed diametrically opposite to his, with his obvious heavyweight enjoyment of food. Did they sit at the same dining table? We asked ourselves. They certainly must have eaten different foods, we agreed. Perhaps *he* lived off a great platter, and *her* off a teaspoon.

He rode the best-looking heavyweight hunters and his bombastic manner and strict control of the field out hunting only added to his 'larger than life' reputation. However, as is often the way, small and determined, his wife kept him in her charge. Dodo herself was the picture of tiny elegance hunting side-saddle with skill and old-fashioned grace, quite correctly hiding her face behind a veil.

Sadly, in 1958, aged only fifty-five, Major Beaumont died suddenly. There was a large funeral, which was attended by all the hunting folk. His favourite horse was led to the graveyard, built on his own land, Harristown, beside Carnalway Church, outside Naas. The horse was fully saddled with the owner's shining boots reversed in the stirrups. The moment was especially poignant when the famous Kildare Huntsman, Jack Hartigan, blew 'Gone to Ground' on the hunting horn as the coffin was lowered into the ground.

The following day saw one of the most memorable hunts of the Kildare Hounds. It turned out to be a day of strange co-incidences, and almost eerie chance.

Patrick, Bunny, and Diana with her boyfriend/best friend Donough McGillycuddy and Desmond Guinness were all out hunting that day and at the second covert draw, Brophy's of Herbertstown, the hounds picked up a scent immediately. Most of the field saw a large fox exit the wood. With a huge joint cry, the hounds followed closely on the trail.

Away they went at speed. The riders found themselves galloping flat out for thirty-five minutes, jumping non-stop. This was no usual hunt, which was normally a stop/start affair, while the hounds cast about for the scent every now and again.

After approximately 7 miles at this hectic pace, the faster horses and riders at the head of the field found themselves halted at the outside wall surrounding the Carnalway churchyard, where Major Beaumont had been buried the day before. They saw the hounds leap over the high wall, and then fall into complete silence on the other side, as they milled around the grave. They could pick up no further scent. It was an extraordinary scene, and everyone went very quietly home.

12

BUYING TRIPS AND BARRYMORE

When it came to finding ponies for her own very young children, our mother knew exactly the qualities she was looking for. She had two golden rules:

A. The children must never lose their confidence, so it was essential that no 'pullers' were allowed; we had to be able give the pony instructions, to kick to go forward, and pull the reins to stop; all the basic rules to be able to feel safe and that we would not be run away with. It is much easier to be brave if you are in control.

B. She would never buy a horse or pony that reared (stood on its hind legs); it was too dangerous.

Our part of the bargain was to learn to ride with 'soft hands' that never grabbed at the reins and hurt the pony's mouth. This way it learned to trust you too.

Later, when it came to buying trained hunters, she believed that the cleverest horses came from the Wexford countryside. She had friends there who looked out for any reliable hunters, suitable for us children and for others. Ned Cash, our local Kildare horse dealer, knew this, so nearly everything he showed Mother was either said to be a Wexford horse, or that it had hunted in Kildare or Meath.

Our part of Ireland was one of the trickiest to hunt over, and required a clever, thinking horse. Often it had to work out for itself the best way to take a particular ditch. All the rider could do was to firstly, give it time to think for itself where it would land on the other side of a ditch, secondly, kick for encouragement, and lastly, fling their weight forward on landing without grabbing hold of the reins, which would pull the horse backwards into the ditch.

Mother's tips on what she looked for in a horse:

1. 'No foot, No Horse' was her motto. Some horse's feet are the wrong shape, and there will always be trouble.
2. You must be able to fit your fist between the horse's jawbones. This provided good breathing room, and made it easy for a horse to be trained to bend its neck.
3. It must not be 'back of the knee' (not a straight line down behind the knees), as this made the horse more likely to' break down' (go permanently lame). A fault often found in heavier horses.

By the early 1960s, we had progressed onto horses, and a proper horse business was afoot. The reason for all the buying, training, and selling of young horses, was to pay for our horses and their competitive needs; besides, Mother and April adored buying and selling, and both had a good eye.

To make way for new purchases, every year after training, the young horses were sold. Most of the buyers were English attending the Dublin Spring Show (in May), and Horse Show (in August). Smaller horses went into Unmade Polo Pony Classes; there were show hunters, and young jumpers with promise. The big money was for the jumpers, where Irish breeding was foremost in the world.

Once a crop of youngsters had been sold, Mother was free to go on her buying trips down the country. These were the days when small farmers could add to their income each year, by breeding from the progeny of an original old farm mare. They would use a local stallion, which either did the rounds of the farms, or the mares were brought to him. A farmer soon learnt that there was a keen market and a good price if he crossed his mare with a thoroughbred stallion.

Most of Mother's young horses came from Mr Costello, of Co. Clare. He kept a thoroughbred stallion for the Ministry of Agriculture 'for the improvement of the farmers' livestock'. He had hundreds of acres of mostly boggy land, with some mares of his own; he also bought in many of the foals by his own stallions.

The youngsters could be seen in the fields, and were herded into narrow lanes, where Mother could choose a few of the three-year-olds for further inspection in Mr Costello's yard.

In the 1950s, and early '60s, the youngsters would arrive by train to Hazelhatch Station. They were unloaded, and then led the 3-4 miles down the hill, along the length of the village, and in through the Castletown gates and up the drive. (Some of them must have been difficult to hold onto, for most had never seen traffic before.) They were immediately put into stables, handled, had their feet done, and dosed with worming solution.

These horses had seldom been touched, so they knew no mishandling or roughness and they usually settled quite quickly.

The worst nightmare was to buy a youngster which was either half-broken, or badly done. A frightened horse will take a long time to train, and can be dangerous. Mother preferred her young horses untouched, and she could guarantee that from Mr Costello.

However, Mother did look elsewhere if she heard there was an especially nice youngster down the country. But it was tricky for her. Everyone wanted to sell her their horses as she was a well known buyer.

One day, arriving at a strange farm with a companion, she enquired about a particular young horse, deliberately not telling the farmer her name, otherwise the asking price would rocket. Mother liked the horse, and they began to haggle. 'I'm not sure, he's a bit "back at the knee", and he could have more shoulder' she started.

There was a pause before the farmer replied, 'Sure, it's only the way he's standing ... I'll turn him around.'

Mother looked doubtful, muttering to her companion, 'Well, if the price is right, I might consider it.'

'Sure he's a grand horse; sure, he'll be a champion. I'll take £200 and not a penny less.' Then the farmer made a fatal mistake, 'Sure isn't Lady Carew herself coming to buy him tomorrow?'

'I *am* Lady Carew', Mother replied, turned on her heels, and departed – no sale.

A very old Irish tradition, straight out of superstition and folklore, but it is still practiced today, is 'a luck penny': A luck penny is a discount on the selling price, a small sum of money given back to the buyer after a deal has been agreed, designed to bring luck to the animal and its new owner. In effect, two deals are haggled over.

First you argue over the price of the horse, and then you argue again over the luck penny. This could be anything from £10, £20 to £200, depending on the agreed selling price. There is no set percentage; it is up to the seller to haggle it down; and for the buyer to haggle it up. Hardened horse buyers love the ritual of it. 'I'll buy it if you give me a good luck penny', usually seals the deal.

Patrick asked to buy a horse called Tawny Port from Chris Collins, a friend and very successful amateur jockey, who also evented in England. It was only a year before the next Olympic Games and Patrick did not have a suitable horse to ride on the Irish Team. Seeing Chris Collins just complete a good cross country round, he asked him if he would sell him the horse he was riding. The deal was done for £5,000, a hefty price. 'Would you give me a luck penny?' asked Patrick, hoping to get a few pounds off the ticket.

'I'll do better than that,' Chris replied sportingly, 'every fence he hits in the show jumping phase, I'll give you £100 off the price.'

Tawny Port knocked down seven fences that day, so he cost £4,300.

The following year Patrick rode the horse at the Olympics, and had a marvellous round. He also came seventh at Badminton. He rated Tawny Port as one of the most talented horses he ever rode, with Ballyhoo a close second.

Eventually the horse retired to hack out with Patrick's father-in-law, Col. Cubitt.

One of the first horses Diana bought on her own judgement came out of a chance meeting with the famous hunting priest, Father McMahon. He persuaded her to drive to Co. Clare (with her cousin, Maureen Owen, for company and protection), so he could show her a nice horse a farmer had for sale.

The two girls turned up at the priest's house, and had to wait a while because the priest had been exceedingly late back from hunting the day before.

'Now, this farmer,' he said looking at Diana, 'I know him well; he's a grand young fella. Ye can get the farmer as well as the horse if you like; he's looking for a wife.'

They piled into the car, and drove a long way. 'How far?' asked Diana. They were on the main road to Cork. His reply was, 'Sure, the further ye go, the mainer it gets.'

She bought the horse, not the man, and called it Darby O'Gill. Diana described it later as 'As mad as a hatter.' So, they were not always successful buys.

One of the early horses Diana trained on her own was a coal black thoroughbred called Jester, which did well in the show ring, and was sold very successfully to Walter Gilbey, of Gilbey's Gin.

The Gilbeys became friends of Diana's, and Walter brought the fabulous Gilbey Coach and Four Horses, plus the grooms in livery, over by boat to the Dublin Horse Show. Every day they paraded the coach and horses around the main arena, with Diana and me on board.

In 1958, Dan King, the head groom, retired to live near Mallow, Co. Cork. He knew Diana was looking for her next challenge. He reported that a beautiful little horse, in a field near his house, had taken his eye. He was bought for £240, and in the autumn of Diana's eighteenth year, the half-wild, grey, five-year-old arrived at Castletown. He was given the name, Barrymore. From the beginning, he had an air about him, something different. He was always a little aloof; as if he knew he was someone special. He developed into a Champion Show model and, once his energy and brains were channelled, became one of the world's best show jumpers.

Diana and Barrymore on the front steps. (Courtesy of L.G. Lane)

He was described, during the Olympic Games in Mexico in 1968, in a newspaper article: 'The most beautiful male was Barrymore, the white stallion from Ireland.' Diana adored him – her all time favourite, though he was not a stallion.

During his first jumping year, the family decided he could be offered for sale at the Dublin Horse Show for £1,500. Otherwise he was never to be sold, and luckily he never was.

Between 1961 and 1969 (when he retired) he had competed in fifteen countries and won in eleven, being placed everywhere except in the Olympics, when he was injured.

He would bow and salute on command (bribed by lots of sugar!). However, his 'compulsive dancing' to music made him unsafe in parades behind the band and his country's flag. He would take enormous leaps into the air.

Diana received a letter after Barrymore had gained his greatest individual victory, the Grand Prix of Ireland, which said: 'I was sorry for the wives and girl-friends of the bandsmen as Barrymore cavorted behind them.'

Tom Tynan arrived at Castletown as head groom in 1957, and his wife helped in the house in later years. They had six children and lived in the basement flat, next to the stable yard. Previously, Tom had trained winning point-to-pointers (racehorses) for Col. and Mrs Newell, of Reedsland, Co. Meath, whose father had been Master of the Kilkenny Hunt in the 1930s.

Tynan had homespun methods to treat the horses. There was his secret bottle of liniment for the horses, which he put on any enflamed legs, but never on a cut. Anti-phlogiston poultices were normal to use to draw out infections, but sometimes he also recycled cowpats for hot feet, and it was not unknown for some legs to be bandaged with cabbage leaves. But mainly he turned out to be an artist at long-reining young horses, training them before they were mounted.

As the years passed, Tynan often travelled abroad by boat and train with the horses he had started off on their careers to become international jumpers for Diana. He proved himself to be a wonderful groom; and even in foreign lands, the fact that he could neither read nor write did not seem to worry him at all.

On these trips, they took most of their own horse food with them, which Tynan guarded well. Mother always made sure he was sent off with his own big tuck-box of goodies to keep him going – biscuits, sweets, and smokes. On one trip, they were on the boat with Marion McDowell's (a fellow Irish team member) groom Danny, who said: 'I'm grand, I have me packet of tea!' That was all he had.

Tom Tynan, his wife and six children looked out from their basement flat onto the front of the house. The whole family was clever; the eldest daughter, Vera, worked in Dublin to supplement the family income, and became a teacher. 'We always had food on the table,' she remembers, 'but money for shoes and extras was hard with the six of us.'

Years later, the two eldest boys owned their own cabinet making company, with forty employees; the younger girls married abroad. But Tom had another extraordinary talent up his family's sleeve.

Their youngest child, Jim, was a curly red-haired boy. He was a child progeny at the piano. We considered ourselves musical, as we progressed through our music exams and played to anyone who would be patient enough to listen, but the sounds coming from the basement was beyond description. Tiny fingers were flying up and down the full range of piano keys; Beethoven, Mendelssohn, Grieg, and even Rachmaninoff flowed through his body as he swayed up and down the bench to be able to reach the notes – the faster the better. The impression that the boy left with us will never be forgotten. Unsurprisingly, he became a well-known concert pianist and teacher.

When Tynan eventually left Castletown, he helped his brother to rear Connemara Ponies in Carlow.

Tricks were not solely taught to Barrymore; Chunky, Diana's cocker spaniel was overweight with all the tit-bits he received from his sit, beg, lie down, and 'dead' postures. His tricks extended to shut the door, big woof / little woof, sugar lump on the nose, finding something hidden, and sit and wait out of sight. The black and white dog was our constant companion around the house, out riding, and even along the roads.

If we were going around the edge of a corn field, Chunky would take a short cut, and 'fly' through the middle, jumping up above the stalks every three or four strides to see where we were. With his long hairy ears flying upwards like wings, his ears were covered in matted burrs, and his long coat had wedges of fur and mud lodged in it when we got home. It took longer to clean the dog than the horses.

He must have sighed at our antics when we built him jumping courses of propped-up books, boxes, and toys. The greatest challenge was to get him to jump something very narrow, like a salt seller. Poor fellow was sent back time after time to do it again. But be careful, as tricks can go wrong.

One of Diana's jumping horses, Pepsi, learnt to do a small rear on command. In an international competition she rode into the area, halted, saluted the judges at one side of the arena and then the Royal or President's Box on the other side. (Ladies bowed in the saddle, and male competitors took off their hats.) The crowds cheered as Pepsi added his own salute – a small slow-motion rear. That was all great fun, until Patrick rode the same versatile Pepsi, in a Three-Day Event. The first phase was the dressage, and Diana was watching. Up the centre line Patrick and Pepsi went perfectly and did an excellent straight halt. Patrick took off his hat to salute the judges and, on cue, Pepsi did his special little rear (expecting much applause). However, a rear is a big crime in dressage. The clever horse realised too late that his party piece was not wanted; he was only trying to please.

The following year, at a show in Scotland, Diana saw a well-known Irish show jumper called Meta being exercised before the Foxhunter (novice) competition, which was a qualifying event for the important British Championship held in London, in October, at the Horse of the Year Show. This class was for horses that had not won more than £40. I was to jump my little all-round horse Paraguay in the same competition.

The family got into a great excitement about Meta, because there was no doubt that the mare was the same one that was currently the All-Ireland Show Jumping Champion! She had a distinctive white sock on her hind leg and a white star on her forehead. Meta proceeded to jump a clear round.

After a family consultation, Diana sprang into action, and objected to the judges, 'As an Irish family and competitor, none of us has ever raised an objection in show jumping before; but this chestnut mare, called 'Lough Foyle' in this competition, is in fact the current All-Ireland Champion Meta!' Diana also said she would contact the Irish Authorities, and said that it was up to them to inform their Scottish counterparts.

In those days, horses were registered to compete in shows under national show jumping rules with only the basic details, such as name, age, colour, height, and sex, recorded.[55] The owner of the mare had declared that 'Lough Foyle' was bred in Scotland, and was a true novice, which they had recently bought for their son. The competition continued, and 'Lough Foyle' won easily.

During the next few days, with the help of Mother, Diana rang the Irish Show Jumping Association, and they told us to object on their behalf. They queried the horse's old owners, who said Meta had been sold to Switzerland at the Dublin Horse Show.

The next big show was the important Edinburgh Horse Show. And, once again, there was 'Lough Foyle'! But the white sock on her hind leg had disappeared, as had the small star on her forehead. They were obviously trying to disguise her! She proceeded to win the Scottish semi-final of the Foxhunter competition. The following day, she went on to win the cup for the Champion Jumper in the show, beating all the top horses over really large fences. Everyone could see she was obviously not a novice horse. The family were greatly anxious. What else could they do? The horse was still competing.

However, by lucky chance, the mare's old rider turned up at the Edinburgh Show. Billy McCully had ridden Meta as a young horse in Northern Ireland with success, before she had originally been sold to a Southern Irish rider. Billy also recognised his previous mount, and informed the judges.

Within a few days 'Loch Foyle' was disqualified from her Scottish successes, and the owner was warned off for a year or more, with much publicity.

However, the crime *did* pay on this occasion, for the very next year 'Loch Foyle' had great success representing Great Britain in the Under 18 Junior European Championships, competing in the wife's name!

COMING OUT AND PARTY TRICKS

Changing Times ❧ *Finishing Schools* ❧ *Changing Rooms* ❧ *Learning to Drive* ❧ *Debutante Presentation at Court* ❧ *Queen Charlotte's Ball* ❧ *Boyfriends and Diaries* ❧ *Prophet's Thumb Mark* ❧ *Lethal Bog Ditch*

The years of 1957 and 1958 brought more domestic changes at Castletown. Nanny Maura caught pneumonia and developed a bad heart, and could no longer manage the ninety-eight steps to the top of the house and, to our distress, had to leave us far too soon. She spent two months in hospital recovering, before she went on to be a nurse in England. Maura returned to Celbridge in retirement, to the cottage and one acre on the Kilwogan Bog Road, which had been given to her father when he retired from his position as groom, by our father.

Aged thirteen, I was packed off to school in England. Miss Colls, the governess, retired to a home for governesses in Dublin, where she kept her RDS Library books and her beloved radio. Diana often visited her for tea and she came back for Christmas's at Castletown.

About the same time, Diana, who was now seventeen, went off to a 'Finishing School' in Paris; a kind-hearted sister, she sent me parcels of French lollipops paid for out of her pocket money.

What is a Finishing School? What did they 'Finish'? Now there's a question! At Castletown, we had never made our beds, ironed our clothes, or even boiled an egg, so why did our parents think that we had no need of cooking, housekeeping, domestic or even child rearing skills? Perhaps they thought we might marry a Duke each. (We didn't! And in any case, most of the available Dukes were somewhat spoilt young men, bent on marrying a fortune of their own.) To our parents, it was inconceivable that once we were married, we would not have tribes of servants of our own. That was how Mother had been brought up, and she must have wanted the same for her daughters. But how times had changed! So, in turn when we disappeared off to get French experience, her only word of advice was not to say '*Je suis plein*', which literally translated says, 'I do not want any more to eat' or 'I'm full up'. Us girls soon learnt that it also meant 'I am pregnant' in French – a phrase designed to put any French Madame into a complete spin. The two Finishing Schools 'equipped' us with *some* French and a lot of fun, skiing, and traipsing around art galleries and museums.

Diana found herself amongst about nine other girls, and after six months in Paris, she now acknowledges she did not learn much. Being strictly brought-up, she was horrified at some of the customs they were expected to learn; the worst appeared to be the French table manners. The same knives and forks were used for each course (and often the same plates). The habit was to wipe the cutlery on a piece of bread to clean them as best you could, and then to rest the offending articles on low props called 'dogs' on the table in front of you, while the next course was piled onto your plate.

Her teacher was some ten years older than her pupils, and her duties were to escort them around the sights, to the theatre, and to the opera. They had the cheapest seats way up high in the gods, but were not allowed opera glasses to be able to see any performance properly.

She taught her girls with absolutely no enthusiasm and it became obvious that she was employed in a job that she completely disliked. This thin young woman was quietly dressed, and the girls wrote her off as a lost cause. She carried all the hallmarks of a future spinster ... or so they thought. To the girl's amazement and disbelief, she went away for a week's holiday and returned proudly sporting an engagement ring.

POEM — DIANA'S FRENCH FINISHING SCHOOL

My parents decided to send me away
To finish me off and to teach me to say
'Good morning' in French, and they hoped, a lot more.
But they didn't know it was on the fifth floor
And by the time you've arrived up at the door
You've nearly collapsed down on the floor.
But the door opens wide and into the arms
Of Josephine you fall, with all her black charms.

She cooks our meals, and a house maid, and all
And in spite of her nails our love does not pall
For the food that she cooks and serves every meal
'Cept chocolate pud for which repulsion we feel.
The beautiful puree loved by Fiona
Is not the same as when served by her Ma,
And even *quelquefois* revolting rice pud
There are faces all round, not as *jeunes filles* should.

The head of the place is Mamselle de Trudon
A terrible Frog, an enormous great Gorgon
'*Venez a table!*' The great war cry we hear
'*Dites donc mes enfants*' is another we fear.
A row is forthcoming, p'haps at night
Fiona, Diana and AP do fight
With brollies and pillows. And why? Cos a bag
On a chair must hang, our dear Di will be shag.

Marie Antoinette is the minion and slave.
And she must tell tales her glory to save.
She is our chaperone, though always lost
In Paris with us, which is much to her cost.
Because we grow angry and growl at the poor thing
When we've walked half an hour to hear a man sing.
She's twenty-three and unmarried which is odd
For a French girl, even with looks like a cod.

Back at home we were allocated new and larger bedrooms. Diana and her fiercely protective terrier Dotto moved into the old nursery, and I was given Miss Colls' room; both were at the front of the house. At last we had views of the sweep of the front drive, the hedge (with Patrick's hole in it), the pointed crooked yew trees, cut and trimmed by hand-and-wobbly-eye, the row of pampas grasses (no longer there) and the iron railings running along beside the drive.

We could see over the front field. The trees' branches were weighed down with age, used for decades by the cattle as a safe haven from the flies during summertime, and the lake where the swans fought each spring. There were grassy humps along the sides, where dredging had left an inviting slalom track for the lambs every spring. We loved watching their antics as they raced up and down the line of humps – it was as if someone had said, 'Ready, steady, go!' and they all started together.

We could look out over Sarah Siddon's Tea House (the Temple), on the other side of the ha-ha and above the wide footpath beside the river Liffey, where long ago St Patrick walked on the old main road to Dublin alongside a companion to carry him across the river in the shallow places. (Sarah Siddons, an eighteenth-century actress, was a close friend of Thomas and Louisa Conolly, and often stayed and acted at Castletown. Her admirer, King George III, had been in love with Sarah Lennox, Lady Louisa's wayward sister.) And we could see far off to Speaker Conolly's hunting lodge, the infamous Hell Fire Club outlined on the distant Wicklow Mountains, a scene of eighteenth-century mysteries and devilment.

Then, ever practical Granny Lauderdale announced she was going to teach Diana to drive. She parked the car in the middle of a large field, explained the gears and pedals, and left her to it. The nervous learner soon got the car stuck astride the only bump within sight, from which Granny patiently extracted the car, 'Just quietly, try again.' And she was away!

In those days, nobody took a driving test in Ireland; you paid your ten shillings for a licence, and the roads belonged to you. Almost immediately, Diana added a trailer to the car, and relieved Mother from much of the fetching and carrying of horses.

What adventures we had! One day, Diana and I set off with the car and trailer to take a horse down country. Our lack of education showed its ugly head, as we perused a likely looking signpost saying 'Cul de Sac'. We had been told the farm was on the first left, so down we whizzed, with the trailer rattling along behind us. Paris or no Paris, we hadn't a clue that the sign meant dead end. At the end, there was no place to turn, Diana had only just learnt to back the car out of the garage, let alone master the considerable skill required in backing a trailer.

We spend a good hour or more unloading the (luckily) patient horse, tying it to a tree, unhitching the trailer, turning it around by hand, and then finding a gateway to shove it into. Diana took twenty attempts at going backwards and forwards, before finally succeeding in turning the car. Then the car had to be driven past the trailer, and hitched up again. By now we were totally exhausted, and it was rapidly growing dark. The horse was delivered rather late. On the way home, driving at night required another new skill, much to do with switches, knobs and levers ... difficult.

A driving test might have been a huge help, but a French dictionary would have been more useful![56]

Driving one summer's day, Diana lost one of the four wheels on the trailer. The tyre had been changed, the nuts had not been tightened, and there was no spare wheel on board. The unfortunate equine occupant of the trailer was thoroughly shaken, but not injured, and luckily was standing on the side, which still retained two wheels.

Very gingerly Diana drove home with three wheels on her wagon, it all seemed to go well, except around the corners. Unwilling to face a rocket about her driving, she managed to come home via a different driveway, keeping the empty wheel socket on the blind side of our parents' view from the house.

Later she went back to retrieve the wheel, having seen it come off in the rear-view mirror. It had bounced merrily on its way, and was found in a nearby wood, some 5 miles away.

By the time I got my driving licence, five years later, my parents insisted that I took proper driving lessons in Dublin. But these proved to be even more hazardous, what with having to dodge the red-haired Instructor's amorous hands. He posed such a menace, that I had to bring a friend as my chaperone.

In 1958, Diana went to London to attend her 'coming out' season. Each year a new set of noble daughters, called Debutantes, were summoned and presented before the Queen in Buckingham Palace; just like many of their mothers and grandmothers before them.

Individually, the court usher would shout out their name, and they would approach the throne and curtsey deeply, in homage to the sovereign. This 200-year tradition came to an end in that year, shortly after seventeen-year-old Diana, her cousin Anne Maitland, and their Grandfather Lauderdale's goddaughter, Zia Foxwell, had been presented.

Diana described the endless queuing outside the Palace, much to the curiosity of passing tourists. Their socially conscious parents seemed to be keen to get in on the last chance for their daughters to receive the upper-class stamp of Royal society.(Perhaps they thought the ceremony itself would automatically bag a coronet of a passing Prince or Duke later.)

The girls would always be accompanied by their parents, and a qualifying sponsor, who had herself once been presented at court. One girl had her great-grandmother sponsor in tow – she was in her eighties, and so frail that she had been granted a special privilege to bypass the queue and enter the Palace through a private door. Incredibly, a whisper spread amongst the other families, apparently the old lady had not been back to Court since she had been presented to Queen Victoria.

The old-fashioned dress code of ostrich-feather headdresses, long white gowns with a train, and long white gloves, had been updated by 1958 to a less dramatic 'day dress with hat'. Parents, who accompanied their daughters, were also told what to wear. There were moustached fathers in top hats, black or grey, tailcoats, grey waistcoats, and striped trousers. Some were military men and followed the instruction that swords should be worn; mothers were swathed in mink coats.

The Debutantes themselves wore flared or gathered dresses, with calf-length skirts in all colours. But for that year, light wild blue silk was voted the favourite; it was worn with long kid gloves, and a closely-fitted petal or feather hat. Hairstyles were mostly short, curled, or styled in a bouffant.

When Diana arrived at the Palace she was handed two embossed cards with her name. Her official court summons was checked, and her parents were swept away to be seated in the audience section of the Ballroom. She handed the first card to the Lord Chamberlain (Head of the Queen's household) on entering the ballroom, and sat with the other girls waiting her turn. At last, the court usher shouted out 'The Honourable Diana Conolly-Carew.'

Diana remembers:

> *I walked forward towards the dais where the Queen and Prince Philip sat on twin seats under a crimson canopy, with the Queen's aunt, Princess Alice of Athlone sitting on a lower dais to the side. The Mistress of the Wardrobe, and several Ladies in Waiting were seated behind the royal party.*
>
> *I had rehearsed it all for weeks beforehand. I did my deep curtsey to the Queen, and took three steps sideways to curtsey to Prince Philip.*
>
> *I then handed over my second card, and passed through into a reception party being held in the state rooms next door.*

The curtsey itself started off as a wobbly art, which had to be mastered beforehand. The technique involved a leg-lock; the left knee locked behind the right knee, allowing a graceful slow descent, with head erect and hands by your side. On Presentation Day, any tendency to wobble was definitely frowned upon, after all you had a highly attentive and critical audience. The grand-dame of the Debs' Curtsey was a Madame Vacani in London, she had taught the technique to generations of nervous girls.

One mischievous participant in that last Presentation ceremony described her moment of royal approval, 'I stood for a split second in front of the Royal Family on the dais, before dropping down to perform what must have looked, from the rear, very like a hen laying an egg.'

At the reception in the magnificent state rooms afterwards, the girls were reunited with their parents, and politely sipped tea and ate chocolate cake.

The point of all this was for a young lady to gain entrance into the so-called rarefied life of the Court Social Scene. Had she not been presented at Court, she would be excluded from the Royal Enclosure at Ascot, and other sporting events including Members Tents, Royal Garden Parties, Cricket at Lords, the royal enclosure at the Henley Regatta, and the best seats at Wimbledon. Official Passes to the Royal Enclosures, as well as to each other's 'coming out' dances had to be approved and issued for events throughout the season. There was no sneaking in.

In 1958, some 200 girls stayed in London to attend parties and the endless succession of events, which made up the season; they often found it exhausting, and it seemed like a full-time job.

The rest of the Debs returned to their homes in the country for their own dance, and many did not complete the full London Season.

There were three extensions to the London Season. First there was the Debutantes' 'coming out' dances were held in their own houses around the country, where neighbours were roped-in to accommodate weekend house-parties of invited guests ... very often total strangers to the host and hostess. Then secondly, the Irish Season was held during every Dublin Horse Show week at the beginning of August. Then, finally, the Scottish Season directly following, in August and September, with Grouse Shooting, Highland Games, and Highland Balls. Most girls went to them all.

Almost all of the London girls held their dances in the big hotels, and some had more than one. Diana and her cousin Anne shared a dance at the Hurlingham Club, and a second during the Dublin Horse Show week, at Castletown.

The Season in Scotland was very different from London. Many of the Scottish Debs curtseyed to the Queen at Balmoral. The Royal Caledonian Ball was held in London, in May, shortly after the Queen Charlottes Ball, at the Grosvenor House Hotel. This had all the formal splendour of Highland evening dress. The men wore kilts, sporrans and ceremonial daggers in their socks, with 'all orders and decorations worn'. The girls wore tiaras, full-length dresses with their clan tartan sashes worn from the waist, across the breast, and fastened with a large brooch on the left shoulder.

Being half Scottish, Diana and her cousin Anne were both chosen to dance in the demonstration set reels, which involved many rehearsals beforehand, even though they already knew the steps. As the swinging, daintily balletic sweep of the four-some and eight-some reels kept the dancers on the balls of their feet, their fast light joyful footfalls wove their patterns in and out of a circle.

In truth, most Debs did not find a husband during the season, but many cemented life-long friendships. The season was a sort of club; they were all in it together, there were good moments, embarrassing moments, and good to laugh and look back on years later.

The last comment we should leave to the *Daily Express*, which wished to remember the passing of the Debutante era. They ran a competition to write 'An Epitaph for a Deb.' The winning lines published were:

> A sparkling debutante lies here,
> Daddy found her very dear.

Queen Charlotte's Ball originated during the eighteenth century, when wigged aristocrats accompanied their daughters to be presented to Queen Charlotte and George III.

The ball was held towards the end of May, and was the second most important event in the Debs' busy calendar (after the Presentation itself). It was the first spectacular ball of the season, and was treated as the court's official Initiation Ceremony. Always held in the Great Room at the Grosvenor House, it was staged as a re-enactment of Queen Charlotte's Ceremony of the Birthday Cake.

A chosen few were selected to parade down the staircase, two by two, in waves of white, and to escort a vast cake down the length of the ballroom. It seemed a somewhat feudal custom as Queen Charlotte was obviously not present. The rest of the Debs found themselves obliged to curtsey in ranks to the cake as it passed by.

The girls attended the ball with their parents in tow. One distinguished guest was cruelly described as wearing a tiara of jewelled feathers, apparently 'like a headdress reminiscent of some celestial poultry yard.' The fathers, by tradition, tentatively escorted their daughters in the first dance.

During the earlier years (the 1950s and '60s) it had been all the rage for young girls to keep lockable five-year dairies, and keep their intimate secrets safely hidden from marauding schoolmates or teasing siblings. Girls read their juicy passages out to trusted friends (usually school-friends), who gasped at their shocking antics; though the less gullible secretly thought that most of it was pure wishful thinking! Most of these diaries were never completed, simply because the re-reading of your imagined indiscretions four years later, became an obvious proof of your state of juvenile make-believe; too painful to own up to, while you were, by now, growing-up.

However, letters exchanged between the sexes were an important backup to your stories. Our early teenage years were filled with the odd family dances, and shy friendships with neighbours' sons who were on the same circuit of parties, sports days, and hunting. It was not at all a case of us picking out a handsome 'fella'. In truth, the boys had the field to themselves, and you felt a quiet acceptance mixed with a certain glow of relief when someone you knew quietly took your hand and offered to take you to the food table for something to eat, as well as dancing with you for most of the evening. There was nothing sensational about it all, we were all very young, and only too grateful not to be deemed a wallflower. *If* that person liked you enough, he might write to you while he was

Father, aged ten, on a visit to Castletown, *c.* 1915. His mother, Catherine Conolly (5th Lady Carew), is sitting on the right with his grandmother, Sara Eliza Conolly (Shaw) and his Neville cousins. (Courtesy of Chris Shaw)

William, 6th Lord Carew and Lady Sylvia Maitland hunting with the Lauderdale Hounds in Lauder, Berwickshire, Scotland. This photograph was taken just after their engagement was announced.

The wedding at St Margaret's Westminster of 6th Lord and Lady Carew, with Ormerod twin cousins as pages. (Courtesy of Portman Press Bureau)

The front gate, drive and church at Castletown.

The indoor staff awaiting the arrival of our parents. The housekeeper was Mrs Crookshank, shown here with her two dogs which are buried in the pet cemetery beside the garden path. (Courtesy of Chris Shaw)

Parents dressed for hunting with Patrick in the pram, with Father's youngest brother Uncle Peter Carew and Aunt Bar.

Major E.M. Conolly (Uncle Ted), our great uncle, who owned Castletown from 1900-1956. He is riding to hounds with his hunter, which was destined to pull the plough when it retired.

Father driving the tractor during the Farming Strike of 1946, with a police escort. Tom Mooney is on the far right. (Courtesy of the *Irish Press*)

Our parents at Queen Elizabeth's Coronation in 1952, where all the guests wore their coronets. (Courtesy of Norman Van Dyk)

Our mischievous grandpa, the Earl of Lauderdale, with Diana riding piggyback.

The wedding of the Hon. Patrick Conolly-Carew and Celia Mary Cubitt, 1962. Gerald Conolly-Carew was best man and the bridesmaids were Diana Conolly-Carew (back, far right), myself (sitting on the left) and Camilla Cubitt, now HRH Duchess of Cornwall (back, far left).

The engagement of Sarah Conolly-Carew and Ian Macpherson, taken on the front steps of Castletown.

The wedding of the Hon. Sarah Conolly-Carew and Ian Macpherson at St Bartholomew the Great, Smithfield. (S&G)

A house party for the Dublin Horse Show. Guests included: Edmond, Lord Fermoy; Patrick; Tim Long; Jeremy Smith-Bingham and Reg Hanbury. Sitting on the side: myself, Diana, Oliver Worsley (brother of the Duchess of Kent) and others. Seated: Bunny, our parents, Lady Mary FitzAllan Howard and others and Chunkey, our cocker spaniel.

Diana and Desmond Guinness in fancy dress. (Courtesy of *The Irish Times*)

away at school. How exciting! But you had to be aware of what was called 'letter escalation'. What started off as 'Dear ...' in the first letter, would end with 'Love from ...' A girl would be careful to answer with exactly the same greetings. The actual contents of these letters were often completely mundane ... 'We had rugby today. I scored a try' (as if).

The second letter would be 'Dearest ...', followed by 'Much Love.' And on it would go until you had a very much more daring 'Darling ...' and, 'All My Love'; all in the space of one term-time. How lovely! A girl might think. You soon came down to earth with a bang, however, during the next holidays, when you went to the next social occasion and found yourself face-to-face with the same sweet boy. You hardly recognised each other. His face had now erupted with acne, and it looked suspiciously as if he was getting ambitious enough to want to grow a few untidy whiskers in odd places around his face. You, in the meantime, had shot up and were looking most uncertain; knowing that you looked decidedly gangly, and not at all comfortable about where to hide away your ugly larger hands and feet. Both of you started to look at the other in a new light that wasn't all roses.

Occasionally you found a boy at Harrow was writing to a girl at my school. Sometimes the boy concerned was too shy or too inexpert to compose his own letters for himself; and the same often applied to the object of his affections. Years later, brother and sister compared notes, and found out that Bunny had been writing a letter for his friend at Harrow, while I was composing the reply from his girlfriend! Both Castletown siblings were so busy inventing feelings to put down on paper for their respective friends, they had little regard to the safer slower method of not writing 'Darling' in the fourth or fifth correspondence. Unsurprisingly, that particular friendship did not last the next holidays either.

Diana has always been a letter-writer, and once memorably caused chaos and not a little offence by writing to two boyfriends on the same day, and putting the letters into the wrong envelopes. She never made that mistake again! When she was a little older, her teenage boyfriend was a more constant and caring person, with beautiful manners.

Donough McGillycuddy lived locally, near Kill. He was an only child until ten years old, when a brother was born. He had many Kennedy cousins, who attended the same parties, and often the same hunts as the Conolly-Carew children. Donough was keen on beagling (on foot), as well as foxhunting. Currently, he is the head of the old Irish clan McGillycuddy of the Reeks. His grandmother's cousin, an Australian, was known as 'Banjo' Patterson, who wrote many ballads including, *Waltzing Matilda*.

Donough's Kennedy uncle owned Weston Airport and was chief pilot when Aer Lingus was first formed. Diana soon became intrigued with the extraordinary relationship he had with his mother. She seemed very dramatic and star-like, and rather scary; 'Shush!' she would say crossly to the young – they were obviously disturbing her by their very presence. Donough was trained to call his mother Tiggie, rather than Mummy! It was a progressive type of bringing-up that was a constant surprise to Diana.

They too wrote to each other, but theirs lasted for several years as she grew up, and a lot of her memories are now taken from these letters. They have been kept and treasured by Donough, who recently produced them from South Africa, where he now lives.

He was a great pen pal, with long letters following his school exploits and discussions about when he and Diana might meet again. He was not on the horse jumping circuit like Diana, who found that her highly competitive side provided a totally separate life from all the rest of her friends. Through all her teenage years, she poured out her thoughts in these letters, including comments on her French Finishing School, her 'coming out' season in London, and the highs and lows of her competitive career.

Re-reading them now, she admits she lived very much in her own world, with a quiet dreamy mind. Although later she had one boyfriend after another, she was quite shy, and always felt surrounded by lovely people, animals, and surroundings – all the time accepting the home discipline without thought. While other girls of her age liked to gossip and tell the latest scandals, Diana did not seem to notice.

In my turn, from the age of fifteen, I was allowed to go for a meal and to the cinema in Dublin, by one or a group of Trinity friends. This was the only entertainment around, other than organised family parties a few times a year. The only other excitement was Alfredo's, the daring nightclub off the Quays. But, this was accepted as being far too grown-up and very strictly out of bounds until you were older.

At eighteen, Diana was given a life membership to the Royal Dublin Society, which cost £24 3s, and our parents bought her a hunter at the RDS, Ballsbridge Sales, for 170 guineas. He was a seven-year-old chestnut gelding named Simon, about 16 hands, with a hollow scaring on his front shoulder – a well-healed old injury. He also had an indentation you could fit your thumb into, called a 'Prophet's Thumb Mark', on his neck. In old folklore, this was a sign of an enchanted horse. Horsemen often took this symbol seriously, as a lucky sign of an exceptional horse.

Her first full-sized hunter had ideas of his own though. The first time she rode him with the Kildare Foxhounds she was wearing her newly acquired Hunt Member's coat, and Simon bucked her off into a large puddle in front of about 100 other riders.

He learnt to do one amazing thing. Out hunting, if rider and horse could not get over an obstacle together, he would wait like a statue while Diana dismounted and scrambled to the other side. She would than call him over and he would push his way through on his own, before waiting patiently while she remounted, despite the noise of the chase and galloping horses around him.

Simon proved to be very versatile. One year, Patrick rode Simon on the winning Kildare Pony Club Evening team at the Irish Championships; and the following year Diana was winner of the individual Irish Pony Club Associates Championship with him.

When the boys came back from school in the holidays, Diana lent Simon to Bunny for a day with the Meath Hounds. As luck would have it, the bank of a ditch gave way as they took off, and despite a huge effort, Simon landed short on the far bank, and slipped backwards into the ditch, throwing Bunny clear on the far bank.

A ditch can be a dangerous jump if you land in the bottom with a horse on top of you, scrabbling to get out. Unbeknown to anyone, this was a lethal bog ditch, with deep water and sinking mud at the bottom. Simon landed on his feet, but immediately started to panic, because he was sinking fast. Bunny crept down the bank, took hold of the reins, and held Simon's head above the water as he sank. Luckily, the Meath Hounds turned towards them, and a message that a horse was trapped in the bottom of the ditch, was relayed to the Master, Col. Joe Hume Dudgeon. He and several followers came to help, while the hunt continued. Under Col. Joe's directions, plenty of reins and stirrup leathers were tied together, to form a sling to fit under the sinking horse. Someone jumped in, risked being trodden on, but managed to feel around the horse's girth to fix the sling. Everyone pulled, and the dear horse was pulled out, plastered in mud, cold, and shivering badly.

Most people were shortly reunited with their bits of tack, and went off to catch up with the hunt; but not the Colonel. He insisted that Simon be led to a nearby pub, where he poured a very large whiskey down the horse's throat. Then, covered in rugs and bandages, he was taken home in his trailer. Simon had swallowed a lot of water; however, his legs were unhurt. He was fed on soft food for several days, and put in a paddock each day instead of taking exercise.

Two weeks later, Diana and Simon appeared out hunting, everyone was delighted to see the old hunter again and Simon was excited to be back. Away went the fox, away went the hounds, away went the field (the riders), but Simon refused to go within several yards of the very first ditch, even with other horses giving him a lead. Diana patted him and took him home.

Later, she telephoned Col. Dudgeon, and told him what had happened. He knew of the special bond between Diana and her horses.[57]

'Don't get upset,' said the great Horsemaster, 'Simon has great confidence in you. He knows he is the best. He has simply lost his nerve temporarily. Do *not* jump him at home, but *do* take him out hunting two or three days each week. Make a big fuss of him, plait his mane, dress both of you up in your best, and go to the meet. Sit around, and when the hounds move off, put him back in the trailer, and take him home. Do it again; this time ride as far as the fox-covert and wait while the hounds hunt in the wood. Tally-Ho, away goes the hunt, but you bring Simon home. Keep doing that for several more days. The next stage, is to set off with everyone else at full speed, with Simon enjoying the gallop; but do *not* go anywhere near the first fence. Take him home again. After about four more outings, Simon can start hunting very carefully.'

Lo and behold, Simon sailed happily over about four small ditches, and went home again.

Diana rang the Colonel to thank him. 'Well done', he said. 'Now don't take him for a week, get him very fit and fresh, but don't jump him at home. Then you can ride him as before, but don't attempt something huge.'

Simon was thrilled to be allowed to hunt again. The 'gentleman' had regained his courage, and was as good as ever.

For fun one day, she entered him as a Show Hunter at Balmoral Belfast Show. The two male judges looked at his face, and looked again. 'Very sorry', said Diana. She had decorated his forehead with a little star ... with her lipstick! He got no rosette that day.

He had his own laugh another day; he had been memorably entered in the Ladies Side-Saddle Class, with a very smart expert on board, but he wasn't having any of that and he bucked so much he was disqualified. Diana once had a bet she would hunt him in a headcollar, but Mother forbade it.

14

HUNTING

The winter of 1957/8 arrived, along with the news that Diana was to become the Joint Master of the North Kildares, a local Harrier pack of hounds, which were stabled at Straffan House in three old Bear Pits. This was the same hunt that our father had served as Joint Master with Col. Dudgeon after the war.[58]

Coming just after Diana's Debutante season, the English social newspapers got hold of the story. This was something unusual! There was a lovely picture of Diana and Simon on the front of *The Tatler* magazine, under the heading 'The Youngest Master of Hounds in the World.' She was eighteen.

To go hunting with a pack of Harriers was less grand but more fun and social than the Kildare or Meath Foxhounds. The hounds chased hares, foxes, and even deer (and on one memorable day, all three). They were less organised, and hardly ever had a 'kill'.

One year, after the Hunt Ball, hounds were put into a field of kale. There was no sound from them for a long time; then there was a burst of music as somebody's favourite cat shot up a tree! That was not allowed.

It was a very small pack of hounds (twenty couples), which hunted twice a week from late October until the end of February, running across the country which still had no wire in the fences in those day. The main difference was that with Harriers, you would be sure to have a run. There were always hares about, even though they usually ran around in a great circle. It was entirely possible to stand on the top of a hill and watch the hare and the hounds run around the base.

There is the story of the eleven-year-old son of the Master of a different Hunt, who had been given a brilliant new pony, and on his first hunt his father's directions were to closely follow the whipper-in. Off went the hunt, and, as luck would have it, the whipper-in's horse fell into a deep ditch. The rider was still on board; hanging around the horse's neck, with his breeches in disarray and slipping a good deal further down his body than they ought. The small boy had been following too close behind, and couldn't stop. In an instant, light as a feather, the pony jumped on and off the whip's exposed white bottom, and crossed safely. All ended well. The whip and his horse managed to clamber out of the ditch. But he was left with perfect hoof-marks on his posterior.

In previous years, when Desmond Guinness became Joint Master of the North Kildare Harriers, he was a stranger to the countryside and had no trailer. His contribution was to pay for some of the food for the hounds, part of the wages for the whipper-in, and to stable one of the hunt horses at Leixlip. With no transport, he had to hack his own steed to the meet twice a week, leading the Huntsman's horse. Having only two hands, it was difficult because he had no clue where he was going. With the reins of both horses in one hand, and a map in the other, he would set forth, always hoping no signposts had been turned the wrong way around, which only went to make the whole exercise highly confusing.

The other Joint Master, Patrick Ellis turned up one day at the meet on time, with an empty trailer. 'Where's my horse?' asked the huntsman, looking vainly in the back. Slight oversight! Nobody minded. Everyone went back to the inn for another drink while it was sorted out.

The meet was usually at a pub, in the days when drinking hours were not restricted. People imbibed both before and after the hunt. But after their hard day's hunting, we never kept our horses waiting long hours in a trailer before returning home.

One year, Mother broke one of her own golden rules by agreeing to lend my beloved Paraguay to the Kildare Master's daughter, who had no regular horse of her own; I was away at school. His nickname was 'Little Donkey' because of his colour, and his short legs. However, the family who borrowed him had a habit of leaving their horsebox outside the pub after the hunt and drinking for hours. After this treatment, twice a week for two weeks, poor 'Little Donkey' went into a rapid decline, refusing to eat, and beginning to look ill and thin. We took him home, where he immediately ate again, and was never lent to anyone else. He had pined, and could not put up with this sort of treatment. (Sadly many horses were forced to.) He stayed with us until he died many years later.

Other Hunts

Kildare Hounds (started by our ancestor Thomas Conolly at Castletown)
>Masters – Sir George snr Lady Brooke, Major Beaumont, followed
>>by Thomas Long.
>Huntsmen – Jack Hartigan and Thomas Long.
>Whippers-In – Eamon Dunphy, J. Lenehan and M. Hartigan.
>Numbers – seventy-one-and-a-half couples of hounds.
>Hunted – four days a week.

The Ballymacad
>Masters – Mr and Mrs C. Cameron.
>Secretary – M. Gilsenan.
>Numbers – forty-four couples.
>Hunted – two days a week.

Meath Hounds
>Masters – Lt Col. Joe Hume Dudgeon, Brig. B.J. Fowler,
>>Capt. R.P.H. Elwes.
>Secretary – Major F. Leyland.
>Numbers – forty couples.
>Hunted – three days a week.

North Kildare Harriers
>Masters – *Previously*, Lt Col. Joe Hume Dudgeon, Lord Carew,
>>Mrs Nancy Connell. *Later* P.J. Ellis, Hon Desmond Guinness,
>>Diana Conolly-Carew.
>Secretary – Mrs P.D. Ellis.
>Numbers – twenty couples.
>Hunted – two days a week.

Tara Harriers
>Masters – G. Briscoe Capt. S.H. Walford
>Secretary – Mrs Briscoe
>Numbers – nineteen couples.
>Hunted – two days a week.

Fingal Harriers
>Masters – R.N. Craigie, Mrs H. McDowell.
>Secretary – Mrs Craigie.
>Numbers – seven couples.
>Hunted – two days a week

Those not hacking to a meet, would turn up in all sorts of conveyances. Small ponies clambered out of the back seat of cars; flat-backed vans with no sides, with a horse swaying precariously behind; a horse tied to the bumper of a car (not too fast); a cattle lorry with the horses' heads out each side. Perhaps, the horses were too tired to notice the extra swaying on the way home after a final session in the pub at the end of the day?

Generally, huge fun was had by all, and nobody bothered much about dressing smartly. The masters and whipper-in for a Harrier Pack wore green hunt coats with shiny hunt buttons, but the rest of the field could be in anything. There

Lawn Meet of the Kildare Hunt at Castletown. The huntsman Jack Hartigan is in the centre, with our neighbours, Henry and Charlie Clements behind him.

would be Hunt Members in tweed jackets (strictly no pink (red) coats), the local farmer's boy with his wellington boots on his old cart pony, the odd gypsy pony, a racehorse qualifying for a point-to-point, the vicar on his trusty cob and the lord of the manor with his children.

The 'cap' money for the day's hunting was 2*s* 6*d* and the annual sub was £10.(Nowadays, it can cost £60 for a single day's hunting). The Hunt Secretary collected the 'cap' money and carried a lot of silver in her pocket to give out to the 'herds' or to the farmers.

In winter, the cattle were usually sold after fattening on the rich Kildare or Meath grass. When the Hunt was nearby, these animals had to be put into fattening sheds, or smaller fields out of the way. This was a considerable inconvenience for 'the herd'. When the Hunt passed through the master's land, he would hold open a nearby gate, and get his tip, 2*s* 6*d* or 5*s*. 'Sure, I'll patch the gaps, Sir!' he would say, meaning the holes the Hunt followers had left in his hedges.

The North Kildare Harriers often hunted all day long. There were many strong hares, which proved almost impossible to catch and frequently the hounds had little rest. We would hack for miles to meets, and home again. It bears little relation to the distances our ancestors used to ride in order to hunt, or even ride to town for some shopping,

The ride from Dublin to Castletown was an hour on a fast horse, and two hours at a more leisurely pace, now it is only thirty minutes by car. In the eighteenth and nineteenth century, they often rode 20 to 30 miles to a meet, and back again at the end of the day. Sometimes, the horses went up with grooms the day before, and were stabled at the meet, while the riders arrived by carriage on the day.

In our time, if a horse tired or was a bit lame before the end of the day, we had to stop and try to work out where we were, and the shortest way home. It is a lonely old road if you make the journey 10 miles longer by setting off in the wrong direction. I have absolutely no 'bump of locality', but soon learnt the best method was to drop your reins and allow your horse's instinct to take over. It was more likely to know the way home than I was. This method didn't always work though. If the horse was lame, you had to get off and walk. If the horse was seriously lame then a local farmer would put it up, for it to be collected the following day.

After a good bath, there would be a boiled egg for tea in the dining room on hunting days. Hungry and tired, you imagined it all the way home. But your horse always came first. It had to be washed down if the legs were muddy, offered another drink, lightly tied up and 'thatched' with straw underneath his rug if he was still sweating, given a soft meal (hot bran mash) while you paid attention to see if there was any cuts or scrapes, then bandaged if necessary, before being given a full haynet. Then the eggs and lots of sweet tea for you!

Two hours later, your horse was given his main meal. (It is important not to feed a horse a big meal immediately after a hard day's hunting.) The horse was always checked again late at night.

When the trailer was used for far away meets, the horses saddle would be taken off, and replaced by a sweat-sheet and light rug to keep it warm. Just a little chilled water was allowed before he loaded up, and a haynet was tied up for the journey home.

Our horses were used to Kildare and Meath country, where we jumped ditches. If you got an invitation to hunt with the Limerick Foxhounds, you *could* take your own horse, but it would take an exceptional horse to jump every different type of fence. Years ago, the obstacles you met out hunting in Limerick were completely different. You could find a wire fence in front of a bank, which the Limerick horses jumped over and scrambled onto like sure-footed cats, before it tackled a descent on the far side, with another wire fence to negotiate.

Conversely, a Limerick horse would have no clue about the technique of jumping any of our deep Kildare ditches. You gave your horse plenty of rein to put his head down to look at the steep angle of the near bank of the ditch, to judge for himself how far down he could slide, before launching himself onto the far bank. One of the greatest dangers lay on the landing side, where the steep bank required the rider to stay forward, and not to loose balance and grab hold of the reins, or he would pull the poor horse backwards into the bottom of the ditch. We always wore a strap (or martingale) around the horse's neck, and were taught to hold onto that to keep our balance, instead of onto the reins.

It sounds dangerous, but good horses and ponies could be trusted to make their own decisions about when to take off, and how far up the bank they must land.

Some ponies were so clever, you saw tiny riders with their arms flung around their necks, hanging on with their eyes tight shut; and still they came safely across.

Frequently we might 'pilot' a novice rider on their first day out hunting. The ditches always posed a problem, so we organised practise sessions at home first. One equestrian was our student cousin, Tom Carew, from Suffolk, who was virtually a non-rider. But he proved to be a natural horseman. His first day out hunting went well – even if somewhat lacking in the steering department. He was seen to be having the odd argument with various bushes on either side of the lanes as we galloped along, 'I never knew how difficult it was to avoid other riders, gates, and tree branches!'

Early one spring, Diana was asked to stay and hunt with Lady Molly Cusack-Smith in Galway, who was somewhat eccentric. She hunted her own pack of hounds – the Birmingham and North Galway Hunt. It was good hunting country over low stonewalls, and there was always a stable full of good horses. There were not many out that day, and Lady Molly was busy with her adored hounds. The weather was too warm for much scent, and the hounds could not find a line. One dog hound came to a wall, and obviously thought it was too high.

'He's a very brave old hound, and will soon retire', said Lady Molly. Herself a large and somewhat stiff lady, she struggled to get off her horse before helping the hound over the wall. Then Lady Molly looked at her tall horse, 'Too high', she muttered. So Diana got off and helped Lady Molly to mount. Before Diana could hop back up onto her own horse, a handsome young local dentist thought he should also do the honours, and jumped off his horse, grabbed Diana and a gave her a leg-up too!

From our very earliest years, we proudly went off to hunt on our ponies or horses, with our sandwiches for the day. On the right-hand side of the saddle, on the seat edge, there were two silver-coloured 'D's, about 3in apart. On these we attached a leather sandwich-case, which held two compartments, one with sandwiches wrapped in greaseproof paper, and one with a glass container filled with our Mi-Wada diluted orange drink. In later years, Mother used to follow the hunt and hand out extra sandwiches as we rode past her on the road to another covert.

Certainly, the Conolly-Carews loved to raid the autumn bramble bushes for big ripe blackberries, but their greedy ponies (and sometimes their horses) loved them just as much!

In some hedges there were much-prized sloes; these made the favourite drink 'Sloe Gin'. It was either that tipple, or Port, that the grown-up hunters carried in their silver flasks.

The sloes were difficult to find, and were to be picked and brought home if possible. If the hunt was in danger of disappearing off while you dismounted to collect them, you would have to try to remember which hedge they were in, and return the next day to pick them.

John Huston was one of the great film directors of our time (*The Maltese Falcon*, *Moby Dick*, *The African Queen*, and many others). He rented nearby Courtown, to hunt and to provide sport for his Hollywood friends. Other hunt members and all the locals turned out to watch, as he often took famous film stars hunting with the Kildares. A regular visitor was Peter Viertell, a well-known scriptwriter and producer, who had become engaged to a film star.

The couple decided it would be grand to have a Hunting Wedding before Christmas, and duly announced it to the press. However, it was very difficult to find a priest to marry them, because they had both been married several times already.

However, the unlucky couple had to postpone the wedding until after Christmas, as a terrible tragedy had just befallen the Kildare Hunt – a young lady was killed out hunting.

In the meantime, they asked Major Beaumont, the Master, if he would give away the bride. Being a very upright man, he was dumbfounded, and did not consider it quite proper. Perhaps he secretly hoped that Fate would intervene, and that he would be able to cancel the Boxing Day meet due to bad weather. To his dismay, the day was perfect and the wedding went ahead, followed by the hunt. Hundreds of hunting people turned up, all agog, and most of them drank like fishes.

Originally, it had been planned that bride and bridegroom would ride to the first covert after the marriage ceremony. But the bride had flu, and the plan fell flat.

Diana felt a little dizzy from the drink, and she and a good number of others went flop into the first ditch.

About this time, Diana was selected to compete on the Irish Team for the Junior European Championships (under 18s) at the White City in London, riding an experienced eighteen-year-old horse called Tubbernagat. This well-known mare was leased for £300 for the summer (the amount of money she had won the year before). Diana and Tubbernagat had instant success. They won three important prizes at the Dublin Spring Show in May, and Diana felt on top of the world.

They had a big win in the Championship at the Belfast Show, and were selected for the Irish Junior Team to go to England. They came first in both qualifying competitions in London, and carried forward a favourite's chance of the Gold Medal. There were eleven in the final, with ten prizes.

They entered the ring, were announced on the loudspeaker and then everything stopped as Princess Margaret arrived. The National Anthem was played and Diana began to canter around. Again her name was announced, and she set of. But alas, amongst all the interruptions, the official starting bell had not yet been rung. She was promptly eliminated. Heartbroken, she ended up as the only one without a prize.

Diana had made exactly the same mistake as most riders do at some time in their careers. It is very easy to do. There are numerous outside noises, which sound like the starting bell and, if you are not concentrating properly, you can easily think the starting signal *has* gone.

15

THE BARGE-HORSE, DUBLIN HORSE SHOW AND HUNT BALLS

In 1956/7, catastrophic ideas were expressed about selling Castletown, and buying a smaller house; the necessary repairs were becoming impossible for our father to finance.

A new house, called Dunsinea, was nearly bought with the help of Grandmother Ivy, but a snag appeared in the final deal. Whatever actually happened, Castletown was not sold, and the money from Scotland was used to make essential repairs. Somehow, we continued on for another ten years in our beloved old house. But the writing was already on the wall. Two incidents involving the roof showed the dangers of leaving repairs too late.

One morning, while Diana was still snug in bed before getting up for 8.30 breakfast, two workmen were working in the rafters above. Suddenly, she saw plaster and a cloud of dust descending in front of her as a man fell right through her ceiling, yelling mightily, caught by his armpits! He was hastily pulled back up, shocked but unharmed.

On another instance, Mrs Murphy was sick in bed in the servants' wing. Our father and Mr Mulligan, the plumber, were inspecting the roof above. 'Sure, the lord's leg came through', she reported. She was showered with plaster, but not hurt, and neither was the lord!

With the awful thought that we might have to leave Castletown one day soon, I continued to pump my father for more and more family stories. Of Lady Louisa, of the great brown bear (that we had all played with), of Speaker Conolly's early life ... At last, he relented, and gave me the key to the attic. He showed me letters and deeds tracing back 250 years; and then left me to it.

Over the next ten years, on every holiday my hobby was deciphering those strange handwritings and reading ancestors' letters (particularly Lady Louisa to her sisters, and vice-versa).

In 1959/60, Patrick had his twenty-first birthday party and we danced in the dining room, because the Long Gallery chandeliers were thought too fragile to hold the weight of wild stamping feet.

Having left school at seventeen, and after RMA Sandhurst, he was commissioned into the Royal Horse Guards (The Blues). The regiment is one of the oldest, and guards the Queen on ceremonial occasions, mounted on their black horses with shining armour.

Ireland's 1959 Event Championships were held at Castletown. Mother had bought a horse for Patrick to event, which had been competing with the late Major Eddie Boylan. Despite being told that the mare had originally towed a barge up the canal at Robertstown, and despite the fact that she refused twice on the cross country course that day, there was something Mother and Patrick liked about her.

She was called Ballyhoo, she was strong and keen, and had some experience in England in smaller riding club events with her owner, who had given Eddie Boylan the ride for larger novice horse trials. The deal was done for £500.

Almost immediately Patrick struck up a remarkable partnership with the mare, who loved to take command of her young rider and jump anything he aimed her at – the bigger the better.

From this unlikely beginning, Patrick and Ballyhoo stepped straight onto the Three-Day Event Team representing Ireland at the European Championships the same year.

A Three-Day Event has dressage on the first day, cross country on the second day, and show jumping on the final leg.

In those days, the cross country was run in four sections; roads and tracks (trotting along country lanes) to the start of the steeplechase phase, followed by more road and tracks (which was usually the first phase again, but going in the opposite direction) and lastly 4 miles of cross-country jumps. It all had to be completed within in a tight time schedule, with penalty marks for excess time.

Patrick describes a near disaster at his First Badminton Three-Day-Event in 1960. At the end of the steeplechase, he had been advised it was a good thing to get off and walk or run beside your horse for a while, to give it a rest. This he attempted to do. Unfortunately, Ballyhoo had other ideas. With a shake of her head, she broke free and galloped off up the lane. This looked like an ignominious end to his fledgling international career. As luck would have it, a rider was approaching from the opposite direction, and that rider was Richard Meade, a family friend riding on the British Team. 'Good Heavens, that's Patrick's horse!' He caught Ballyhoo, and brought it back to him.

Both competitors went on to complete the Three-Day Event without suffering any time penalties on their roads and tracks.

For seven years, Patrick and Ballyhoo were on the Irish Team continuously, completing six consecutive Badminton Three-Day Events (over the largest fences in the world), being placed seventh in 1962, and third the following year. We used to walk the cross country course in horror each year at the size of the fences (you could drive a car through the middle of them, they were so wide).

They also had success at the first ever Burghley Three-Day Event in 1961, where they were third individually, and won a Team Silver Medal at the 1962 European Championships there.

The *Evening Telegraph* report on Burghley Horse Trials, 16 September 1961, read:

> *Yesterday's Cross Country Course was so difficult, that Col. Frank Weldon (who finished 4th), and who was the Captain of the British Olympic Team, remarked, 'The ideal Cross Country Course is one that puts the fear of God into the rider, but leaves the horse unharmed. The Burghley course meets these requirements. However, it is possible that it was too severe for the standard of competition; but that is not the fault of the organisers. It was not foreseen that so many good riders would fail to complete.'*

Anneli Drummond-Hay who won the competition on Merely-A-Monarch, said, 'I was horrified when I saw the size of some of the jumps.'

Ballyhoo and Patrick were third; and his friend and fellow officer in the Blues, Jeremy Smith Bingham, came second.

The dressage section was never Ballyhoo's strong point, but the more difficult the cross country, the better it was for her. She was eventually retired at the age of fifteen, in order to breed from her. She was strong, with good sound legs, a great heart, and spirit that made her a devil in the stable. She had the spark and fire that made her one of the world's most consistent horses.

But Ballyhoo had other ideas about a husband. Eventually, aged nineteen, she consented, and bred five foals in consecutive years. Incredibly, every one of those foals inherited her great spirit, and they all went on to compete in Three-Day Event's internationally. Three represented Ireland, and two represented Great Britain.

Each year, Castletown sent six to ten horses and ponies to the Dublin Horse and Spring Show. Some were youngsters to be shown and sold; others were the family jumpers. All competing horses got a RDS grant to travel by road or rail. At the Castletown end, Hazelhatch station had roughly-fitted stalled wagons in a siding, where the horses were loaded from a concrete ramp. At the other end, there was another railway siding across the road from the RDS, at Ballsbridge, where they disembarked.

Each year, Patrick (and later Bunny) started bringing army friends to Castletown for the show. He brought his Labrador dog, Remus, on the plane from London, paying £4 for the seat beside him. One guest was John Draco, who was quite foreign-looking – a practical joker who liked to dress up as 'Count Ivor Hostieck' and parade around with a monocle. While at Sandhurst, his favourite trick was to bring his own coffin in his car. Pulling into a garage, he jumped out of the car, opened the lid of the coffin, '5 gallons please!' he said, and shut the lid again.

The Dublin Show was always an exhausting week with dinner parties and Hunt Balls every night, with the imperative that the Castletown guests had to get out of bed early the next day in order to go to the horse show at Ballsbridge. The partygoers, looking bleary-eyed all day, somehow managed to perk up spectacularly at night.

Family and guests alike were woken the next morning by Mrs Anderson and Mrs Mooney arriving in their bedroom with a brass jug of hot water, which was placed in the washstand for shaving and washing in a large china bowl. (There was no hot water in the bathroom taps before 4 p.m. each day.)

Once rudely woken, the revellers would be bundled into one of the cars, to get to the show by lunchtime, where we had a mountain of picnic goodies to eat, and more alcohol. The homemade cream cheese was always the star of the show, until one year when it made everyone ill.[59]

The guests were required to wake up and cheer when a member of the family did well jumping; in fact, they were Diana's own cheerleaders every year.

The horse show itself started on the following Tuesday, and for five nights there was a Hunt Ball each night. Each foreign embassy with a competing team hosted a cocktail party. These were obligatory for all the international foreign team riders, who were required to attend with their *Chef d' Equippe* (Team Manager). They were held in the evenings, which usually produced a scramble in order to get ready in time, having competed all afternoon.

The biggest of these embassy parties was held at the beautiful British Embassy, near Leopardstown; but the loveliest setting was the Italian Embassy, with its superb house in Lucan. In those days, the Italians had most of their success on Irish horses (especially the d'Inzeo brothers).

The most famous dance was the Louth Hunt Ball at the Shelbourne Hotel, which was held on the Friday night after the Nations Cup 'Aga Khan' Competition. All the teams attended, and the winning team were especially feted and cheered.

Every Hunt Ball provided a free table for the foreign riders, with as much as they could eat and drink thrown in. The following day was the last, and it hosted the most important individual competition, the grand prix. This meant, for that one night of the week, they could drink as much of the hard stuff as they wished! They were only responsible for their own ability to perform in the next day's competition, with no other team mates to rely on them not having a hangover.

With most teams staying at the same hotel, the Shelbourne, for the whole week, there were pranks and games that followed, naturally. One story relates to the saga of the long rows of newly cleaned riding boots, lined up to attention outside the bedrooms in the early mornings. They attracted the attention of one mischief-maker, who quietly ran up and down the corridors changing them all around. However, after a mighty fuss from be-stocking protestors, the boot-man was sent for, and managed to save the escalating international incident. Very efficiently, he sorted them out. Each bedroom number had already been chalked on the sole underneath each boot.

Another dance on the same night was the British Legion Ball at the Gresham Hotel, where our parents attended as President Royal British Legion Ireland, and President of the Ladies Section. These parties were famously wild, with much throwing of food and anything else that was not nailed to the floor. The cleaning bill must have been as expensive as the hire of the rooms.

There were Hunt Balls for the Kildare's, as well as the North Kildare Harriers at Castletown at other times of the year, everyone wearing their best bib and tucker. One time, we remember, the best society tailor in Dublin bought himself a ticket, just to see his clothes dancing.[60]

Even Castletown's precious print room saw its share of action, where anyone could use the large billiard table. We hoped our ancestor, Speaker Conolly, would not have minded that we used his old bedroom next door (our library) for Roulette, organised by Capt. Spencer Freeman of Irish Hospital Sweepstake fame.

One particularly memorable Castletown Hunt Ball was in January 1963, when we had nearly 500 people dancing in the dining room. Each member of the hunt or farmer was allotted two tickets at 25s each. We created a nightclub in the basement with cleverly painted walls, illustrating hunt members sitting around a heavily laden food table, depicted as foxes, which was painted by a neighbour John Jobson. We took great delight in seeking out flashing lights and loud music; and were completely unaware there was the dead body of our butler right next door, in the room that is now the ladies' toilet.

Our new butler, Carroll (with the heavy breathing down the telephone) became too ill to continue. (There was a family rumour that he succumbed to the charms of a stable girl once too often.) He was taken poorly two days before the ball. He professed to having no family, and was feeling unwell, so he handed Mrs Murphy his Post Office Book, 'In case anything happens to me,' he said.

It was kept a complete secret, but he died the night before the dance. Mrs Murphy had found him as she went to bring Carroll his supper in bed, and went and told Mother and Granny Lauderdale the sad news. They decided to leave him locked up there till the day after the Ball. After all, there were no instant communications like mobile phones in those days, and they considered it quite impossible to warn all the several hundred ticket holders. They decided it was too late to cancel the Hunt Ball, but they kept it secret from Father, because they knew he would have attempted to have cancelled the whole thing. We children never knew the story until years later, and nobody spilled the beans to our father. The butler's bedroom was locked, and the ball continued.

The Nightclub Fox Mural (painted by our neighbour John Jobson), depicting members of the hunt as the foxes, including Diana with her arms in a sling after an accident out hunting. (DG)

He did not exactly rest in peace, because his bedroom was right next door to the dungeon Night Club, along the bottom passage. There were flashing red light bulbs, and thumping music all night.

The next day, the local women came to lay him out, and discovered a hoard of money underneath his mattress. The word got out that a butler at Castletown had died rich and suddenly the house was invaded with 'long lost relatives', claiming the money.

During one Winter Hunt Ball at Castletown, Ornella Rignon, a beautiful young Italian Contessa was sent by friends to stay with us to forget her Italian lover, Col. Franco Boski, who was much older and who had a fast reputation with the ladies.

Ornella, with her lovely ash-blonde hair was dancing with Paul Nicholson, twice winner of the Aintree Foxhunters Chase, who was greatly enjoying the company of the beautiful Italian girl in his arms. 'Excuse me', said a foreign voice; and Ornella danced away in the arms of her forbidden lover, Col. Franco Boski. He was immaculately dressed in tails and white tie. Mother felt responsible, and did not want Contessa Ornella and Col. Boski to disappear like Cinderella, so she asked Boski to stay overnight. He was given a small room, a long way from Ornella, on a different floor. At the end of the dance, he was shown his room.

Full of mischief, some members of the family put some string across the staircase, intending to catch Boski if he crept out to visit Ornella in the middle of the night. However, we caught an unfortunate maid instead, who broke her leg

The Italian Contessa Ornella Rignon seated on the right. Mama was fearful she would disappear off at midnight like Cinderella, with her forbidden lover. (Courtesy of *The Irish Times*)

the next morning. The dressing down we received from our parents was terrible. Ornella married Boski shortly afterwards. She show-jumped internationally for Italy, and the marriage proved a great success.

When Diana was jumping in the international competitions at the Dublin Show, she stayed in a rented flat for the week. It had cooking facilities, and was near the RDS. She was with approximately three girls and two boys, students who were looking after the family horses at the show; each one was usually given a ride in one of the Show Classes.

The head groom did not compete, but he and his male assistant slept in rooms above the grooms' canteen at the RDS. It was pretty rough, but they enjoyed it. The competing horses stayed up for the week in loose boxes on the showground.

Each competing country's embassy held a cocktail party, and the Teams were expected to attend, dressed in their best. These parties were eventually phased out over the years, as more and more of the riders became professional and did not wish to attend. So, the riders' social scene crumbled.

At the Kildare Hunt Ball at Castletown one year, one of the greatest characters of the Irish horse world, Ned Cash, attended, dressed immaculately in white tie and tails. He had been brought up tough and rough, and had once admitted to grave-robbing when he was younger; but now he ran the best-known dealing yard in Ireland, with horses he bought by the lorry-load, and sold from his base in Clane, Co. Kildare. He famously built his stables using the local church as a lean-to wall, and ignored the protests.

Not having sufficient fields to house all his horses, he often left some roaming freely along the roadsides, eating the long grass and the succulent hedge sprouts.

He provided most of our hunters at Castletown, and many of the Irish Army Show Jumpers. He would always take any unsuitable horse back, and replace it with another. His business grew, until he had clients from all over the world. He knew which horses might become good enough with proper training, and usually asked a sensible price. His sons could retrain any horse, and were extremely successful point-to-point riders – young Ned later went on to show jump for Ireland.

The morning after one of the Hunt Balls at Castletown, Ned Cash senior was discovered by our mother, in the red drawing room, fast asleep, naked; with his ample body spread all over the French gold-lacquered sofa, and a crate of empty beer bottles under the table. His pink (red) hunt coat was respectfully draped around the seventeenth-century painting of General Ginkel; his waistcoat adorned the Chinese cabinet painted by Speaker's Conolly's wife; his trousers were riding piggy-back around the neck of a bust; his tie and socks hung around various door knobs and bell-pushes in the wall, and we did not care to ask Mama where his under-breeches were, or any other unmentionables. Hurrying out, she called the butler, who politely, guided the last remaining reveller back into his clothes, and pushed his car out of a muddy field.

In the early 1960s, George Ponsonby, from Kilcooley, partook a little too liberally in the good food and drink provided at lunchtime on one memorable pheasant shooting day at Castletown.

Before the afternoon shooting was due to start, George and other guests were caught by Papa, decorating the busts and statues in the front hall with lipstick! The more modest statues got flourishes of red hair and red buttons; the nudes were enhanced with circles around their bosoms, and impressive red nipples. They were caught red-handed! It was, of course, a joke; but our father was furious. The lipstick was in danger of permanently marking the stone, and it took a long time to remove it completely.

A generation earlier, an elderly Ponsonby owner of Kilcooley Abbey used to select one of the plumper housemaids to take to bed as his human hot water bottle (presumably his wife had merrily passed on). One cold evening in the winter, it was very dark. The master of the house, in his four-poster bed, found that his human hot water bottle was extremely smelly. The odour finally roused him; he got up, fumbled in the dark to find a bottle of perfume. He unscrewed it, and unceremoniously poured the contents over her. It was not much help really – in the morning he discovered he had poured blue ink all over her.

Another story about the Ponsonby's, involved the IRA. They came to Kilcooley to look for Tom Ponsonby one dark night. He heard them coming, and disconnected the electricity, leaving the gloomy big house in complete darkness. He grabbed some soft shoes and a flashlight, and cooly played hide and seek with them, hitting a few intruders before melting away in the dark, flashing his torch on and off to confuse them. They got spooked, and scarpered off as soon as they could locate the front door.

16

ACCIDENTS AND SUCCESS

At the age of twenty, Diana developed pneumonia, and suffered severe lung damage. At the time, Grandmother took her on a recuperation cruise to South Africa. But her energy levels were never the same again. Lack of oxygen was to affect her for the rest of her life, which meant she always had to rest between show-jumping rounds, or after any real exertion.

Nobody could possibly foresee the repercussions eight years later, when she was competing in the thin air at the Mexico Olympics.

As years passed, Diana's successes became more varied. She was an elegant and successful show rider, as well as competing in the show jumping.

In the early 1960s, a young relative of Barrymore was purchased by Diana. He was a large chestnut, with a good jump, and they named him Ballyfine. He was trained by Diana, who showed him at the Dublin Horse Show, where he won the coveted Supreme Champion Hunter. That same year, Ballyfine and Diana won the Novice One-Day Event Championship at Castletown; then they went to England to come second in the Working Hunter Class at the horse of the Year Show. He was shaping up to be a top class event Horse, with a promising future. That winter, Diana sold him to Patrick, to be his eventer.

One day, Patrick took him out hunting with the Fingals, and jumped a blind ditch, and poor Ballyfine flopped on landing, with a crack. Patrick thought he had dropped his whip, but the crack was Ballyfine breaking his leg. Luckily Professor Martin Byrne, the vet, was out hunting that day. 'I'm so sorry Patrick; we're going to have to put the horse down,' said the vet, who always carried his humane gun with him, for accidents in the hunting field were not unknown. But the gun would not work, to add to the agony. Eventually the grim task was done.

Shortly after Ballyfine's Champion Hunter win at the Dublin Horse Show, the family were at dinner, when the telephone rang.

'I want to sell you another champion,' said a rough Irish voice, 'it's by the same sire as Barrymore and Ballyfine.'

'Thank you very much,' said Diana, 'what's the price?'

'The price would be right!' says the voice.

'How old?' asked Diana.

'Two years.'

'I don't really want a two year old … what sex?'

'Sure, it's a filly.'

'I don't want a filly,' replied Diana.

'Ah, sure you'll come and see her, she'll be a champion. I've never tried to sell her to anyone else. She's a chestnut, the same colour as your great champion!'

About six weeks later, the man telephoned once more, and Diana eventually agreed to go and see the filly; it was some miles away. Diana, on a buying trip on her own, felt in the need of a girlfriend as guardian. They met three large jovial and somewhat rough-looking men, who made them feel welcome and took them to a shed. They opened the door, and a tiny golden-coloured pony with a white mane was revealed. It was more like a delicate wild deer, than a horse. 'Isn't she great?' the men said. Diana stood and looked; 'great' was hardly a suitable word. The owner got the sad message that his 'Champion' was no world-beater, and after some time, Diana decided to buy her anyway, for about £60.

Mother was keen to see the little horse, but Diana wanted her Grandmother to see it first, when she came to stay shortly afterwards. So, Diana hid her in the old broodmare stables about a mile away in the pheasant field, and she would ride there and back twice a day to feed and handle her, and to tame her a bit, for she was still wild.

Shortly afterwards, the filly escaped into the Great Wood! Then a beautiful white Welsh Mountain Pony stallion, from the US ambassador, Raymond Guest's, stud farm at Ballygoran, also escaped. All on his own, he came across country and joined her, cavorting in the woods.

The Hunt was due at Castletown the following week. So a huge and very funny round-up was organised, with as many riders as they could muster, with Diana and myself pretending to be cowboys (our favourite horses quite frequently wore Western bridles for fun).

A very embarrassed stud groom from Ballygoran turned up on a bicycle, smartly dressed with gaiters and brown boots; and led his well-trained escapee home again, trotting along beside the bicycle.

What fun it had been, trying to catch the mare and the stallion! It took all day. Granny Lauderdale was given the pony, which was very sweet, but no champion. The mare was sold after it had been trained and broken-in as a children's pony, and later in life, bred a winner at the Dublin Horse Show.

Here is Carmel Locke's memories of Castletown:

I was fortunate enough to be accepted as working pupil at Castletown in 1963, which was wonderful for me as it enabled me to pursue my lifelong ambition of working with horses. I wanted to be able to look after my own horses one day.

I was very excited on my first day. I was taught how to muck out the stables, feed, water and groom the horses, and I was allowed to exercise one or two. Mr Tynan, the head man, gave the orders about what was to be done, and who was to do it. He was a good tutor.

The girls who were there were Christine Middleton, Ann Myers and Peggy Wyldbore-Smith. We all pulled together most of the time.

Lady Carew would call into the stables frequently. I was very fond of her. I did not see a lot of Lord Carew, but when I did we chatted about local goings-on as I was from Celbridge. He was a lovely gentleman.

It was a great delight to meet Diana. It was wonderful to watch her ride. Hers was a real expertise. We got on very well and I learned a lot from listening to her and watching her. It was very happy place to be and I loved it and looked forward to going in every day.

A very vivid memory I have locked in my heart is the day Capt. Patrick and his wife arrived back to Castletown. What a handsome couple. I personally had seldom seen anyone so beautiful as Capt. Carew's wife, Celia. There also was baby Virginia, who we admired at every available opportunity. She had a young lady to look after her, called Mary Kenny.

Paraguay and Paddy were the horses I was allowed to ride, and I loved them dearly. Diana took me on my first ever hunt on Paddy. It was brilliant. She also took some of us girls greyhound racing. Whilst I was at Castletown a young lady brought her horse to be stabled there. It was Hilary Sterling and her horse Major Raffles. I had quite a lot to do with Major Raffles, and I looked after him very well.

I must not forget the late Miss Joan Reddy and her mare Andrea, which she was always training up and down the avenue. Somehow, she seemed to be a part of Castletown drive just as much as the trees were.

The late Josie Darlington frequently came to shoe the horses. Barrymore had problems with his feet and he had to be very careful with him.[61]

I recall Diana and myself returning from a show with two horses. On the bridge in Celbridge we had an accident, I had to walk the horses back to Castletown and it was quite scary heading up the front drive in the dark.

Amid show jumping events and hunts I was kept busy like everyone else. I was off every second Sunday, as long as there was no event.

The horses, whilst I was there, were Barrymore, Errigal, Freddy, Paddy, Paraguay, and Ballyfine, who was my favourite. I also remember Ballyhoo the lovely mare. There may have been more, but these stick in my memory. They were all very precious and lovingly cared for.

Lady Carew decided that I should go to Scotland for the summer. This was a huge surprise to me as I had never been out of Ireland before. I was to go to Thirlestane Castle, the home of Lady Carew's mother, the Countess of Lauderdale. I was given the responsibility of travelling with the horses on my own.

Thirlestane Castle looked like something from a storybook; one could imagine fairies popping up around it. I settled into my new surroundings and got on with my work experience. It was not quite as hectic as it was at Castletown. Diana took me to the Edinburgh Festival. Then it was time for me to return to Castletown.

On arriving back in Dublin, I ran into serious problems with the customs office over trunks of tack. However, by the time Lady Carew arrived to collect me, I had it all sorted, and she was very pleased.

Quite some time after my return, I became ill, and Lady Carew told me it was too dangerous to have me around the horses because I was frequently fainting. I suppose it made sense, but I was very upset at the time. Gradually, I came to terms with what I thought was just a set back. It was a difficult time for me. Lady Carew suggested I do a secretarial course, but my heart was not in it. I missed life at Castletown, and above all I missed the horses. I continued my riding lessons against medical advice, and still enjoyed the horses.

I had been trying different kinds of medication for a long time when, following a chance meeting with a surgeon Monty Montgomery, I had a brain scan. This was to prove very helpful as it was discovered I had a germ in the brain. Straight away I was put on the right medication and my world was right for me once more.

I applied for a position for a secretary/groom, and I got the position. It was very interesting as I seemed to be responsible for everything. I did not know it then, but my employer was later to become my husband and dearest friend. He was the famous Irish tenor Josef Locke.

I fulfilled my childhood dream and was the proud owner of several horses, and at one stage I had twenty-one donkeys and twelve Dalmatians. It was a story with a happy ending. One could say it started at Castletown. I have many happy memories of the times I spent there, and of the lovely Conolly-Carew family.

Diana, Carmel Locke and
Ballyfine at the Horse of
the Year Show.

'How brave', some people say to the competitors in all daring sports, whether it
is climbing a mountain, or jumping a high fence. But it is not brave; it is a chosen
sport, an extra excitement to face a challenge, and a rather nerve-wracking high
before the action. The brave ones are those who are truly afraid. They see only
disaster and failure ahead, and are certain they will hurt themselves before they
start; but they gather their courage anyway, and give it a go. They are the brave
ones.

Everyone was nervous before a big competition, but the adrenalin helped you
to perform better; waiting your turn was as exciting for the horses as for the
riders. They trembled too. Generally, once you had entered an arena, it was down
to business for both of you. If your horse was a youngster, it could be difficult to
make it concentrate on the fences ahead, instead of ogling the crowds and the
waving flags.

Patrick needed to be well warmed up, and sometimes accused himself of
not performing well during the first part of a show jumping round. One year
he tried an experiment before the Limerick Show. He played squash for three
hours before the competition, and thoroughly warmed up he won the show
jumping championship.

Outside influences can sometimes affect a performance of even the
most experienced horses. Patrick describes the Olympic Games in Munich,
where he was the first to go in the competition. He entered the dressage
arena on the first day, and as prescribed, came to a perfect halt in the centre
to salute to the judges. The vast banks of spectators in the stands all around

burst out clapping and stamping their approval, and Patrick's horse became so apprehensive he very nearly fell off. The organisers had failed to inform the crowd they had to keep quiet during any dressage test. They were well instructed for the rest of the competitors, but it was too late for Patrick. He completed the Three-Day Event, but his dressage marks could have been much better.

Accidents did not occur just out riding, they also happened whilst out shooting.

During the winter holidays, when Granny Lauderdale came to stay, there was a family shoot arranged, to which the local parson, doctor and other friends were always invited. At Castletown, there were not the great number of pheasants you get in a professional shoot nowadays, but the local worthies were very keen novices, because they seldom had a chance to indulge in the sport. Ivy Lauderdale (who was a good shot) was ever practical upon these occasions. She kept a wary eye on them, insisting she should stand near a large tree, so she could dodge behind it if the next-door gun swung in her direction.

As girls we hated shooting, but Patrick and Bunny have always enjoyed the sport. They were taught their shooting etiquette with a high stick planted on each side of them, so they could not swing their guns around, and 'pepper' the next-door gun.

As children, the words: 'You are not a good rider until you have fallen off 100 times', were drilled into us. But it helps if you learn to roll yourself into a ball as you see the ground coming up to meet you! Falls and accidents are part of everyday riding life. Of course, we did not realise until years later, how difficult it was for our mother to watch us going cross country. She had seen her own fiancée killed steeple-chasing years before, and now had to see Patrick going around Badminton Horse Trials. We can only imagine how she felt.

There were three main causes of accidents; hunting, jumping, and young horses (playing up, or on the roads). Though, something like an excitable horse throwing its head up can easily break your nose. Even something as simple as a car horn could cause panic.

Our mother had a habit of driving a large blue car at speed down the avenue when we were exercising young horses. She would drive past us giving a cheery hoot and often sending a spray of water from the puddles towards us. The result was chaos and sent horses in every direction.

One day Diana innocently picked a leafy branch along the front drive, to serve as a fly swot for her horse's ears, which caused it to loose its nerve later. The horse panicked outside Gleeson's ice cream shop on the other side of the bridge in Celbridge because it felt the reins touch its ears as she remounted, and it started plunging forward with her hanging only half-on – she was within a hair's breadth of being flung into the path of a passing lorry, somehow, she was lucky that day.

In 1952, the great Irish lady champion, Iris Kellett, caught tetanus (lockjaw) after a simple fall when her horse slipped. Her recovery was painful and slow, but she returned to be the Ladies European Champion in 1969.

It was the careless and unnecessary accidents you blamed yourself for. Diana was furious when she came back from a show jumping trip abroad, to learn that a girl groom had jumped one of her potential new stars over several fences, and had badly hurt its legs jumping into the concrete-based water jump, which had practically no water in it. The girl had been under strict instructions to exercise it only, not to jump it.

Luckily, it was fairly rare for a horse to be killed. But the riders all had their share of breaks. Many years later, Patrick almost lost his life in an accident in the United States, by a fall from a golf buggy! He was due to be the President of the Ground Jury (senior judge) at the Atlanta Olympic Games in 1996. The year before, Atlanta ran a test event over the same terrain, and Patrick was flown out to judge it. Before a competition, the judges have to inspect the cross country course, and give their approval. If a fence is considered too difficult, it is modified. He was being driven in a golf buggy around the course, and they were approaching some fences down a hill into a wood. The driver of the buggy lost control, going faster and faster, and was heading for several large trees. Patrick had the option of bailing out, or hanging on and hoping for the best. The wheel of the buggy caught the root of one of the trees, and went over. Patrick was thrown out, breaking many ribs and puncturing a lung.

It took four hours to get him out, and to work on his increasingly life-threatening injuries. He was taken to hospital and operated on. Some four weeks later, he was declared fit enough to travel home. Some three days after returning to Ireland, his lung filled with water, and he was rushed to St Vincent's Hospital in Dublin, where he nearly died. Cutting down along the lung area to release all the fluid, his heart stopped on the operating table. He was resuscitated, but remained in hospital for a further two weeks.

As a result of the accident, Patrick lost 90 per cent capacity of one of his lungs, which has affected him for the rest of his life.

He did, however, go on to judge at the Olympic Games at Atlanta the following year.

Another incident to do with the administration side of the Olympics came at the time of the Los Angeles Games, when Patrick was president of the Equestrian Federation of Ireland (FEI), and chairman of the selectors for the Irish Team. It transpired there were not enough accredited places attached to the team, but they decided that they needed his experience; so he travelled as the Irish team farrier!

At the start of the Games, upon hearing of this unlikely happening, Prince Philip (who was president of the FEI) wrote a joke invitation to a meeting of all team farriers at 11 a.m. The only person to receive the invitation was Patrick, and naturally he was the only one who turned up. Prince Philip had set him up!

One of the main hunting hazards we encountered in the Kildare was a horrible ditch, called Laragh Brook. It was a wide, deep, quite fast-running stream, and claimed many casualties over the years; it was one obstacle we preferred not to have to jump. The canals were dangerous too and usually never attempted; though it was quite possible to swim your horse across.

Very often the canal ran alongside the railways line, and this was the reason for one of the most horrific accidents in our time.

If hounds got onto a railway line, the country trains would stop to watch the hunt. But it was a dangerous situation; the huntsman had to extricate them immediately in case a train could not stop. It was not unusual for hounds to be killed. One hunting day, Paddy Desmond, the whipper-in of the North Kildare Harriers, saw the hounds on the railway, and the only way to get to them quickly, was to swim himself and his horse across the intervening canal. But he had forgotten that his horse had been 'tubed' (a breathing hole made in its throat – an operation that was not unusual for broken-winded horses). Paddy and the horse got into the canal, and the horse drowned.

It was usual to come home scratched from bushes and brambles, and covered in mud. It wasn't a disgrace to fall out hunting; you wore your piece of Kildare mud proudly, like a battle honour. Unfortunately, a clod of mud that flew into my eye, one day out hunting, contained a piece of wire, and has caused me problems ever since.

Falls whilst jumping are part of the game and they were usually fairly harmless. During one memorable day with the Meath Hunt, off came Diana, and her horse went flying alongside the rest of the Field, disappearing fast into the distance.

'We'll have to catch Diana's horse,' someone said reluctantly, for they were in the middle of a very good gallop across the fields. Very kindly, they did – but the run was so good that they kept going with it!

Diana's spectacular fall off the Bank at the Dublin Horse Show.

Over the years, I suffered a broken nose, concussion, and a cracked coccyx. But in later years, Diana very nearly paid the ultimate price for being fearless across country. It happened when her horse hit a root, and they slipped to the bottom of a deep ditch together. She got off, and started to clamber halfway up the tall bank on her own.

'You stay there!' she called out, but it was not her usual horse. Unlike Simon, it did not understand. It plunged up the bank on top of her, scrabbling to heave itself out. Her neck was nearly broken, her spleen was removed, her pancreas was split, and, cruelly, there were severed nerves to her neck, which has meant her balance has never been the same again.

Out hunting one day, when I was little, I called out 'Hard Luck Charlie!' as Mick flew over the top hat of the smart hunt secretary of the Kildares, Charlie Clements, who had just fallen in the ditch in front. I am not sure if it dented his pride a little, but I was firmly told to honour your elders and betters.

Charlie's wife Mary, his brother, Henry, and sister, Kitty Clements, all hunted twice a week, and were our neighbours and great friends at Killadoon. Kitty had bred generations of thoroughbreds to race, and would hunt the youngsters herself, even though she was getting on in years. One particular horse was a problem for her, it was young and a bit strong for her to manage; its brakes did not seem to work. Eventually, she was very proud to have resolved the problem in her own fashion. It would only pull up when she said 'Sugar.'

Being told she shouldn't take such a risk, Kitty always replied that her dearest wish was to die while she was out hunting. Why shouldn't someone want to go, doing the thing they like best in the world?

Richard Meade, a family friend who was at Cambridge University, came to stay at Castletown to hunt. His parents were successful Connemara Pony breeders in England, and his father was the Master of the Monmouth Hunt. Richard was a lovely rider, having already won the Boys Pony Club Eventing Championships in Great Britain. He confided to Diana that his ambition was to have a good enough horse to event, but he feared he could not afford one.

Later, while taking an Equitation Course at Col. Dudgeon's Establishment, he bought a horse that Diana did not like at all. She doubted it would fit the bill. 'If it isn't any good, I'll try to find another for you with the right sort of talent,' promised Diana. He took it back home, and it did not prove a success, so Richard contacted her. Diana looked and advertised, but the only likely candidate seemed too expensive; however, Richard came back to Castletown to try it. What could be done?

Diana thought of Kitty Clements' homebred thoroughbreds. Kitty's young horses were never sold, and were rather powerful and full of energy, too much for her. Among them was a beautiful little horse called Barberry, which was too small for the tall Kitty. Diana had an idea! Would Kitty (who was a great hunting enthusiast) lease Barberry to the son of a Master of Foxhounds? Charming Richard was introduced, and he tried the horse. It went superbly.

Fearful the horse might get hurt, Kitty hesitated; but eventually a deal was struck, with a signed agreement that neither party could sell the horse without the other's permission, and Kitty parted with the finest horse in her stables.

Apart from getting badly staked out hunting with an Irish friend, Susie Lanigan O'Keefe,[62] all went smoothly with its training. They went on to win at novice level, and then on up the grades, until they were picked for the British Olympic Team. They did wonderfully, and Kitty received a memorable telegram after the second day: 'In the lead at the Olympics!'

They knocked some show jumps on the last day, but Richard and Barberry won a Team Gold Medal.

That started Richard's career as the No. 1 male rider in England, and would result in further Olympic medals on other horses, including an individual Gold Medal in the 1972 Olympic Games. He was a fellow team member with the European Champion, Princess Anne. She eventually married another team member, Mark Phillips.

17

FRIENDS

We first knew the Reddy sisters, Joan and Una, when they showed and jumped ponies to great success at the Dublin Show; Una went on to be an accomplished side-saddle rider. Their father owned the Ever Reddy Garage in Dublin, and had lost his money during a depression in Ireland. Thereafter, they lived in different houses belonging to the bank after they were repossessed. For many years they lived in a lovely house in Lucan.

Joan, the elder sister, was rightly very proud of her six months training at the Spanish Riding School. She rode with a stiff, very correct classical seat in the saddle, with long reins, but without much participation from the horse. Perhaps she didn't get as far as lesson two, where you pick up the reins more tightly.

They became great family friends, and fell into hard times when their mother died. Shortly after, they came to live in the round house at the Gate Lodge. Sadly, they died some years ago.

There were three vicars in Celbridge in our time, Canon Elliott, Chancellor Brandon, and Canon Strong.

Chancellor Ernest Brandon, whose father was a vet, was appointed from 1951-1963. On his first day in the parish, he wanted to pay his compliments to the Lord of the Manor, and caused a stir by landing in the front field in a two-winged light plane, for his first visit to Castletown. He came from Weston Aerodrome[63] nearby, and was greeted by Murphy, the butler, running into the front field, anxiously waving a white 'flag' (undoubtedly a hastily acquired pillow case), following strict instructions from our father to show the pilot where to land, and which direction the wind was blowing. Chancellor Brandon married Cherry, a gifted artist and designer, the following year, and they had a daughter, Faith. They all enjoyed their hunting.

Ernest had a weak heart from cross-country running during his scholarly days at Trinity College Dublin. During more leisurely times, he was to be found holed up at Castletown, playing chess with Papa.[64]

They lived in the Rectory, which had been built near the Celbridge Mill in the 1800s, by Sarah Eliza Shaw's uncle (she was our great-grandmother and the wife of Tom Conolly, the American Civil War gun-runner, and friend of Napoleon III of France). But the house was cold and leaked badly, and twice Cherry developed pneumonia, and Ernest's breathing and bad heart were badly affected.

The Parish Council decided they would build them a new smaller house, on land donated by the Conollys. It would be paid for by the sale of the old Rectory, and it would take some time to build. In the meantime, Ernest, Cherry, and Faith moved into a caravan in their own garden to keep dry and warm. Ever a busy man, it was some time before Ernest paid his first visit to the new Rectory building site: 'Would that be the garage you're building?' He could not believe it was so small; a fraction of the size of the big old rectories that he was used to.

The Brandons were keen to become members of the RDS (Royal Dublin Society), which supported Ireland's agricultural life, gave concerts and lectures, and had an extensive library. They were told the fastest route was to exhibit something at the shows. Cherry had always loved her hens, so they showed them with great success as new members. But while still exhibiting their chickens in the showring, Cherry had her prize black cock stolen for cock fighting by travellers, who were passing through on their way to Ballinasloe Fair.

After Ernest died, Cherry continued her artistic talents as a main designer of the intricate patterns and colours of Armani scarves and accessories, frequently travelling to their design studios in Milan and Rome.

Their daughter, Faith, rode for Ireland at dressage, and married Peter Ponsonby of Kilcooley, a 4th cousin of the Conollys. Faith now travels abroad as an international dressage and eventing judge.

Harry McDowell, a genealogist, and his wife Joan bought the Old Rectory for £8,000 in 1963. It took two years, and another £8,000 to restore it. Now renamed Celbridge Lodge, it is a typical Irish gem. Unfortunately, Joan passed away during the writing of the book, but thankfully Harry continued to be our adviser.

We have much to thank him for, as he was one of the discoverers of the Old Secret Castle papers, which had been hidden at Castletown. For 250 years they lay underneath an abandoned lift shaft (not an obvious place to look), and had been left behind when the house was sold. These papers have provided me with the basis of this book.

Nancy Connell, from Leixlip, was a much loved friend who gave children's parties each summer for all the children of Leixlip, with tea, games, and presents. She told lovely stories, and once, when asked her name by one brave law officer, she replied, 'I'm Nancy Connell, well known to the police.' She was particularly proud that one of her relations was buried in the sand up to his neck by the IRA, and drowned when the tide came in. This harassment by the IRA was judged a bit unfair, because the family had impoverished themselves feeding thousands of poor during the Famine.

The Drummonds from Courtown House nearby, gave wonderful parties every year on the weekend before Christmas, and invited everyone from nine to ninety years old.[65]

Young Lord Fermoy (an uncle of Princess Diana) became a firm family favourite and a frequent visitor during the Dublin Horse Show. He was a brother officer of Patrick, and was a fine jazz pianist. While staying at Castletown once, he got mislaid at the end of one riotous dance in Dublin. The next morning, my father and mother were worried, and contacted the police, who said, 'We've got a few, but no one of that name!' He eventually turned up in a taxi, not at all sure where he'd been.

Another of his exploits was to ride in the Grand Military Gold Cup Steeplechase at Sandown, representing his regiment, The Blues. However, the day before this important race, he failed to pass the Household Cavalry riding test. Two of his brother officers were also due to ride in the same race the next day, and they met to discuss tactics. They generously offered to assist him throughout the race, but eventually would be trying to win.

It turned out, the winner was Edmund Fermoy himself, in a record time. After that, they did allow him to ride in the Household Cavalry Parades.

Another friend was the late John Fowler, who, with Diana, dreamt up a novel way of raising money for a charity. It made history for its own particular brand of lunacy, even in Ireland! It was summertime, and they announced a midnight steeplechase to be run at Punchestown, Co. Kildare. For £3 a head, the revellers would be able to dance till midnight in the noisy disco, and eat an ox-roast. Then the twelve intrepid jockeys would climb aboard and have their steeplechase. The riders were required to wear fancy dress on the floodlit course. All the top jump jockeys sportingly turned up. One of the intrepid riders was Bob Davies, a well-known jump jockey, who rode Pendil for the English trainer, Fred Winter.

His problems started well before the race, when he was twice thrown in the makeshift paddock. As the runners moved off into the darkness (the moon was hiding behind a cloud), a thousand or more spectators manoeuvred for a favourable position in the eerie, shadowy grandstand. There they waited, peering into the gloom for a sign of the runners … until an announcement came that the race was being held on a different course 500 yards away.

When the lunatic race finally began, Bob Davies was immediately buried at the first fence, and struggled back to consciousness to see the three leaders (all dressed as fairies) thundering towards the last jump, with another jockey, Mouse Morris, out of control without a bridle, heading towards the same fence from the opposite direction. Somehow, the four managed to clear the obstacle without colliding, but Bob Davies decided it was time to hang up his boots and find another profession.

At the end of informal dinner parties at home, amongst close friends and students, our father's favourite party-piece was his decanter measuring trick, when he placed a glass ship's decanter on the dining room table, and challenged newcomers to guess its height. This was an unusually tall round shape containing Madeira wine, with a very narrow top for pouring, and exceedingly wide at the base for stability onboard ship.

Out would come his napkin: 'I'll prove to you that the measurement around the top of a proper decanter is the same as its height.'

'Impossible!' came the replies.

But, he was right, for the eye is deceived by the width of the glass rim at the top.

During parties, the grown-ups played Bridge, and, for once, were polite to each other. Papa had a separate bedroom, and he and my mother shared a bathroom in the middle. One day, in the middle of a Bridge party, Father asked me to find something in the bathroom cabinet. Rooting around on the glass shelves, to my horror, I found a packet labelled 'Fast Teeth' (denture fixative powder). Knowing nothing at all about grown-up dental secrets, I spent the next several days intently watching my father's mouth. Was he talking faster?

One year, just before the Dublin Horse Show, on a night when parents were out, several daring young men suggested an attempt at table turning; calling upon the spirit world to create a phenomena. Had we not grown up surrounded with stories of the Devil, and the White Lady? If Squire Conolly could challenge the Devil, why not us?[66] We were easily spooked, but thought this quite thrilling. Ten of us sat around the sitting room table, with our fingers lightly on the top, in full view. Someone started an incantation and we scared ourselves witless when the table started to rise into the air. We dropped the table and scarpered in every direction, and never tried it again!

In 1961, I went skiing with Diana and some Trinity friends. I could ski because I had been at school in Switzerland. But Diana found herself being 'run away with' by disobedient skis down a slope, but was caught bravely in the arms of a large man.

Our student friends often came for informal 'bring a bottle' dance parties in the Green Drawing Room,[67] where we provided a huge help-yourself hotpot. Some of them came for evening shooting parties in the Big Wood. We placed them in good positions, and left them to it, waiting for the thousands of pigeons coming home to roost at night. We made sure each one had a torch, for if the moon was not bright, they could easily get hopelessly lost; or worse, shoot each other. (Luckily, they did not hit many of the unfortunate birds.) Despite coming from a sporting family, where the arts of shooting and fishing were highly praised, we two girls hated the killing of wild animals ... perhaps we had seen too much of it.

Among our Trinity friends was Van Cowdy. She had a King Charles spaniel, who always came too. Some 300 years ago, King Charles II had decreed that his favourite breed of dogs should be the only ones allowed in Trinity College, Dublin. With her tongue in her cheek, Van arrived at the door, plus dog, and claimed her rights under the law of King Charles to bring it in. The guard consulted with other guards, other guards consulted with a big-noise, and eventually he replied, 'By law, I can't stop you ... but please DON'T!' So she didn't.

Van broke her leg badly when her fiancé Peter Moore[68] fell off a sea wall and landed on top of her and she was in urgent need of some tender loving care, so it was suggested she came to stay at Castletown for all the nursing and attention she might need.

Her biggest memory is being carried, feet first, up the front stairs, and struggling desperately not to fall out of the stretcher, head-first 50ft down the stairs. Obviously the tender loving care did not cover the transit period when her student friends were transporting her.

Her bedroom, on the top floor, became a high-spirited party area, with bottles and games, and a pair of debagged trousers thrown out of the window; all innocent high jinks. The unoccupied trousers flew past our parents' window just below, and got stuck in the middle of the hedge in the basement ditch. Outside went Rupert Mackeson (whose mother was Diana's godmother) into the ditch below, without his offending trousers (nobody would lend him any). He thrashed about amongst the bushes searching franticly, just below our parent's window. Up went the window, 'What's happening?' roared my father.

Van later shared a flat with Lady Ann Maitland, our 1st cousin. Ann was very strictly brought up in London. Years later, she remembers that era, and is still a little astonished at her own behaviour: 'Imagine! I threw food around at the Horse Show Hunt Balls!'

One of the Trinity group, Keir Campbell, asked Diana to the Trinity Ball in Dublin. He turned up resplendent in full-dress Highland kilt. The newspaper the next morning, reporting the goings-on, said her skirt was longer than his.

Yet another of Diana's student friends hired a horse from Ned Cash, at Clane. He had cheap rates for students from Trinity. They were out hunting near Ned Cash's yard one day, when the student's horse slipped into one of the larger ditches. The rider scrambled up onto the bank safely, and the horse quickly did the same – and disappeared after the hunt without its rider.

'Don't you worry,' said a bystander, 'wait a few minutes and I'll get you another horse!'

The Trinity man waited while the bystander went over a couple of fields to the road, picked up his bicycle and sped the odd mile to Clane, saw Ned Cash who gave him another saddled and bridled horse, which he led by bicycle to the young student, who was by then waiting on the road. He mounted his second horse and finished the good hunt, albeit some way behind the rest of the field. At the end of the run, the famous Kitty Clements, a great goer then in her late sixties, rode up to him leading his original horse, 'Yours, I believe', and handed him his first horse. Now he had two!

18

ETIQUETTE AND THE DOWAGER

Our parents often gave, or went to, formal dinner parties, with the guests in white tie or black tie for the men, and long dresses or skirts for the ladies, with jewellery on display. The etiquette was complicated, and had to be practised at home. The hostess led the ladies in, followed by the gentlemen, with the host last. Guests were placed around the table, where there was often a written card with their name.

Each gentleman was required to change who he talked to when every course was served, starting with the lady on his right during the first course. The lady on the left had all his attention for the second course, and then he turned back to his right-hand side again. This etiquette was strictly followed, despite the fact that one of them was frequently much more interesting than the other.

The food was served from the left-hand side, starting with the lady on the right of the host, and then the host was served, and the food went on around the table. If there were a lot of guests, service started at each end of the table at the same time.

You were faced with a barrage of cutlery on each side of your place, and several different sized glasses. The correct way was to start on the outside with the knives and forks (check what your hostess was using), and not worry about the glasses, because they were filled up for you as the meal progressed. The last man to be served was often a junior member of the family, and this place was known as 'starvation corner'.

For the ladies down the line, it was often tricky to know how much to take on your plate (there was always a large dowager who heaped her plate ahead of you!). With a quick calculation of how many other guests there were to be served, it could average out at very little each. If you were lucky, your hostess said merrily, 'There's another dish', so you could tuck in.

Originally, the custom was to start eating when all parts of the course were on your plate, so it did not get cold – but not before your hostess had begun. Nowadays, it is more frequent for all the guests to wait until everyone is served before they start eating.

The ladies departed for the Drawing Room for coffee and liquors and a bathroom retreat to freshen up; leaving the men to the growing raucous noise of tall tales not fit for women's ears, sometimes for a very long time.

At one such dinner party, Diana was catapulted into the company of grand old fogies, without the support of other young. Our mother had developed flu, and at the last minute, could not attend a White Tie and Long Dress Dinner Party at Dunsany Castle, given by a Lord and Lady Dunsany. He was a very tall, slightly forbidding, aloof figure, who wore a monocle. Mother said that Diana must go in her place, and mind her Ps and Qs. With a quick dash to Mary Norris's hairdresser in Celbridge for a wash and set, Diana tried to rise to the challenge. Young and uncertain, Diana discovered that all the other twenty guests were Ambassadors and their wives; a lot of very important bigwigs. After drinks in the drawing room, the butler announced dinner.

When everyone traipsed into the dining room, ladies first, the host began placing the guests, showing the chair on his right-hand side to one of the grand ladies, and then indicated to Diana, and said, 'You sit on my left.' Diana froze. Brought up with protocol instilled into every corner of her being, she could not believe that the youngest and only unmarried female in the room should sit beside the host. There must be some mistake. Again Lord Dunsany nodded towards the left-hand chair, and Diana had no idea what to do.

'Go on!' hissed her cousin, April Drummond, giving her a poke (she was obviously getting hungry). So, red-faced she had to sit beside her host, whose monocle was on a cord around his neck, rather than in his eye, where it should have been – then he could have seen properly. Randal Dunsany talked during the first course to the lady on his right, and as the second course was being served, he swung around to converse with the reluctant lady on his left, Diana. He went through the rigmarole of screwing in his monocle, and said, 'So, tell me, how is your daughter that show jumps?' he asked. He thought Diana was Mama.

'That's me,' she replied wishing to retreat.

The pecking order of guests around the dining table could make or mar a formal meal. The position of honour (on either side of the host at one end, and the hostess at the other) were usually reserved for the grandest, or most senior guests. But the waters often became a bit muddied when this rule was applied to members of the Diplomatic Corp. The Ambassador who had been longest in his post took precedence, even if he came from Outer Mongolia. This sometimes caused bruised egos, and the sulks.

Raymond Guest was a new US Ambassador, a millionaire, well-known racing man, and a personal friend of the American President. His wife was a princess and not pleased to be placed away down the table, and hardly talked to anyone. But – rules are rules!

An interruption during a dinner party was very rare, but sometimes it could not be avoided. Our parents were attending a formal dinner party at Rusborough House nearby. Mother sat next to the host, Sir Alfred Beit. The butler came up to the host, and hissed urgently through his teeth, 'Speak up, my man!' encouraged Sir Alfred loudly.

'Excuse me, Sir', he lisped, 'the house is on fire!'

There were no more courses that night.

On occasion, Castletown was open to members of the public, usually in aid of the nurses. Knowledgeable friends, and sometimes we, acted as guides. We had queues down the avenue to see the decorations in the Long Gallery copied from the Vatican; and especially for the intriguing, disturbing story of the Devil, which has drawn visitors from around the globe ever since the 1760s.

Monarchs, emperors, dukes and duchesses, politicians and all the guests down the generations came to hear the story, and had to judge for themselves how Castletown could possibly be involved in such a strange, disturbing tale, which goes something like this:

Squire Conolly (in the mid-1700s) had his own private pack of hounds,[69] which he first stabled in the old Dongan house in the farmyard, and then, behind the new church at the entrance gates.

At a meet one day, a handsome stranger on a superb black horse requested to join in the Hunt, and rode up close to the hounds all day. As was tradition, at the end of the day all riders repaired back for a convivial noisy dinner in Castletown's dining room.

'Sit beside me,' said Tom Conolly, intrigued to know more about this dark stranger. Indeed, the anonymous guest had strange tales to tell, and was clearly becoming agitated. In those days, at less formal dinners, the host kept the bottles of wine standing upright on the floor beside his feet, aiding constant replenishment of the glasses. Glancing down to reach for the next bottle, Tom Conolly saw a disturbing sight. His guest had kicked off his hunting boots, to reveal animal-like cloven feet gracing Castletown's dining room carpet. It was the Devil himself!

The local clergyman was summoned. However, after much argument and frustration, there was nothing he could do to persuade the Devil to leave! Along came the priest, who cursed him roundly, and threw the Bible at him. The Bible bounced off him and cracked a large mirror (the damage is still there to this day), and the Devil disappeared beside the fireplace, where the marble hearth has had a forked crack ever since.

The Devil story was written down at the time, and signed by all the participants who sat at the table. A narrative poem of the incident became well-known some years later.[70]

Strange as it may seem, none of us ever felt a bad presence in Castletown; in fact it was a lovely family-orientated, friendly house to live in. Certainly, floorboards creaked, shutters rattled, and we shouted at each other from great distances. But we knew we must never tell Castletown's very own Devil story to our guests, until they had been staying at least two days.

The Devil's Crack in the Dining Room fireplace. This features in Castletown's infamous Story of the Devil, with Squire Conolly and his guests. A Bible hit the Devil, and he disappeared down the crack. We had a house rule for our visitors: we never told the Devil's story to new guests until they had stayed for at least two days, so they would not get spooked.

The house openings for the public were stopped in the early 1960s, because we considered the place was too dusty.

Mama threw everyone into a panic one July morning. She had received a letter from the Nurses' Garden Scheme, thanking her for her old promise that the gardens at Castletown should be open to the public the following weekend. It enclosed an advertisement for the occasion to remind her.

As Castletown, in our time, had never had any formal flower beds, nor any herb garden, or fountains, or a maze, or anything that would detract the eye from the ascetic beauty of the outside of the house – we had a problem! We wondered who had suggested there had ever been a formal flower garden? Yes, there was landscaping down to the river, ancient trees galore, wonderful walks with temples and secret byres, but no flowers. There was the walled 10-acre garden half a mile away, but by the 1960s, it no longer had eight gardeners to keep it in order. What were we to do?

Grandmother Ivy was staying and, ever resourceful, she clapped her old battered hen hat on her head, and got down on her Dowager-Countess knees, and began scrubbing the Long Gallery floor. 'If we are going to have to show the visitors *something*, it had better be the house.'

Grandmother had us all at it. Diana and I were designated to do the front staircase, and we got a taste of what the maids had been through, endlessly cleaning and polishing every brass stair-rod and every column on the banisters, all the way to the top – a nightmare.

Mama gamely attempted to enclose her curly fair hair in a scarf, but didn't get it quite right, it kept slipping, so that soon went. She retired to the market garden, to have an argument with the weeds. Why was the cleaning of the house so memorable to us? Because we had never done it before!

The Garden Scheme organisers arrived early on the big day, and announced that the visitors must get to see *some* garden, so we organised lifts in the cars there and back to the walled garden.[71] The house opening was a great success, but it was not what our green-fingered visitors had come for. All day long, we ferried them up and down the garden drive, ever polite, there was not one word of reproach, until the very last return journey. I was at the wheel, when someone bravely asked, 'Where's the flower garden?' I had been expecting this, and replied, 'It's not open today.' Goodness knows what they thought.

The colonnades on the stable side of the house came in for much unorthodox use. At one time, Diana attempted to grow mushrooms in the darkened room in the corner; unfortunately she forgot to water them. Grandmother arrived for a visit and, as usual, took charge. She watered them well, and then the whole family disappeared off to Scotland for their six weeks annual holiday. There may well have been a wonderful crop of mushrooms, but we never knew.

That colonnade room came in for all sorts of other uses over the years.

Some years after the mushroom fiasco, Patrick married Celia Cubitt, a daughter of Col. Guy Cubitt.[72] Patrick brought Celia and their new baby, Virginia, to stay for a few months at Castletown. Celia describes how they were occasionally expected to juggle baby duties with horse competitions at more or less the same time:

> Any able-bodied member of the household would jump horses in the Sunday Shows. We would set off with up to ten horses and a picnic lunch, and often would return home after ten at night. The baby had a pram with detachable wheels, which went in the boot of the car. On arrival, the pram was assembled and any one available kept an eye on the baby while I rode.
>
> On one occasion I was feeding the baby her bottle when I was called to jump, so she was passed to my mother-in-law with her bottle, who was called on to present the prizes, and when I returned to the car, the baby was very happily accepting her bottle from the sixteen-year-old stable lad.

Celia used to dangle the receiver of the baby monitor over the balcony of the hall while they were in the dining room. If the baby awoke, her wails would echo like a banshee round the house. Everyone felt certain it could be heard in Celbridge. The little one was not yet talking; in fact she said and gurgled very little.

Most days the pram was parked in the colonnades, where she got fresh air, but still remained dry if it rained. On one occasion, there were baby chickens in the room beside the pram, under a heat lamp. For several weeks all went well. At last came the day when she said her first words! It wasn't 'Dada' or even 'Mama.' It was 'Cluck ... Cluck ...'

SUCCESS, LEAVING HOME AND DISASTER

At the end of my schooling, at fifteen, I was sent off to a Finishing School, but it was not to Paris, Florence, or Rome to learn French or Italian. Oh no! I was delighted to find myself in a Swiss Alps School for young ladies, in Les Diablerets; skiing morning, noon, and night, with a smattering of French thrown in.

'*Mon Fertile*' seemed an unfortunate name for a bevy of girls eyeing up the boys on the ski slopes. In fact, the only pest of the male species we encountered was the eight-year-old son of the ski-lift owner. He was very small, and all day long he whizzed straight down the slopes from top to bottom, never bothering with a snow plough, or a turn of any sort; a constant hazard. We were sure he would break his neck, or ours. We were wrong. He was Jean Claude Killy, the future Olympic Gold Medallist, and World's No. 1 skier in the 1970s. His advantage was that his parents didn't have to pay for the ski-lift each time!

My 'coming out' season hardly existed. Upon leaving my Swiss Finishing School, aged seventeen, and before competing with two horses in the Irish team for the Junior European Championships, I took my first steps towards independence. I elected *not* to sign up for a full London round of dances and social events; especially as there was no presentation at court in front of the Queen any more.

I was always more aware of people and comments around me than Diana was. Perhaps I had a typically younger sister judgemental attitude. One sat back and watched your elder sibling mix with some very nice young people, but others were very false, loud and rude behind her back. I believed it unforgivable, for instance, for invited guests to pester the maids. I was not a telltale, and I reckoned I would not be believed anyway. But it did make me very wary. I'm afraid I looked on the hawking around of noble daughters as a sort of symbol of an unnecessary, outdated era.

But my parents were patient and tolerant, and treated me to a magical evening at Castletown, when I had my own 'coming out' dance during the Dublin Horse Show week, where I could invite all my own friends to stay. But then my somewhat jaundiced view of the London scene was firmly 100 pre cent verified by an incident during one of the two London 'coming out' dances (given by friends) which I *did* attend. And I have never afterwards heard of such blatant rudeness.

Sally at her 'coming out' dance at Castletown.

I was dancing with one of the troupes of 'Debs Delights' (young men), when he suddenly came to a crashing halt in the middle of a jive (or something I was really enjoying) – he left me standing alone in the middle of the dance floor with the words, 'Oh! I can see Mary over there. Sorry about this, but you can't compete against a lady and a fortune.' And he disappeared to ask Lady Mary to dance with him. If I remember rightly, I gritted my teeth, and swore revenge. You see, I was only an Honourable, with no fortune. I decided that this young man had obviously looked up my credentials before he asked me to dance; otherwise how would he have known? Looking back on the incident, it was hard to believe this happened in the twentieth century.

I never did get my revenge, but I finally swore never to go to any more Debutante dances again.

Starting to rattle my gilded cage, I became all too aware that all my schooling had taught me little that might help towards making an independent future; after all, I had never even had to make my own bed. Mama had been aware of my growing desire to make my own way in the world, and now consented to let me take a secretarial course in Baggott Street, Dublin, instead of doing the London season. The plan was for me to work in either Dublin or London when I had completed my course.

If this acceptance was a surprise, it was probably a welcome one all round. My parents must have been secretly relieved they did not have to fund an expensive London season. They never talked about money in front of us, who were unaware of the growing financial difficulties at home. The expenses of a Debutante were well documented:

A minimum of six dance dresses
One of them long and white, for Queen Charlotte's Ball.
Two or three were coloured, long and formal for the grander Balls around London. And the others could be short, for dances in the country.

Several day dresses
These were in silk or chiffon, suitable for Ascot, Henley, 4th of June at Eton etc.

Sets of shoes, gloves, handbags, and hats (to match)
These were all bought or dyed to go with the various outfits.

There was also a whole raft of specially fitted underclothes and girdles recommended for Debutantes, with extremely complicated openings (which many a girl claimed had been specifically designed to deter any drunken fumbling in the dark when nobody was looking).

The girls were given a make-up lesson, usually in places like the Elizabeth Arden section of Harrods, and shown how to look after their skin. They were sold little pots of extremely expensive Elizabeth Arden Twelve-Hour Night Cream, which magically tried its best to repair overtired eyes, and horror of horrors, an occasional skin-eruption on the face. Cream powder and a little rouge was used, just like their mothers, to endeavour to give the face that perfect roses and cream complexion. Unfortunately, this face powder would come off onto a gentleman's black dinner jacket, if you were unwary enough to want a hug. So there were no hugs.

Most of the dresses were bought off the peg in departmental stores like Harrods, though a lucky few had dressmakers back home who were up to the task. Almost as soon as a new fashion or a different cut was illustrated in the press, a Debutante would step out in a very credible copy.

Further costs were cut by one or two ingenious mothers, who managed to have ball dresses made out of their old curtains. If their brave daughters held their heads up, and acted the part, nobody was any the wiser; though some of the old matrons loudly claimed they could sniff out an old pelmet at a thousand yards.

An article in *The Tatler* gave the estimated costs:

Item	Shoestring Deb	De Luxe Deb
Mums' luncheons	£25	£100
Dinners	£60	£600
Debs' teas	£10	£50
Mums' dresses	£80	£500
Ascot tickets	£14	£14
Hairdressing, taxi, etc	£50	£250
Debs' 4 cocktail frocks	£50	£250
" 7 evening frocks	£90	£450
" 2 Ascot frocks	£30	£120
" 6 pairs of shoes	£22	£60
" 4 handbags	£10	£25
" 24 pairs of nylons	£10	£12
" suit	£12	£48
" coat	£15	£50
" Evening wrap	£6	£30
" 5 pairs of gloves	£4	£16
Cocktail Party	-	£600
Dance	£225	£5,000
Total	**£713**	**£8,125**

Today's equivalent would be about £15,000 for the Shoestring Deb, and more than £130,000 for the De Luxe Deb.

Diana and Barrymore meanwhile were by now jumping for Ireland in a number of European countries. The horse had gone from grey to snow white, and looked magnificent flowing over the wide continental fences, with his slight elegant rider. Diana has kept a much-treasured article written about her, and published in the leading German riding magazine, *Sainte Georg Magazine*. She has never before spoken about it. Reporting on the Nations Cup (Team Competition) at the famous arena in Aachen, Germany, it reads:

> *In my opinion, the best style was shown by Miss Conolly-Carew. The rider's legs always stayed in the proper place, as if they had been nailed there, before, over, and after the jumps. The rider is always in free movement, you would never see her hands move backwards at any moment. The rider and horse always showed a picture of perfect co-ordination.*

Patrick rode eight horses eventing at international level. He also show-jumped two horses internationally, and competed in Britain in the Nations Cup for the Irish team. This was a rare feat.

Over the years, Diana rode fourteen different horses for Ireland, all over the world. She competed in fifteen countries; and either won, or was placed, in thirteen of them. She won in USA, Spain, Portugal, Switzerland, Italy, France, Holland, Belgium, England, Scotland, and Ireland. She came second in the North American Championships in Canada, and was placed in Puerto Rica, and in Wales. She also competed in Mexico, and Australia.

Her most treasured gift from that era is the legion of lifelong show jumping friends from everywhere. Her team mates, Marion McDowell, the charming Irish Army Officers, Tommy Brennan, the Hayes', Tommy Wade, Francis Kerins, brother Patrick, Iris Kellett, and her list goes on and on. Many, unfortunately, are no longer with us.

This part of the story is perhaps the best place to explain Diana's earlier claim to have an amateur heart. It applied earlier to her not pushing a young horse too hard in order not to frighten it too soon in its career; it also applied to her semi-amateur era, yet her approach to competing at the top level was both professional and successful.

There was very little prize money in those days. There was none in the Nations Cups. One's only reward was the honour of representing your country. But the Grand Prix, on the last day, was always the most valuable single competition. When Diana won the Dublin Grand Prix of 1967, she won £200.[73]

Later, when the sport started to become professional, many of the riders chose to keep their best horses for the big cash prizes, and not for the Nations Cups. This brought the change in the amateur's rule. Nowadays, there is huge prize-money for Nations Cups worldwide; and the individual winner of the Dublin Grand Prix will earn approx. 50,000 Euros. Also, many top jumpers are almost worth their weight in gold. Some have been sold for over £1 million.

It is interesting to note that the handling of your winnings, while jumping for Ireland abroad in the 1960s, was very different to nowadays. Firstly, the Irish Show Jumping Association selected the horses and the riders, and organised all your travel. They then paid for your international entries, and you paid them back out of your winnings. But the prize money was so small that your biggest aim was to prove your worth by covering all your costs; and perhaps they would send you on another team.

One of Diana's funniest memories is of competing in the Open Speed Competition at Balmoral, Belfast. She was first to go on Cousin Jack, the little horse she later lent to me for the Junior Team. He started at full gallop, and was going so fast she did not notice three men lying fast asleep behind the first fence. However, she never wavered and continued merrily at full tilt. The crowd had been holding their breath, for they had already seen the human obstructions. They loved her panache, and laughed with her all the way around the course.

A large 'caravan' of riders, grooms, horses and all their equipment and food, created a huge amount to luggage which had to be carefully guarded and escorted from one international show to the next. Remarkably, few items were ever lost, mainly because each groom was responsible to keep an eye on their own horse's equipment. But, as the circus moved on, there were occasional muddles.

One year, after the British Nations Cup at the end of July, which was held in London, the horses, grooms and baggage travelled by train and boat to the Dublin Horse Show. Tom Tynan nursed his two horses and their luggage back to Castletown; these included Diana's suitcase with all her riding clothes and bits and pieces. Upon opening her case back home, she discovered a foreign gentleman's military uniform. It looked Portuguese, with lots of smart braid; and though the cases looked alike, this one was definitely not hers!

Luckily, she got her own clothes back when her case turned up at the Shelbourne Hotel with the Portuguese team. History does not relate what the foreign fellow thought of the 'frillies' in his suitcase.

What were the show jumping trips abroad like? Well, one lasting impression was of the many men on the international show jumping circuit; they greatly outnumbered the ladies. Diana described it as something of an eye-opener!

All the foreign riders were in the same hotel for about six days; and the males were naturally delighted to try their chance with the pick of the ladies.

Diana tells us of one memorable adventure to Rome: Two Irish riders were selected to go to the Ladies European Championship in Rome – Marion McDowell with Sweet Control and Blue Heaven, and Diana with Barrymore and Ask Himself. The four horses, Diana's groom, Lesley (now Mrs Lanigan O'Keefe), Marion's groom, Danny, and the two riders, arrived safely several days early. There was great excitement, because it was arranged that all four would go to St Peter's, and have seats to celebrate Mass with the Pope. It was a wonderful ceremony, and packed with people from many nations. The Pope spoke in many languages to welcome the various church missions. Diana had never heard a congregation clap and cheer before.

After the service was over, most of the congregation left; but they stayed to walk around the outer edge of the huge cathedral, where there were smaller chapels on the outer side.

The only Catholic amongst them was Danny. Diana glanced at him – Danny was *smoking*!

'Danny, you cannot smoke here!' she cried.

'It's so huge; I forgot we were still in a church.'

Diana thought he would spit out the cigarette, and put it in his pocket. Not at all! He threw it down and ground it out. Goodness knows which Pope or King might have been buried beneath. Diana was horrified, and Danny picked up the squashed remains.

The Rome competition was held over three days. Both Diana and Marion rode two horses on the first two days. Then they had to choose one each in the final, where two rounds were jumped over an enormous course. Unfortunately, Barrymore was slightly sore, so Diana had to ride Ask Himself, which had never seen that size of course before and was far less experienced. It was extremely hot that day in Rome.

In the first round, Ask Himself jumped the round of his life for a clear, along with one other. In the second round he was jumping magnificently, and went clear up until the middle of the course, and suddenly he seemed to lose his spring, and hit the last six fences in a row. The horse finished completely exhausted, and Diana jumped off, knowing there was something terribly wrong.

He had never been quite sound in his wind (breathing), which had affected him from winning races, but not as a show jumper. However, with the huge effort in the great heat that afternoon on the beautiful garden lawn of Piazza di Sienna in Rome, he had suffered heat stroke. He was taken back to the stables and treated. However, he became ill that evening.

The Italian Liaison Officer could not be contacted, however, a charming English-speaking Polish Officer, competing in the other competitions, came to help Diana. 'I am a vet,' he declared. What incredible luck to have a vet on hand out of hours.

He commandeered a car, and Diana accompanied him to the nearest chemist. He bought what he needed; they both stayed up all night with the horse, and without a doubt saved Ask Himself's life.

The next day the horse was transferred to the Italian Army Show Jumping Unit, where he received vital care, until all the horses and riders were due to fly home some ten days later.

There was one last competition left, for all male and female international competitors. Barrymore was able to jump again, and came up trumps by winning the final international class of the show. Diana was thrilled to find that the Irish Ambassador to Rome was attending in the Royal Box.

After the Rome Show, Marion and Diana competed over the following weekend at the Naples International Show. The jumps were much smaller, and the show far more relaxed. They both won several prizes, including the Pair Relay.

Before the next competition, the Grand Prix, the exiled King and Queen of Greece were introduced to Marion and Diana, along with Barrymore and Sweet Control.

'You have both done very well!'

'Thank you,' they replied, and Barrymore did his special bow and salute to royalty.

The Grand Prix started, and the snow-white Barrymore entered the arena. The bell rang; they sailed over the first fence and then the second. Barrymore and Diana were the best! They sailed high over the next fence ... but ... she had steered him over fence thirteen instead of number three by mistake, and they were disqualified. Being so full of royal praise, they were not concentrating on the course. It brought her down to earth with a thump.

They all returned to Rome, where a plane, which would also take the horses, was booked to take them back to Ireland. Without incident, the four horses, luggage, and four passengers boarded the plane, having signed the papers to leave Italy. The engines started ... and then turned off again. The pilot and second pilot left the aeroplane without a word, and returned to the airport.

It was stifling hot, and very bad for horses and passengers alike, with no air-conditioning.

Diana got out, and found someone who could explain what was happening in English. It appeared that French airspace had been suddenly closed to all planes, as there was almost certain to be an attempted coup against General De Gaulle, 'Maybe it is already happening, said the Italian.

The tired old horse-plane was not fit to fly over the Alps, which might have been the only answer to avoid French airspace. For the foreseeable future, the flight was off. The Italian authorities would have to wait for the outcome of the situation.

The passengers' passports could be re-stamped, but the horses would have to stay on the plane, as no-one had authority to sign them back into Italy. Desperate not to let their beloved horses suffer in the heat, Diana and Marion sat down to think what they could do.

Diana remembered an old friend Count 'Pippo' Cigala, a courteous, distinguished nobleman and a retired soldier. Count Giuseppe Cigala Fulgosi was an important figure in Italian equestrian circles. He was Master of the Rome Foxhounds, and spent part of each winter hunting in Ireland, with many Irish friends (especially the legendary Thady Ryan, owner and master of the Black and Tans). Diana had been in conversation with him at the Rome Show, and had explained about her sick horse.

'Here is my card with my private and business addresses and telephone numbers. Contact me if you need any help at all ... I would be honoured to help the Irish!' Then he had joked, 'The King is dead (Italy is a Republic); the Pope is Communist; so contact me, the Master of the Rome Foxhounds!' Perhaps, he was just the man to help.

So, she spoke to his secretary, who luckily spoke English well enough to pick up on Diana's fractured French (which had proved invaluable on many such trips) and realised there was an urgent situation. The Count rang back in a few minutes. 'Relax, I'll sort it out, I'll be at the airport shortly.' The lovely man, as the Irish say, fixed everything.

The horses were duly signed back into Italy, but where to put them? Count Pippo suggested the kennels and stables of the Rome Foxhounds, only a mile away down the famed old Roman Road, The Appian Way. This road was lined with crumbling statues, and was the main prostitute pick-up place, with dozens of the girls decorating the route, even in the middle of the day.

'You can lead the horses down the Appian Way,' he suggested helpfully. He also offered to take the most essential luggage in his car, enough for the four people, and the four horses; the rest would be safely left on the plane.[74] There would be plenty of horse fodder at the Kennels.

They sorted out which luggage they must take, unloaded the horses from the plane, and set off down the road, each leading one horse. A memorable walk! The horses looked at the statues in amazement, the prostitutes shifted from foot to foot and stared at the strange group of horses being led, no doubt wondering why anyone should walk beside a horse instead of riding it.

When they arrived at the kennels, Danny stayed with the horses once they had settled them in, quite happy, as he found one of the other grooms there was Irish.

Count Pippo Cigala took the three girls to his beautiful apartment in Rome. 'Marion and Diana,' he announced, 'you two sleep in my big bed, and Lesley can take the Spare Room.' He was a bachelor in his late fifties, with a great eye and charm for the ladies. 'However,' he added with a twinkle, 'I shall stay with friends till we get you safely on your way home. I wonder what my maid will say in the morning, when she comes to wake me and finds two ladies in my bed!'

He was wonderful, and took them out to eat in quiet places where it did not matter that they were not smartly dressed, and showed them the sights of Rome. He paid for everything, and ferried them to and from the stables to keep an eye on the horses. Luckily, they knew he could afford it, as they had already changed their winnings into pounds.

A few days later, the French crisis was over, General De Gaulle was secure once more, and off they flew, thankful to arrive back safely in Ireland.

Just before they left, Pippo Cigala twinkled at his three lady guests, 'I love my apartment with its wonderful views of Rome; now you can see why I enjoy *this* view ... I can look out and watch the nuns of the convent below, walking in their garden.'

My most memorable international competition came when I was sixteen and I was selected to compete in the Irish Junior European Team. The other three riders were Marion McDowell, Deborah Eakin, and Helen O'Connell. When I left Castletown on my great adventure I had a girl groom and two horses. my own sweet little horse called Paraguay and Cousin Jack, kindly lent to me by Diana and who I had ridden in the qualifying competition for the team.

The man in charge, the *Chef d'Equipe* of the team, was called Bill. His job was to look after the riders, nurse them through their nerves during their first international experience, advise them on problems, make the entries for each class, walk the course with them, and generally be their mentor and guide. Bill travelled with us alright, but once he arrived, he seldom came out of the bar. We thought it funny at the time, but not for long.

Unfortunately it was also Dublin Horse Show Week, and Diana and Mother were needed at home. So there was no family support to fall back on. Luckily,

I found an old family friend, Mrs Smith-Bingham, who happened to be at Hickstead and who agreed to help us.

All the teams from Europe were royally treated and put up in the Grand Hotel, Brighton; but the girl groom was not so lucky. As was normal, all the grooms were billeted in caravans near the stables. I got a panicky phone call from the girl groom, who was forced to keep her caravan firmly locked at night against drunken male intruders.

Cousin Jack and I came third in our first Junior European competition, but Deborah's horse went lame, and she had to ride my favourite little hunter, Paraguay. His springs were not really good enough for that level of competition, but he tried hard and only hit one fence.

The following day, I rode him in a minor competition, and he thought there were dragons coming out of the double ditches at the far end of the arena. He would not go within yards of these terrors. 'Some Irish Hunter,' I mumbled into his mane. It was pointless hitting him, he had a bee in his bonnet that day; maybe

Sally and Cousin Jack at the Junior European Championships at Hickstead. (Courtesy of John Nestle, *Riding Magazine*)

he hadn't liked someone else jumping him the day before. (The only time Diana jumped him; he felt unsure and stopped with her.)

Then we discovered to our horror, the Team Competition was going to include the wide Hickstead Water Jump. I had never jumped a water jump. Never mind ... Cousin Jack would know how!

All week the gallant horse carried his rider, and never hit a fence, but time after time I messed the water up for him. The first time, I gave him the same instructions as for an upright fence – we landed plop in the middle. The second time, I left it to the horse – and he was so busy waiting for instructions, we got wet again. By now, I longed for Diana's help.

When in doubt, gallop at it! Away we went for the last time, and laughed at the almighty splash we made.

Bill, the mentor, retreated from the bar, and blearily travelled home with us; it was not Ireland's finest hour.

Most international riders travelled with two top-class horses when representing their country. Diana's number one was usually Barrymore, who jumped in the larger competitions like the Grand Prix's and the Team Events. Her second horse was usually a speed horse, like Errigal, who won many foreign show jumping classes going flat out against the clock, over slightly smaller fences. Over time, she refused small fortunes for both of these horses, because, unlike most of the others in the yard, they were never to be sold.

Now that Diana had made her name, as she says, 'If you have one good horse, it improves a rider, and this enables you to train others to the same level of success.' It provided her with the opportunity to obtain good prices for some of the other promising youngsters she had trained.

This started, in 1961, with Diana reaching her majority, when she was given £100 by our grandmother, Ivy. This was a 'carrot' incentive brought in to discourage any young members of the family from smoking before they were twenty-one. With her £100, she added to her kitty by enrolling grandmother as a sleeping partner, and began buying one or two horses every year to train and hopefully sell on at a profit.

As each one was sold, half of the profit was given to her parents who had paid for all its keep, and grandmother got back her investment. The first three young horses sold well, making enough profit for her to buy the next ones on her own.

Ever since the war, our father had pursued his interest in the welfare of Irish ex-servicemen returning home from France and Germany. They often had horrific injuries, little money to support their families, and unsuitable housing. He was a hands-on figurehead for the British Legion in Ireland. In 1960, he became National Vice-Chairman, and three years later was appointed National Chairman of the British Legion, his office was at their headquarters in Pall Mall, London. He was the first Chairman who did not serve in the First World War.

He dealt with every aspect of ex-servicemen's lives, from the poppy factory in Richmond, to dealing with local councils in persuading them to provide better housing. For the first time, he brought journalists in to explain how the poppy money was spent; and one article in a Sunday glossy magazine was headed 'Call me Bill', explaining his relationship with the applicants that came to the British Legion for help.

He visited war graves in many of the countries involved in the Second World War, including the USA, Canada, Africa, and Holland, to assist with the organization of their ex-servicemen.

At the same time, our mother, having a life-long interest in the Irish St John's Ambulance Brigade, became one of their instructors for new recruits. Diana was roped in for practise sessions, and remembers being bandaged round and round, so tight that she could not move or make a noise. They all wandered off for a tea break during regular exams ... and forgot her.

Two of the leading lights were the Miss Overend's, who were described as 'small determined ladies'. One of them serviced and drove their Rolls Royce car until she was well on in years. They lived on a farm on the outskirts of Dublin, eventually realising that they were getting too elderly to work the land. When they sold it, there was a proviso that the farm was not to be built over. Over the following years, a good many builders tried to buy it. Today, the land is preserved as the famous Airfield Children's Farm. This farm provided the pets in Children's Corner at the RDS.

Our mother became the president of the St John's Ambulance, and looked elegant in her black and white uniform. She was also chairman of the Women's Section of the British Legion in Ireland.

When he was a schoolboy, Bunny had ridden a pure white pony called Dazzle, which was more like a small horse. Together they developed a reputation for speed, which became Bunny's speciality.

Dazzle was a wonderful hunter, and they were both fast and brave over the Pony Club cross country, and hunter trial courses. In fact, they used to go so fast that he jumped right to the bottom of the quarry, in the Pony Club Championships at Castletown, and had a terrible fall. It transpired that Patrick and Bunny had had a bet as to who would do the fastest time!

When he left school, he joined the 15th/19th King's Royal Hussars, and later became ADC to General Wyldbore-Smith, stationed at Dover Castle.

Not surprisingly, his sport has always been racing. For a while, he was an amateur jockey for the trainer Fred Winter, and trained his own racehorses to run in hunter chases and point-to-points while he was still in the army.

Diana leased Bunny a good old chaser, which did well for him. She also gave him a lovely horse she bought cheaply at the Kelso sales, in Scotland. Bunny hunted the horse in England, and qualified it to run in point-to-points. Granny Lauderdale came to watch their first race. It ran away at the start, and turned a complete somersault over the first fence. 'Dangerous,' said Grandmother, and promptly bought it, so he could not ride it again.

Bunny's greatest successes came when he won the Grand Military Hunters Chase at Sandown, and was second in the Grand Military Gold Cup. He was also due to ride in the Grand National, at Liverpool. However, his horse coughed on the morning of the race, and could not start. He was wretchedly disappointed, and never got a second chance. Back home on leave, he took a squashed saddle, that he had run over with a car, to the saddler. 'What happened to the horse?' asked the appalled man.

Whilst completing my secretarial course I kept on enjoying my jumping, and loved to help with the schooling of young horses at home. However, there was one incident during this period, which just might have changed my mind.

One young grey horse I was training had an exceptional talent. He was called Jumbo, because he was the largest and he was heavy. He had a phenomenal jump, and he obviously loved it. What he liked best was to catapult himself and his rider into the air, six feet off the ground while jumping over a tiny pole. I was like a flea on his back. There was not much control, but I had never sat on a horse with such natural talent. For the first time ever, I felt the awesome power of a potentially top class horse. What a revelation! It was a totally different feeling.

Normally, for its first competition, a young horse from Castletown had an outside rider, like young Ned Cash from Clane. He was strong enough to cope with a wide-eyed animal who had never seen crowds before. But this time, Young Ned had injured his leg at home a few days before Jumbo's first competition; so I persuaded my parents to let me jump him myself.

Well, the steering was difficult; the arena seemed much too small for him; the corners felt too tight to get around. We were in danger of jumping over the cars around the outside on more than one occasion (and no doubt he would have jumped over cars, crowds and all). But when I could point him at a jump, he launched himself skywards like a heavyweight rocket. The power behind the saddle was so astonishing that the only way I could stay in the saddle was to grab a tuft of mane as we took off. On exiting the area, when we had finished, he was so excited by his adventures that he took me for a gallop and we ended up on the far side of an enormous field, threatening to jump an impossible-looking hedge. Luckily, we managed a turn of sorts, and we eventually came to a shaky halt.

I returned to Castletown that evening, and knew I had found a horse worth staying at home for. I had visions of working during the week, schooling the horse in the early mornings, and jumping him each weekend. After all, that was the normal life of a lot of the riders on the adult jumping circuit. For the first time I saw an easier path ahead. But unfortunately for me, I had not worked out that once the horse's unusual talent had been seen in public, it was already worth a small fortune.

The next morning I approached my mother with a request to keep the horse, and said that I would stay at home if I could keep the ride. Mother's response came as a shock. She said the horse was too big for us girls, and he was worth too much money to keep. She had already contacted Joe McGrath, employer of Shamus Hayes, one of the world's greatest riders of that period. Mother suggested he saw the horse, and Shamus was coming to try him that same day.

To test the horse to his satisfaction, Seamus Hayes erected a big triple-bar with sloping poles. Approaching the fence for the first time, he gave the youngster no instructions at all from the saddle, and the horse jumped it easily. Then, to everyone's horror, he turned the horse around, and successfully jumped it backwards! He bought Jumbo for £800, and called him Doneraile.

I was ecstatic for the horse; Seamus would train him far better than I could. But nobody had ever talked to me about the family money problems, so I had no idea at the time how critical this horses value was for my parents. I wish now they had explained. I would have understood more.

Doneraile did go on to become a great international horse. First he became the four-year-old show jumping Champion of Dublin, and then he went on to jump for Ireland with Seamus Hayes, notably coming second in the Hickstead Derby, and winning the 1967 Grand Prix in Holland. He was eventually bought by the top Italian rider, Manchenelli, and ridden at the Olympics.

One evening during my last term at Secretarial College Diana and I were invited by Robert Guinness, from Straffan, to join a group going to the cinema in Dublin to see the new James Bond film *Dr No*. Amongst his friends was Ian Macpherson, a tall balding fellow, who appeared to have more brains and common sense than I was used to. We got talking, he called me slightly scruffy, and I found his straight forward attitude to life – calling a spade a spade – very truthful, open and refreshing. In any event, I quite agreed with him, I *had* got dressed in a minute and a half, and probably had not quite achieved the required sophisticated look.

There was nothing whirlwind about this romance. I was still going to London for the odd Ball, and for my brothers' Regimental Dances in London and in Germany. And, as was usual, I had two or three young men with me, who I trusted as friends and escorts.

Little was I to know, I had just met my soul mate, who has shared my life for the last forty-five years. The only problem was that he had been married. This caused a seismic family earthquake, and finally resulted in me leaving my beloved Castletown to live with Maitland cousins, and to work in London.

Two years later, my parents relented, and we announced our engagement at Castletown

When I was twenty-one, we married in St Bartholomew the Great, in London, and my parents gave us a magnificent wedding reception in the Army & Navy Club in Pall Mall, as well as a little house in Essex as a wedding present.

So, I was living away from Castletown from the autumn of 1962, although Ian and I visited for the yearly Dublin Horse Shows. This was largely why I was not fully aware of the ever mounting financial problems, and the growing impossibility of keeping Castletown's roof and electricity in good working order.

During the Dublin Horse Show of 1963, Ireland selected its first civilian/army combined show jumping team. Previously, the Irish Army alone had represented Ireland in the Nations Cup at Dublin, for the coveted Aga Khan Trophy.

Between 1949 and 1962, there were no wins for the home crowds to celebrate, and this period saw a progressive ground swell of opinion to allow civilians to join the army team. At last, in 1963, the rules were relaxed, and a new-look team was announced: Capt. Billy Ringrose on Loch An Easpaig, Tommy Wade on Dundrum, Seamus Hayes on Goodbye, and Diana on Barrymore. All of them had earned their places. Of the three civilians, the diminutive Dundrum had just won the King's Cup (for men) at the Royal International in London; Seamus Hayes had won the Imperial cup in London; and Diana had won the Grand Prix at Enschede in Holland, and was the leading lady rider at Aachen and come fourth in the Ladies European Championship.

Countrywide expectations for this new team brought approx 32,000 people to the RDS to cheer on the Irish riders.

The parade of the teams before and after the Aga Khan Trophy is still unique worldwide, because of the pageantry provided by the Irish Army band. Each team, in turn, is paraded behind the band and their country's flag, to line up in front of the President's Box, where their country's national anthem is played.

A few of the horses from the various teams had to be exchanged during the parade, for the noise of the band so near them could lead to an accident. That year, 1963, both the chestnut Loch An Easpaig, and the snow-white Barrymore were replaced for the Parade. Billy Ringrose rode a grey, and Diana had her second horse Pepsi, a dark brown.

As usual, each team jumped two rounds with four horses, and only the best three counted for the team score. Ireland was the first team to jump, and Seamus Hayes and Goodbye completed a magnificent clear round. The Germans also went clear with their first rider. Diana and Barrymore dislodged the corral fence for four faults, and the Swiss team rider got his speed wrong, and was penalised a quarter of a time fault. Billy Ringrose felt the crowds give a dejected 'Oooh' as he knocked two fences for eight faults. Ireland's chances did not look good. But the marvellous Dundrum with Tommy Wade tackled the huge fences at speed to go clear. The roof was nearly lifted off the stands with the cheering.

After the first round was completed, Switzerland was leading with their quarter of a time penalty, with Ireland lying second with four faults. At the start of the second round, Seamus Hayes and Goodbye left a hind leg in the water jump, with more collective groans from the stands. Under great pressure, both Diana and Barrymore and Billy Ringrose on Loch An Easpaig improved on their first rounds with thrilling clears.

The position of the teams just before their last riders jumped could not have been more exciting. Ireland, Switzerland or Germany were all in the running to lift the coveted trophy.

Tommy and Dundrum entered the arena, and every Irish spectator held his breath. Dundrum looked tiny beside the fences, as he started his round. He flew over them; he almost appeared to skim the paint off the poles as he answered every call with his personal stag-like jumping. Folklore believed that day, that angels had lifted Dundrum clear over those twelve fences. The cheering was immense. With the other teams lowering poles, Ireland had won for the first time in fourteen years.

There was only one headline in all the Irish newspapers the next morning: 'Aga Khan Win!' Around the country, the winning team members were treated like modern-day pop stars, and signed autographs wherever they went.

That 1963 win, with the first military and civilian mixed team, is credited with creating an enormous boost to the popularity and numbers of show jumping competitions around the country, and with inspiring a whole new generation of young world-class riders from Ireland.

Both Diana and Patrick were in Mexico for the Olympic Games. Diana and her show jumping team were stabled near the centre; but because of the high altitude, with thin air and a polluted Mexico City, Patrick and the Event Team were stationed about 100 miles north, where the conditions were more suitable for the long cross country and endurance test.

Brother and sister off to the Mexico Olympic Games.

All the Irish competitors for every discipline had travelled to Mexico several weeks before their competition to acclimatise.

My brother and sister proudly marched together in the opening ceremony behind the Irish flag. The parade was memorable.

Alas, Patrick's horse Ping Pong went lame, and he was unable to compete, then the poor horse contracted 'grass sickness', and tragically died several weeks later.

Barrymore was much affected by the climate, and slipped and stopped several times over the gigantic show-jumps. At the last double (only two horses went clear over it out of seventy rounds), Diana said, 'Steady!' at the second one, immediately after he had cleared the first, and he ran out the side. Eliminated, Diana's lungs gave out and she collapsed off the horse, after leaving the arena. She jumped again later in the day for sixteen faults, which was the same score as team mate Capt. Campion. What Diana did not know was that the gallant little Barrymore had broken a blood vessel in the first round, where he finished lame; and later proved to have jumped the second round with a cracked pedal bone (in the hoof).

After Mexico, Barrymore was confined to his stable for four months. The next spring he was restored to health. He was second in the Dublin Spring Show

Championship, and won at Westport, beating Iris Kellet on Morning Light, who, a few weeks later, won the Ladies European Championship with amazing riding on a very difficult horse.

The sixteen-year-old Barrymore was retired, and lived out his life at Castletown. He was later buried in Diana's garden, which was organised by Patrick because Diana was too upset.

Over 140 years ago, in July 1868, the Royal Dublin Society ran the very first Irish show jumping event on the lawn of Leinster House in Dublin (now Ireland's parliament, the Dail). It was advertised as a 'Leaping Competition', and was judged over four days, with just one jump each day. A horse had to clear the one fence to progress to the following day.

Day 1. HIGH LEAP   4ft 6in timber obstacle, trimmed with gorse.
Day 2. WIDE LEAP   A water tank of 12 feet, with gorse-filled timber.
Day 3. STONE WALL   Loose stones built up to a narrower top.
Day 4. THE FINAL.

By the third day, 'leaping' had become a spectator sport. A crowd arrived when it had been rumoured there would be a 6ft stonewall. There were only nine horses left to take on the challenge. After the second round, just three progressed to the final day; when 6,000 people turned up to watch them battle it out. The winner was Shaun Rhue, ridden and owned by Richard Flynn, a sheep farmer from Strokestown, Co. Roscommon. He sold the winner for £1,000[75] to Tom Conolly of Castletown, who hunted him.

Nearly 100 years later, in 1967, his great granddaughter, Diana, from Castletown won the main show jumping event at the RDS (at Ballsbridge), the International Grand Prix of Ireland.

Castletown, once again, became the home of the Champion Jumper of Ireland.

20

DECISION TO SELL, A FAILURE AND DESMOND GUINNESS

Having only very little domestic help coming in each day from the village, the cooking arrangements got so difficult and they became quite hazardous. Our parents and Diana had never had a cooking lesson in their lives. Fending for themselves, they seemed to be living on chicken from dubious sources, which they put straight into the oven. Somehow they survived! When in doubt, mother probably stuck to her marmalade sandwiches.

Mrs Mooney (the wife of Tom Mooney a farm worker) came five and a half days a week, whizzing around her chores at full speed. When visitors came, the wife of the groom, Mrs Tynan, came to help, and they both ran around the house making beds and tidying.

They vied contentiously for the 'tip' left behind by the guests. The first one in the next morning got the whole pot. 'A lovely man,' muttered Mrs Tynan, as she won the race to scoop up the 5s tip left by any of the male guests.

The constant repairs to the house became overwhelming. The roof leaked in several places, and buckets stayed on permanent guard duty underneath each drip into the bedrooms. Everyone in the house became custodians of a number of allotted buckets to catch the leaks. Diana's main area of responsibility was outside Grandmother's bedroom. The knack was to not let them overflow. This caused much dashing about, especially if a drip got worse. She had to gauge how long she could leave it. A whole day? Half a day? Perhaps a couple of two hours?

Conolly's Folly, and its suggestive shape. It was built by Speaker Conolly's widow Catherine to give employment during the Famine years. The deeds were handed over in an American ceremony and Mariga Guinness is buried underneath its arches. (Courtesy of Thomas Gunne)

The Hellfire Club, originally Speaker Conolly's Hunting Lodge, a site of much devilment in the 1700s. It can clearly be seen on the horizon from Castletown.

The front staircase, showing the stunning plasterwork on the walls. (Courtesy of Thomas Gunne)

The Dining Room with the screen on the far left. The food was assembled behind the screen before serving. This was where Mother crept up on the housekeeper, who she suspected of stealing the drink. (DG/SM)

The Print Room, planned and designed with fashionable cut-outs by Lady Louisa and her sisters. Our billiard table can be seen in the middle. This was frequently used when we had male guests staying.

The spinet piano in the Long Gallery. One of the first pianos made for Lady Louisa Conolly – with family photos on the top. (DG/SM)

Sally playing the piano in the Hall.

Tom Tynan, a master craftsman at long-reining young horses. This photograph was taken near the current footpath leading from the car park to the house.

Diana and Ballyfine in the infamous water jump during the Castletown Horse Trials. He was the Dublin Horse Show Champion Hunter and it broke her heart when he died shortly afterwards in a hunting accident.

The wedding of The Hon. Diana Conolly-Carew and Baron Alexis Wrangel in Celbridge Church, Castletown.

Diana and Capt. Billy Ringrose, fellow Irish Team members, at the Rome International Horse Show. (Courtesy of L'Anne Hippique)

Diana and Errigal jumping on a snow-covered ice rink in Switzerland, where the horses needed special long-grip studs. She is wearing an arm sash for the Lead Rider of the Show. (Courtesy of L'Anne Hippique)

Patrick and Ballyhoo (the ex barge horse) receiving the trophy from HM the Queen for the Services Show Jumping Team at the Windsor Horse Show. (Courtesy of *Windsor, Slough & Eton Express*)

Diana and Barrymore trotting into the Dublin Horse Show arena after winning the Dublin Grand Prix. (Courtesy of J.F. Connor)

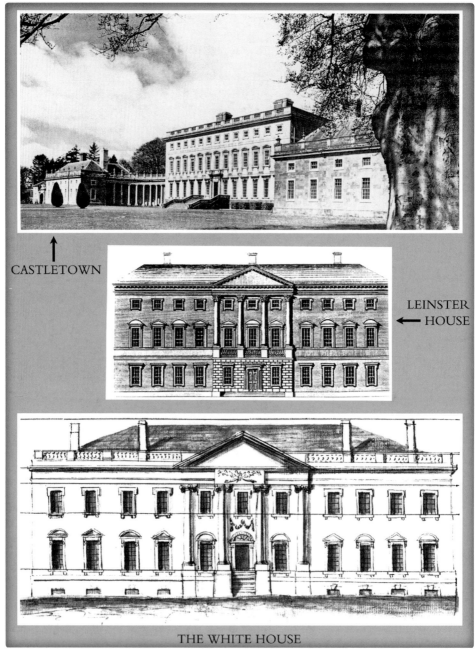

CASTLETOWN

LEINSTER HOUSE

THE WHITE HOUSE

Jackie Kennedy came to see for herself the uncanny likeness that the White House, in Washington, had to Castletown. It is accepted that Castletown is the 'grandfather' of the White House. Built by an Irish architect who copied the Castletown and Leinster House designs, the White House has a great many of Castletown's features, but with one storey less, and fewer windows.

Some leaks were on the first floor, so the rainwater from the roof had already travelled down through the upper floor. The house was in a very bad way.

In 1963, one afternoon, Desmond Guinness telephoned my father. Could he bring Princess Margaret for tea in half an hour's time? Panic! The house had to be opened up, and a decent tea produced.

The family lived in a typically untidy Irish mess; there was no staff to clean up behind us. Hats, sticks and gloves were strewn all over a downstairs table, wellies were left as they were kicked off, and coats were piled and dumped on the back of an old coachman's chair till the chair became invisible. The sitting room on the first floor became a hunting ground for articles in newspapers, pens, missing playing cards, odd pieces of puzzles, scissors, sellotape, pieces of gift wrapping paper, and scrapbooks. Only Mama kept her sewing table in order.

The formal rooms on the ground floor were kept tidy, simply because they were not used; but they were rarely dusted or swept in those days. The house was very dirty.

The family ran maniacally around giving anything we might see a 'quick lick' – a sort of old cloth passing at the run. There was no time to change clothes or to smarten up. Princess Margaret arrived, and did a tour of Castletown, with the Long Gallery, the story of the Devil, and all, she even asked to see Barrymore in the stables.

She had been in the Royal Box, and had seen him come second in the Queen Elizabeth Cup (The Ladies Championship of England), in London.

Diana brought him out to the front of the house, and was very proud of him when he bowed down low (another trick), in his best royal manner.

During 1963, Father consulted the family about the increasing costs of the repair and upkeep of the house. He had received an estimate of £150,000 to repair the roof, and to re-wire the house. Whereas, in the olden days, more land and outside estates could be sold to keep Castletown going, 300 acres of the farm had already gone.[76] There was only the house and 500 acres left of Speaker Conolly's great estates.

At the time, Patrick, still in the British Army, had hoped one day to return to live at Castletown. With no other option to save the house, the awful decision was taken to sell and the preparations were put in hand.

To understand the deepening financial crisis, it is necessary to recap on the increasing costs.

In the early years, when Uncle Ted Conolly came back to live at Castletown, between the two world wars, he appointed a farm steward named Hill, and took on many farm men at a time when there was very little employment in the country.

The steward and the men settled into their various roles, and all went well for sixteen years – but too slowly for Ted Conolly and his land agent. The estate needed more productivity. Already, the farm was not paying its way and helping to offset all the costs of the main house. Ted warned the steward that he was not keeping his eye on the farm workers' work rate. Nothing improved, and Hill left. A new steward was hired, who had a reputation of chasing his men to greater productivity. He pushed them too hard, so they downed tools and walked out!

New workers were taken on, but they took too long to settle in. For twelve years, the new steward ran most of the financial side of the farm, getting approximately £45 each week to pay the men's wages. He was also being reimbursed for machinery parts, seeds, cattle bought, and all the rest of the farm requirements. He was in a position of trust – as was the head gardener, who handled and accounted for the garden money excellently, each week.

When our father took over the house and estate, the initial investment from Mother's family in Scotland, was soon eaten up by urgent repairs. There was new farm machinery needed (the first tractors, binders, conveyor belts for bales etc being from the late 1940s and early '50s), barns needed to be built, fences made, the three-quarters of a mile front drive to be tarmaced for the first time, and there was constant upgrading of the cottages on the estate, as well as renovations on houses owned in Celbridge, Leixlip, and Maynooth.

But as the years went on, it became harder. This point is clearly shown when a vast electrician's bill came in for wiring the workers cottages and the Castletown outbuildings. In settlement, Father handed him the deeds of the old Courthouse building in Celbridge. Woods were cleared, and timber sold; thousands of Christmas trees were planted; field drains were put in and, where possible, fields were ploughed for the first time, and fertilised.

In the garden, which had always paid its way over the years, new ideas were tried, such as bringing Dutch experts over for advice on growing tulip bulbs. There were also acres devoted to the mass growing of daffodils, which the family helped to pick, box, and send off. Early forced strawberries were specially grown in the greenhouse for other house parties and dinner parties during the April Punchestown Races. They were grown high up on long shelves, out of the reach of children! A huge amount of out-of-season tomatoes from the heated greenhouses became too costly to produce in later years, when cheaper imports flooded the market. The same eventually applied to grapes, peaches and nectarines.

Outside there were apple, pear and plum trees all netted and trained along the high walls. There was also a vast rhubarb patch, which seemed to take over its corner of the garden, and carrots were grown in rows, pulled, and stored in pits.

Diana and I helped pick hundreds of gooseberries for market on summer evenings. The knack was not to get too badly pricked, because wearing gloves made the whole process too slow. (The punnets were carefully weighed, and we earned decent pocket money at a penny a punnet.)

For the last two or three years, the garden was rented out, with an arrangement that Castletown received produce from it.

Our father was very serious about the estate, and very well organised. He was considered a kind and fair employer (perhaps too kind), who seldom raised his rents. He took professional opinions on any changes, but it was not always good advice. As the figures on the house and farm accounts started to dig deeper into the red, as time went on, the horses (which were meant to cover their own costs) made matters worse.

Eventually it simply was not possible to pay for the upkeep of a 250-year-old house like Castletown, just from the income of an 800-acre farm and market garden. Castletown needed major renovations, or the wonderful historic house would fall down around us.

ESTATE WORKERS 1963-1966 (LIST COURTESY OF MICHAEL GRANT OF ST PATRICK'S PARK)

Employer	Lord Carew
Agent	Mr Peter de Stackpoole
Steward	Harry Mercier
Cowhand	Bob Stanley
Ploughman	Patrick McGarry
Assistant Ploughman	Michael Grant
Herd	Tom Losty
Farm Hand	Tom Buggle
Head Groom	Tom Tynan
Dairy Maid	Mrs Stanley
Maintenance Man	Bob Smith.

It later transpired that in spite of a good offer from a German who wished to buy Castletown, before the sale, Father would not accept it. Perhaps the war years were still too vivid in his mind.

Some favourite valuable objects had already been sold privately during the years leading up to the contents sale. Amongst these were several paintings, and a beautiful copy of the *Book of Kells*.

In 1966, the house contents were sold over three days. There was a large amount of furniture and paintings, glass, china, and silverware that we could not take with us, or which would not fit into the new house, Mount Armstrong, 12 miles away. This followed the auction of the house and approximately 500 acres of land, which were purchased by Major James Willson, the former Master of the Kildare Hounds, and his cousin, Mr Julian de Lisle for £166,000.

Desmond Guinness was the under-bidder that day, acting as President of the Irish Georgian Society because there is no charitable trust like the National Trust in Britain, to save important historical houses. He wanted Castletown to become an important flagship for Irish Architecture.

He tells his own story of bidding for the house with his own money:

My family trustees were pressed to sell shares to come up with as much money as possible to buy the house. We wanted to preserve it as the centre for the Irish Georgian Society, which we had founded.

I had someone to bid for me, and sadly it went £40,000-£50,000 over what I had to spend; and Mr Wilson and Mr De Lisle bought it. Besides, £166,000 was a reasonable sum in those days. The new owners publically undertook to repair the roof, and declared they were going to live in the house, and keep it occupied. They spoke to everyone about their plans to have offices in the basement, and run Ireland's finest Polo and Horse Centre.

Before the sale, a special arrangement had already been made with Desmond, to preserve many of the important pieces of furniture and paintings, chandeliers etc., and to sell them to him at a discount price.

The feeling of failure weighed heavily on our father (though he would never show it), as after doing his best for the house, and having previously saved it single-handedly in the fire, the family had to move out. His lifelong habit of lighting one cigarette from another became even more obvious; smoking sixty cigarettes a day to the day he died.[77]

Diana was the one who showed the most open emotion at leaving. She adored the house and just before the family moved out, she became ill, developing a bad attack of flu. She was the last member of the family to leave. Sad, ill, and despondent, she was unable to travel, so Sir Ivan KirkPatrick, a diplomat and friend of the family, offered to take her to Donacomper (just across the river) for comfort and bed rest.[78]

After one year, the buyers had still not paid. Worst of all, Castletown was standing completely empty and uncared for. What our ancestors and our family had striven and strived for since 1729 – to keep the house alive and occupied – was lost. Did the buyers not mind if it fell down? By rights our father should have abandoned the buyers, and put it up for resale. His dilemma was painful. But as an honourable man, he gave them more time.

Desmond describes the unforeseen consequences when the sale conditions were extended:

> *Unfortunately, Bill already had the money that I had paid for the chandeliers, and paintings etc. (and bits and pieces which filled up my own rooms in Leixlip Castle).*
>
> *If he had received no money at all, he would have been forced to put the house back on the open market, or sold it privately to me.*

What nobody realised was that the 'buyers' had only ever been land speculators. In fact, they were using delaying tactics. After the sale, in great secrecy, they immediately sought planning permission for a housing complex over all the land beside the front avenue. They knew they would never be able to pay for Castletown until the planning authority gave them approval.

Worryingly, the local authorities duly passed the housing plans on *both* sides of the magnificent avenue, including the field down to the River Liffey, our ancient 10-acre kitchen garden, part of the woods, and up towards the farmyard.

The poor house stood empty for two years, with trees growing on the roof, and lead being stolen – access to it was not possible, and nobody knew its true condition. By chance, Desmond and two friends were talking about Castletown, and decided they must somehow take a look at the interior. He tells the story:

> *We entered the estate in great secrecy. Miss Pauline Fenno of Boston, a great supporter of the Irish Georgian Society, was in Dublin. She came with me and my bidding agent, who managed to climb in through a window and unbolt the Front Door. This revealed the true state of the house inside. She said, 'Desmond, we've got to save this!'*
>
> *There were dirty newspapers all over the place, some of it wet from leaks. This was truly the first time anyone knew that Castletown had not been touched for two years. It was a shock, and it was a disgrace. The lucky thing was that none of the lovely fireplaces had gone.*

'I have a great idea,' she said, 'let's go into this together with equal shares.'

I was naturally thrilled by her suggestion, and drew up plans to make an offer for Castletown, hoping to halt at least some of the proposed house-building projects.

Not surprisingly, Miss Fenno's heirs were less than enthused by this wonderful plan, and managed to put a stop to it! She had to drop out of the deal. This left me in a terrible position, and if I was to save Castletown, I was going to have to attempt to come up with the whole amount myself.

Thank goodness he managed to do it.

Luckily, the scheme designed for a housing complex on the south side of the avenue towards the River Liffey was, eventually, allowed to lapse during my tenure.

On the north side of the avenue they created a wide strip of grass, and then a continuous mound, providing a satisfactory screen before the housing estate began.[79]

As soon as the deal was completed, Desmond and Mariga Guinness moved two Trinity students, Brian Molloy and William Garner, into the house. With huge dedication (Desmond describes them as 'very brave'), they opened the shutters and the windows to let in the air, cleaned up, began basic painting projects, and lived there without water or electricity, and hardly a lavatory for a considerable time. But the very fact that people were prepared to live in the house meant that thieves could no longer take the lead from the roof, or try to remove the fireplaces, and the voluntary renovations moved ahead rapidly.

The house was bought in April 1968, and it was opened to the public in July, three months later. There was very little furniture, except what Desmond had bought from our father.

Again Desmond takes up the story:

I heard that Jackie Kennedy was coming over to Ireland at that time, so I leaked it to the press that she was coming to Castletown.

Jackie Kennedy came to see for herself the uncanny likeness that The White House, in Washington, had to Castletown. Desmond goes on to say, 'Hundreds of people came to see her, and the house. The publicity got us started. Afterwards, we took her to see Conolly's Folly, and opened a bottle of champagne.'

Desmond tells the inside story of the sale of Conolly's Folly, a few years before:

When the late Lord Brocket was alive, I had a girlfriend at the time, who was his agent's wife. He owned Carton House and Conolly's Folly; and after he died, his second son, David Nall-Cain, was left to grapple with both heavy death duties, and a new Government wealth tax. He discussed with his agent which part of the estate could be sold to raise some of the money.[80] *The agent told his wife, and the wife told me. I put in an immediate bid for it.*

Eventually, the folly was bought for £1,000 by a generous lady in America, Rose Saul Zalles, in order to give it to the Irish Georgian Society. Desmond recounts the moment it was transferred to their keeping:

> *We travelled over to the USA for a grand ceremony of handing over the deeds, in front of the Irish Ambassador and the American press.*
>
> *The big reception room in the Irish Embassy had a grand display of models, photos and paintings of Conolly's Folly. In prominent position were the rolled-up deeds with ribbons and seals galore. This looked all very impressive, and all waiting to be publically handed over to the Irish Georgian Society by their benefactor.*
>
> *The deeds were all completely fake of course, but they looked good!*
>
> *Well, the Irish Ambassador was standing in between us, and he started giving his welcome speech, as required: 'And now I think we can finally say that the marriage between Ireland and America has been consummated.' Of course, everyone burst out laughing, because they knew the suggestive shape of the Folly!*

The saving of Conolly's Folly was a big project for Desmond and Mariga in the early days. It had been struck by lightning, and needed urgent repairs.

Years later, when she sadly died, Mariga was buried under the main arch of the Folly.

Each summer, Desmond had students from Trinity College, America and beyond, who had heard by word of mouth of the project taking place, and who gave up their time to help renovate Castletown.

Some of the rooms on the top floor (our old children's and nursery maids' bedrooms) were made habitable. They worked all day long, and acted out plays in the old kitchen in the evenings. These became extremely popular with the public. Many of the students acted, some sold drinks, refreshments, and took in the money. It all helped to pay for the renovations to the house. Desmond himself acted sometimes, in *Sweeney Todd* and other plays, and once, memorably took the part of a rather drunken clergyman holding an unlikely-looking Bible, with 'Imbible' written on it.

Lecture tours around America followed in order to raise more money. Sometimes Desmond received a large cheque, but mostly very small donations. He now remembers it as 'very hard work.'

In time, the financial support became more organised, and they established about seven Irish Georgian Society Chapters[81] in America. Gradually, they brought in the necessary funds, and required two secretaries, Hazel Mayer and Jose Green, who began working at Castletown, handling the Georgian Society work and dealing with the Castletown Restoration paperwork. Jose Green still works there.

Without the dedication and sheer hard work of Desmond and all his volunteers (some from all over the world) there would be no Castletown to see today.

Over the intervening years, the family have found it very hard to take the criticism about the state of the house at the time Desmond stepped in to save it. For years we have remained silent as to the true reasons. The buyers had given their assurances to everyone. First, Major Willson was going to live in it at one point; that it was going to be a casino, or a hotel. These were public pronouncements reported in the newspapers. Was it really nothing to them if Castletown fell down with neglect? Now our parents are gone, we can tell the truth of their despair at the deceit of others.

The family had jealously guarded both the fabric and the contents of Castletown for nearly 250 years. In the past, we have seen the terrible struggles that each generation has faced to keep the house going – to sell other land all over Ireland to help pay for its upkeep, and to make sure it was lived in as a home.

It was estimated that Speaker Conolly (who built it) had the rents from a fifth of Ireland to keep Castletown in the grand style that it deserved. Once these lands had been either sold, or forcibly taken by the Government's very laudable tenant-owning policy, the death-knell was sounded for many of Ireland's great houses. It can be argued that Land Bonds were issued as compensation, but the political realities overtook them, and they proved to be nearly worthless.

Our father did his best, he married his lovely heiress, and the house was rejuvenated for thirty years between the 1930s and '60s. However, Mother's family had their own stately house to keep going, Thirlestane Castle, in Scotland, which is even larger than Castletown. (When our Grandmother Ivy, Countess of Lauderdale, died in 1972, Thirlestane Castle itself faced a bill of over £1 million to cope with insidious dry rot, and major underpinning to several of its ancient towers.) All houses need repairs, but historic old houses only have a certain lifetime before they start to crumble and die if left without substantial financial support. It is our legacy to help preserve the best of them.

Now we know Castletown's story, let us celebrate the house as it is today, perfectly restored thanks to the Office of Public Works (OPW). This body has had a vast impact on recent Irish Heritage renovations. In this case, they act on behalf of the State and of the Castletown Foundation, which in turn acts as an advisory body to the OPW. For some twenty years, Patrick has been a director and trustee of the Castletown Foundation, so, that vital family link with our wonderful old house is still ongoing, and very much intact.

Now, let us be determined to dedicate our personal time and energies into helping support future concerts, events, galleries, and perhaps *Son-Et-Lumieres*. We must support the complete dedication of the curator and her team of helpers, who have placed Castletown as one of the great international venues in the World.

The great house is in *your* hands.

We still love to have our family weddings at Castletown and the coloured lights illuminate the back steps at Castletown making a breathtakingly beautiful setting for the wedding of Camilla Conolly-Carew and Anthony Newman.

Postscript

Finding the Castletown Papers

The clearing out of Castletown was an endless and almost impossible task. Nearly 250 years of family occupation left many dark nooks and crannies to be explored. When some of the furniture came to be sold, even the auctioneers missed some items. The big double desk, for instance, from the Long Gallery[82] was auctioned off with some old prints from the eighteenth century hidden in its recesses.

A huge pile of old papers and documents with ribbons and seals were discovered by our father, underneath the billiard table in the print room, where they must have lain since the late 1800s, when the billiard table was moved from the bachelor's wing (above the stables). He called in his friend Harry McDowell, from Celbridge Lodge, a genealogist who was used to handling important documents. Harry helped Father sort them out, and made arrangements for their further safekeeping.

Diana was astonished to find a stack of approximately 150 papers piled up on the Study floor. They looked old. 'Take them if you like, said Father, 'they are about to be burnt.'

There were two torn copies of Squire Conolly (Lady Louisa's husband) on his racehorses, painted in 1770 (The originals had been done in 1770), as well as ninety-eight lithographs of the time of Daniel O'Connell, and of our cousin the Duke of Wellington, 100 years before.

After the move, workmen found scrolls and deeds when they were clearing out under the unoccupied lift shaft. These were hastily recovered, and proved to be the story of the Old Castle, which had long been overgrown and forgotten. These priceless documents went to Lena Boylan, the local historian, who re-discovered the existence of the secret castle. She unravelled its history, and subsequently was the author of *The Owners of Castletown*, which has provided the basis for the extensive research that has gone into this book.

The following books and articles were also utilitised:

A History of Celbridge by Tony Doohan

Arthur's Round by Patrick Guinness

Aspects of Leixlip by S.M. Pegley

Battles of the Boer War by W. Baring Pemberton

Ballyshannon by Hugh Allingham

Castletown & Its Owners by Lena Boylan

Castletown, Co Kildare by Patrick Walsh

Celbridge Charter by May of Celbridge CC

Dongan Private Family Papers (USA) courtesy of John R. Dungan, DOS, MD

Galloper Jack by Brough Scott

Guinness Brewery in the Irish Economy

History of the Kildare Hunt by Earl of Mayo and W.B. Boulton

Horses Are My Life: The Story of Ned Cash by Des Maguire

House of Dreams by Stella Tilyard

Irish Houses & Castles by Desmond Guinness and William Ryan

'Irish Georgian Society' *Country Life* (Mar-April 1969)

Irish Georgian Society Booklets (Jan-Mar 1965/68)

Ireland by the Irish by Michael Gorman

James Hoban's Biography Records of Federal Lodge

Journal of Kildare Archaeological Society (1908/1960/1969)

Lady Louisa Conolly by Brian FitzGerald

Leinster House by Tithe An Oireachtais

Leixlip, Co Kildare by John Colgan

Norman Kilcloon by Gerald Rice

Origins of the Carews by Joan Richardson

Show Jumping Legends by Michael Slavin

Thirlestane Castle by James Jauncey

Topagraphical Dictionary of Co Kildare

The Scotland of Mary Stuart by John Skelton

The Concise History of Ireland by M.& C. Cruise O'Brien

The White House: An Architectural History

The White House by William Ryan and Desmond Guinness

The Fall of the House of Conolly

The Anglo Boer Wars by Michael Barthrop

The Rise & Progress of Gardening in Ireland by Joseph C. Walker, MRIA

The Last Curtsey by Fiona MacCarthy

Viking Dublin National Museum

Wellington: The Years of the Sword by Elizabeth Longford

Weather Forecasting by Robin Page

Appendix 1

THE CAREERS OF THE
CONOLLY-CAREW FAMILY

THE LATE LORD CAREW (BILL CAREW)

▸ National Chairman of the British Legion 1963-1966, for which he was awarded the CBE.
▸ President of the Irish Farm Land Association.
▸ He founded, and was the first president of, the Irish Olympic Horse Society.
▸ He died in 1994, aged eighty-nine, and is buried in the family graveyard beside the church at the end of Castletown drive.

THE LATE LADY CAREW (SYLVIA CAREW)

▸ Chairman of the Women's Section of the British Legion, South Ireland.
▸ President of the St John's Ambulance Brigade.
▸ Chairman and president of the Irish Pony Club.
▸ Chairman of the Riding for the Disabled Association in Ireland.
▸ President of the Connemara Pony Society.
▸ She died in 1991, aged seventy-eight, and is buried alongside her husband.

PATRICK CONOLLY-CAREW (THE CURRENT LORD CAREW)

▸ An army officer in the Royal Horse Guards, The Blues. He retired from the army in 1965 to return home with his wife and baby daughter to assist in the sale of Castletown, and subsequently to run the equestrian side of the new family home at Mount Armstrong, Co. Kildare.
▸ He was on the Irish team for the Three-Day Event in both the 1968 Olympic Games in Mexico, and the 1972 Olympic Games in Munich; and was a silver medal winner at the European Championships in 1962. He represented Ireland in

Patrick.
(DG/SM)

two different disciplines: in Eventing for twenty-six years, and also international show jumping, being one of the very few riders to do both.

▶ Rode at Badminton Horse Trials on ten occasions; Burghley six times, and Punchestown Three-Day Event ten times.

▶ *Chef d'Equipe* of Ireland's Three-Day Event Team at the 1976 Olympic Games.

▶ Former chairman of the International Equestrian Federation Three-Day Event Committee for eight years.

▶ A member of the FEI Bureau for eight years, and currently an Honorary Bureau member.

▶ A former Official International Judge for eventing for over twenty years, which included Olympic Games, and World and European Championships.

▶ President of the Grand Jury (senior judge) at both the 1992 and 1996 Olympic Games Three-Day Event.

▸ Patrick is the holder of the FEI Gold medal for Three-Day Eventing; a distinction also held by his daughter Virginia (this is a unique achievement, for they are the only father and daughter to both hold the FEI Gold medal in the same discipline).

▸ Patrick is currently president of Eventing Ireland; director of the Castletown Foundation; council member and trustee of the International League for the Protection of Horses, a worldwide equine welfare body now renamed World Horse Welfare; and former Council member of the Royal Dublin Society for fifteen years.

▸ Patrick married Celia Cubitt, daughter of Col. the Hon. Guy and Mrs Cubitt, and cousin of HRH The Duchess of Cornwall. As a young girl, the Duchess was a bridesmaid with Diana and me at the wedding of Patrick and Celia in 1962.

▸ Patrick and Celia have four children (Virginia, Nicola, Camilla and William) who are all married, and currently have eleven grandchildren.

▸ Virginia married Neil McGrath, son of Anna and the late Paddy McGrath (of the famous horse racing and breeding dynasty), and they live in County Kildare. Neil is a Member and Steward of the Irish Turf Club. They have two sons William and Christopher. Virginia rode for Ireland in both the 1966 Olympic Games in Atlanta and in the 2000 Olympic Games in Sydney on the Three-Day Eventing team. She also won a Team Bronze Medal in the European championships in Rome. She was awarded a Gold Medal for eventing by the International Equestrian Federation.

▸ Nicola married Piers de Montfort, a London investment banker, and they have two boys and a girl, Tom, Harry, and Louisa. She represented Ireland internationally, riding working hunter ponies.

▸ Camilla married Anthony Newman, a chartered surveyor, and they have two sons, Edward and Charlie. Camilla was a guide at Castletown for a time before setting up and subsequently selling two businesses. She is currently a property consultant.

▸ William married Jane Anne Cunningham and they live in Kildare with their four children, Poppy, Patrick, Georgina, and Daisy who are all keen equestrians. William is in property investment and development.

CELIA (THE CURRENT LADY CAREW)

▸ Celia is former chair of the Irish Pony Club, and its current president.
Former member of the Board of Governors of the Kings Hospital School.

▸ A dressage judge and a former FEI International Eventing judge.

▸ She is also a gifted and keen gardener.

DIANA CONOLLY-CAREW (BARONESS WRANGEL)

▸ In 1985, Diana married Baron Alexis Wrangel, son of the last White Russian General, who, with the help of European Allies, rescued 144,000 civilians and led into safety nearly 100,000 of the remaining soldiers of the White Russian Army, in full battle order. He also rescued the top priests of the Russian Church, with many of their treasures, who were being harried, murdered and robbed by the Red Army.

▸ Alexis sadly died in 2005, and is buried in the Conolly-Carew family graveyard.

▸ Diana had an outstanding international show jumping career for Ireland, mainly with Barrymore; but also with ten others horses. She has had the unique distinction at the RDS Horse Show of winning the:

Diana. (DG/SM)

Show Pony Championship
The Hack Championship
The Small Hunter Championship
The Working Hunter Championship
The Supreme Hunter Championship

▶ She won Grand Prix of Ireland, and was a member of Ireland's winning Aga Khan Team in 1963 (being the first lady member of the previous all-army Officer Team).

▶ However, she counts the highlight of her career as being chosen to represent Ireland in the Olympic Games show jumping in Mexico in 1968, on Barrymore.

▶ In the late 1970s, Diana lent her horse Errigal to the Irish Junior (under 18s) Team, ridden by Paul Darragh. The team became European Champions, with Diana as team captain (*Chef d'Equipe*).

▶ Paul Darragh rode Diana's horses to two silver, and one bronze medal in the Individual Championships.

▶ Diana is the main researcher for this book.

Gerald Conolly-Carew (Bunny Maitland-Carew)

▶ An army officer in the 15th/19th The Kings Royal Hussars, 1960-1972.

▶ ADC to Major General B. Wyldbore-Smith at Dover Castle 1964-1967.

▶ Married Rosalind (Rossie) Speke in 1972.

▶ They have three children (Emma, Edward and Peter) and two grandchildren:

▶ Emma, a qualified nutritional therapist.

▶ Edward, a financial consultant with a company of his own. He married Sarah Ball in 2011.

▶ Peter, another financial consultant with a company of his own. He married Posie Hardie in 2006, and they have two children, Lochie and Martha.

▶ Peter rode as an amateur point-to-point rider.

▶ Bunny added the Maitland name when he inherited from his grandmother the Lauderdale Family home, Thirlestane Castle; one of the oldest and finest Castles in Scotland. In 1982, after a massive restoration program he opened the doors of the castle to visitors. Since then, many thousands of visitors have enjoyed over 400 years of the Lauderdale family history in the castle.

▶ Bunny, for several years, played polo on his Regimental Team.

▶ He is a former Amateur National Hunt rider; he came second at Sandown in the Grand Military Gold Cup in 1963, and won the Grand Military Hunter Chase at Sandown in 1968.

▶ He has been a member of The Jockey Club since 1987. He stewards at many racecourses, including, for several years, being senior steward at the National Hunt Festival at Cheltenham and senior steward at the July meeting at Newmarket.

Gerald (Bunny).
(DG/SM)

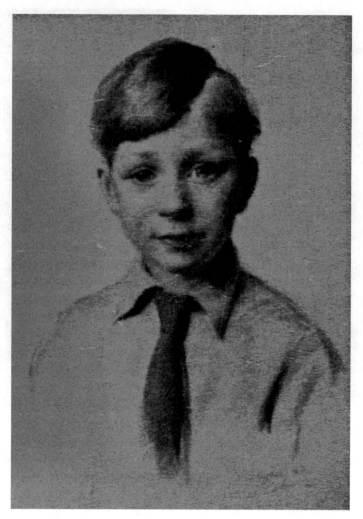

▸ In 2007, he was appointed by the Queen as Lord Lieutenant of Roxburgh Ettrick and Lauderdale.

▸ He is a brigadier in the Royal Company of Archers, the Queen's Bodyguard for Scotland.

▸ A member of the Border Area of the Territorial Army Committee.

▸ Chairman of the Lauderdale and Galawater Branch of the Royal British Legion Scotland, 1974-2004.

▸ Chairman of the Lauderdale Hunt, 1981-2002.

▸ Chairman of the charity International League for the Protection of Horses, 1999-2008; since called World Horse Welfare, of which he is vice-president.

▸ Chairman and host of the Scottish Horse Trials Championships at Thirlestane Castle, 1982-2008.

The wedding of the Hon. Gerald Maitland-Carew (Conolly-Carew) and Rosamund Speke. Patrick Conolly-Carew was best man and the bridesmaids were Virginia Conolly-Carew (right), Nicola Conolly-Carew (left). John Macpherson was the pageboy on the far left.

▸ Chairman of the Gurkha Welfare Trust of Scotland, 1996-2003, and since then, president.

▸ Elder in the Presbyterian church in Lauder since 1977.

▸ Community councillor 1987-2012.

SARAH (SALLY) CONOLLY-CAREW (MACPHERSON)

▸ Married in 1966 to Ian Macpherson and lives in Wiltshire, England. They have three children (John, Caroline and Katherine) and eight grandchildren.

▸ John is married to Lara Meinetzhagen. They have three children, son Alec, and twin girls, Molly and Honor.

▸ John was educated at Harrow School and is a banker, and a great sportsman, recently winning the Wedgwood Trophy 400 kilometre polar race to the North Pole. He has also completed the famous Marathon Du Sables.

▸ Caroline is married to Richard Gray, who served as a captain in the Coldstream Guards, is also a polar sportsman, and is now a banker. They have three children, Daisy, Archie, and Ivo.

▸ Caroline evented with success, and qualified for a Trial for the English Junior Eventing Team.

▸ Katherine married Markus Bolder, and has two children, Harry and Jed.

▸ Katherine evented with success, and qualified for Trials with both the British Pony Eventing Team, where she came second; and with the British Junior Eventing Team.

▸ Sally rode for Ireland in the Junior European Show Jumping Team at Hickstead, coming 3rd in the Opening Competition.

▸ She has been a writer for many publications, with a special interest in medieval fiction, and is your author here.

Sarah (Sally).
(DG/SM)

Appendix 2

THE ANCESTORS

THE ANCIENT CONOLLYS

The name goes back to old Irish history: Conolly – Connolly – O'Connolly – O'Conghalaigh – meaning 'as fierce as a wolf'.

When ancient Ireland was still called 'Fodhla', in the year AD 637, the O'Connollys, the O'Harts, the O'Regans, and the O'Kellys were listed as the Four Princes of Tara, who defended Ireland against a Scottish invasion at the Battle of Magh Rath.

Tara was pre-eminent of the five provinces of Ireland because it provided the justice and laws for the kings, chiefs, and tribes of the other provinces.

The O'Connollys, as well as being one of the four learned 'Law-Givers of Ireland', were recorded as purchasing the harbours on the River Shannon, securing the defences along the border of the vast Kingdom of Meath, which was owned by all of the Four Princes of Tara and their tribes.

The ancient Kingdom of Meath covered a fifth of Ireland in two regions. The eastern half 'Magh Bregia' ('magnificent plain') covered half a million acres of the finest lands, described as 'vast plains of unbounded fertility'. It extended over most of the present-day counties of Meath and Dublin, and included Fingal, along the coast between Dublin and Drogheda, between the Liffey and the Boyne, with the town lands of Kells, Tara, Trim, Navan, Athboy, Dunboyne, Maynooth, Lucan, and Celbridge.

The western region was called Teffia, and was also owned by the Four Tribes of Tara. This covered Westmeath, parts of Longford, and Kings County. The O'Connollys possessed and defended Co. Kildare.

They moved to Co. Monaghan when the Normans invaded Ireland and took over all the fertile lands around Dublin.

After the religious persecutions of the seventeenth century, and the Flight of the Earls, it is believed by historians that many families selected one branch to turn Protestant, for expediency sake.

The grandfather of Speaker Conolly (who built Castletown) left Monaghan, and settled as a Protestant in Ballyshannon, Co. Donegal.

Conolly Family Tree

Patrick Conolly = **Jane**
of Ballyshannon

Rt Hon William Conolly == Catherine, eldest	**Patrick Conolly** == Frances Hewett	**Rev. John**
of Castletown, Co Kildare	daughter of Sir	of Dunton Bassett, of Stretton.	of Co Donegal.

Rt Hon William Conolly == Catherine, eldest
of Castletown, Co Kildare daughter of Sir
Speaker of the House of Albert Conyngham
Commons in Ireland. of Mount Charles,
b. 1662. m. 1694. Knt. d. Sept 1752.
Died without issue
1729.

Patrick Conolly == Frances Hewett
of Dunton Bassett, of Stretton.
Leicestershire,
Attainted as "*of*
Donegal & London
1689". Died. 1713.

Rev. John
of Co Donegal.
born. 1665.
Entered T.C.D.
21 May 1682.

William Conolly MP. == Lady Anne Wentworth
of Stretton Hall, Staffordshire, daughter of Thomas, 3rd
afterwards of Castletown. MP. Earl of Strafford (1st Earl of
b. 1699. m. 1733. d. 1754. new creation); sister & co-heir
of William 4th Earl of Strafford.

Frances Conolly
b. 1697.
==
William Rewse, of
Queen's Square,
London.

Rt Hon Thomas Conolly == Lady Louisa Augusta Lennox, **Katherine** **Anne** **Harriet**
P.C, MP *(Squire)* daughter of Charles, 2nd Duke b. 1734 m.1761 (Henrietta)
of Castletown. Richmond & Lennox, K.G. m. 1754 George Byng. m. 1764
b. 1734. m. 1758 d. 1821. Ralph, 1st Earl MP. Rt Hon John
died without issue 1803. of Ross Staples, of
d.s.p. 1771. Lyssan, Co.
Tyrone.PC,MP
d. 1771.

William Conolly Staples == Anne, daughter of **Louisa Staples** == Admiral Hon Sir Thomas Pakenham
Died without issue 1798. Sir James Stewart, m. 1785 2nd son of Thomas, 1st Lord Longford
7th Bart. of Fort b. 1757. d. 1836.
Stewart. d.1867. *(Aunt & Uncle of* Kitty Pakenham,
who married the Duke of Wellington)

Edward Michael Conolly MP == Catherine Jane 14 other Pakenham children
for Co. Donegal. daughter of Chambre
(Col. Conolly of Castletown) Ponsonby-Barker
(Assumed the Name) d.1861.
b. 1786 . m.1819. d. 1848.

Thomas Conolly MP == Sarah Eliza Shaw **Chambre B** **Frederick** **Capt. Arthur Wellesley**
for Co. Donegal. daughter of Carter b.1825 b.1826 b. 1828
(Tom Conolly of Castletown) Shaw of Celbridge. d.1835. d.1855 d.1855
b. 1823. m. 1868. d. 1876. in S Africa. at Inkermann.
(godson Duke of Wellington)

THE ANCIENT CAREWS

The stories of the Carews go back to the two sons of the Princess of Wales, at the time of the Norman Invasion. Whereas the ancient Conollys were of wholly Irish descendants from the Four Princes of Tara, the original Carews were the sons of Princess Nesta, the Princess of Wales.

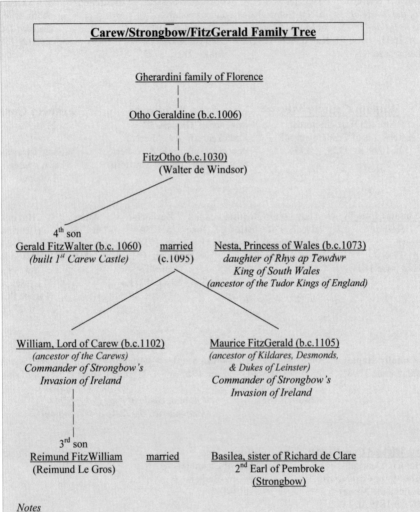

Carew/Strongbow/FitzGerald Family Tree

Gherardini family of Florence

Otho Geraldine (b.c.1006)

FitzOtho (b.c.1030)
(Walter de Windsor)

4th son
Gerald FitzWalter (b.c. 1060)   married   Nesta, Princess of Wales (b.c.1073)
(built 1st Carew Castle)   (c.1095)   daughter of Rhys ap Tewdwr
                                                   King of South Wales
                                          (ancestor of the Tudor Kings of England)

William, Lord of Carew (b.c.1102)   Maurice FitzGerald (b.c.1105)
(ancestor of the Carews)   (ancestor of Kildares, Desmonds,
Commander of Strongbow's   & Dukes of Leinster)
Invasion of Ireland   Commander of Strongbow's
                                                Invasion of Ireland

3rd son
Reimund FitzWilliam   married   Basilea, sister of Richard de Clare
(Reimund Le Gros)   2nd Earl of Pembroke
                                                (Strongbow)

Notes

1. Princess Nesta of Wales – was known as the *Mother of the Irish Invasion*. Her sons, by various fathers (including King Henry 1 of England), were the leaders of the Invasion.
2. Son of = Fitz. Sons generally took their father's Christian Name *i.e. Walter FitzOtho's son would be FitzWalter, Gerald FitzWalter's son would be FitzGerald etc.*
3. Our father, the 6th Lord Carew, was very proud that a Carew was coming back, 800 years later, to old ancestral lands: for the old castle at Castletown was built by the FitzGerald side of the family.

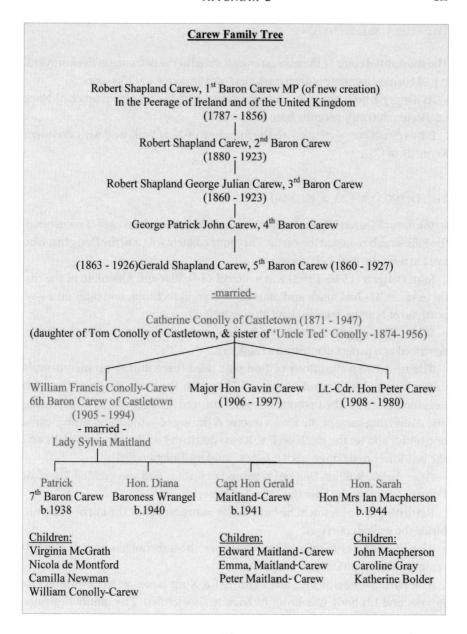

Carew Family Tree

Robert Shapland Carew, 1st Baron Carew MP (of new creation)
In the Peerage of Ireland and of the United Kingdom
(1787 - 1856)

Robert Shapland Carew, 2nd Baron Carew
(1880 - 1923)

Robert Shapland George Julian Carew, 3rd Baron Carew
(1860 - 1923)

George Patrick John Carew, 4th Baron Carew

(1863 - 1926)Gerald Shapland Carew, 5th Baron Carew (1860 - 1927)

-married-

Catherine Conolly of Castletown (1871 - 1947)
(daughter of Tom Conolly of Castletown, & sister of 'Uncle Ted' Conolly -1874-1956)

| William Francis Conolly-Carew 6th Baron Carew of Castletown (1905 - 1994) - married - Lady Sylvia Maitland | Major Hon Gavin Carew (1906 - 1997) | Lt.-Cdr. Hon Peter Carew (1908 - 1980) |

| Patrick 7th Baron Carew b.1938 | Hon. Diana Baroness Wrangel b.1940 | Capt Hon Gerald Maitland-Carew b.1941 | Hon. Sarah Hon Mrs Ian Macpherson b.1944 |

Children:
Virginia McGrath
Nicola de Montford
Camilla Newman
William Conolly-Carew

Children:
Edward Maitland-Carew
Emma, Maitland-Carew
Peter Maitland-Carew

Children:
John Macpherson
Caroline Gray
Katherine Bolder

The two Carew brothers came over with their kinsman, Strongbow, The Earl of Pembroke, who led the Norman Invasion of Ireland.

One Carew brother changed his name to FitzGerald (and his line became the Earls of Maynooth, and the Dukes of Leinster who lived at Maynooth and Carton House as well as in the old secret castle at Castletown); and the other brother stayed a Carew and settled in Wexford and Waterford. Hence, it can be said, the Carews came back to Castletown after more than 800 years, as Conolly-Carews.

THE OLD CASTLE HISTORY

The substantial ruins of the old castle are located at the entrance to the farmyard. It had been deliberately hidden from view and forgotten for 250 years.

Its history is both romantic and mysterious, with the uncertain touch of black magic, and has only recently been discovered.

It has direct connections with the founding of New York, and with President Kennedy of USA[83]

THE DONGANS, EARLS OF LIMERICK

In the days of Queen Elizabeth I, after several law suits and changes of ownership, the FitzGeralds regained the castle. They immediately sold it to the Dongans, who lived in it for the next 120 years.

John Dongan (1546-1592) was a Sheriff of Dublin and Alderman of the city three times. He had made and married two great fortunes, and built up a vast portfolio of bought or leased land all over Ireland.

When FitzGerald's old castle and estate at Castletown were bought, it was described as a perfect gentleman's residence.

The next two generations of Dongans lived there during an increasingly difficult period for Catholic owners of land. In the early stages of the Irish Rebellion of 1641, the Catholic Dongans enraged the Protestants by capturing and converting some of the King's troops. A throng of 'a thousand strong' came one night, and set the castle on fire. It was destroyed, with only some walls and the bell-tower remaining – as it is today – and the Dongans fled.

After 1660, William Dongan returned to favour, and was created Viscount Dongan of Clane, and later the 1st Earl of Limerick.

Returning to Castletown, he built a new mansion beside the burnt-out ruin, inside the walled courtyard.

The present day farmyard buildings are the substantial (much altered) remains of William Dongan's mansion.

The Earl lost one of his sons fighting for King James at the Battle of the Boyne, and his body was brought back to Castletown. The family fled once again.

His brother, Thomas Dongan (1634-1715), became the 2nd Earl of Limerick, and was sent out as British colonial governor of the Province of New York, where he gained the trust of the Iroquois, the five nations of Indians, and took territory from the French. He drew up the New York Charter of Liberties, which outlined freedom and justice for every man. This is still the basis of New York law.

Extract from The Pedigree
of The Maitland Family

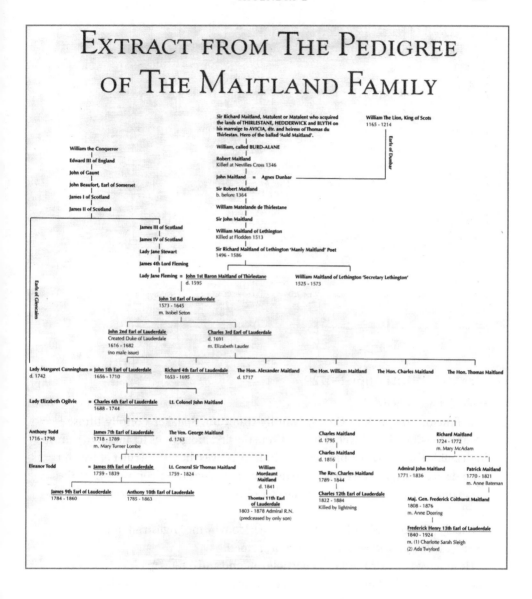

He lived on Staten Island in a country house, in an estate which covered nearly half of the island – he called it Castletown. This name still remains in parts of Staten Island.

He eventually returned to Ireland, and reclaimed his old family home. However, because Catholics were not allowed to own land, he sold it to Speaker Conolly; who chose not to live in the Dongan mansion, but to build himself the finest house in Ireland – the present day Castletown.[84]

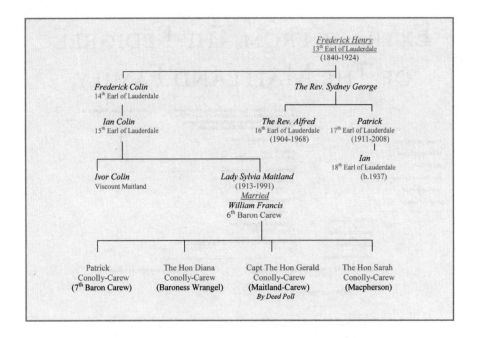

SPEAKER CONOLLY (1662—1729)

He built Castletown.

Following the ancient Conolly family tradition, Speaker Conolly himself became the Chief Law-Giver of Ireland, and the first indigenous Irishman to gain high political office (Lord Chief Justice). Indeed, he was the virtual ruler of Ireland for a decade, despite the early mistrust and jealousies he encountered. At the same time, he was also re-elected Speaker of the Irish Parliament continuously until his death.

Speaker Conolly refused the offer of an earldom by the English administration, in order to keep the trust of his own countrymen.

He amassed an extra-ordinary portfolio of land and estates in order to support the great house he had built, and to generously provide estates and houses for the many members of his own family.

Appendix 3

SELECTIONS FROM THE CASTLETOWN HOUSEBOOK

Face Steamer

A gentle cleansing vapour for the face, to be taken upon the first of every month.

1 tablespoon dried comfrey
1 tablespoon rosemary
1 tablespoon camomile
1 tablespoon cider vinegar
¾ teaspoon gum arabic
20 fresh nettle leaves
Slices of cucumber

Place dried herbs, nettles and gum Arabic in a basin. Add ½ litre boiling water. Lean over the bowl, covering the head and basin with a towel. Steam for 15 minutes. Wipe the face with slice of cucumber. (Not to be used on serious skin disorders, or broken veins.)

Elderflower Cleansing Milk

To remove freckles and light daily grime.

225ml buttermilk
1 tablespoon dried thyme
4 tablespoons dried elderflowers
1 tablespoon honey
½ teaspoon tincture of myrrh

1. *Pick elderflowers in June and July. Put buttermilk, elderflowers, and thyme into a basin over a pan of steaming water. Heat for 30 minutes (the milk will separate into curds and whey). Remove from the heat, stir, and cover with porous cloth. Leave for 2 hours.*
2. *Reheat again over simmering water. Strain into another basin through a double-thickness of muslin. Stir in the honey and tincture of myrrh (the milk will be a greenish/brown colour). Seal in a jar or bottle.*

Cleopatra's Cleansing Cream

> To be applied once a week

4 teaspoons white beeswax
2 tablespoons baby oil
2 tablespoons anhydrous lanolin
4 tablespoons almond oil
2 table spoons rosewater
¼ teaspoon borax
3 drops of essential rose oil (optional) *(do not use this for oily skin)*

*Melt beeswax and lanolin separately. Measure them into a basin over a pan of simmering water.
Blend in almond and baby oils. Remove from the heat. Dissolve borax in rosewater while stirring
in oils and waxes continuously. Slowly pour in rosewater. Put it in a pan of cold water, keep
stirring until mixture cools and begins to thicken. Blend in the rose-oil (optional)
Apply to face and throat. Leave for few minutes. Remove with cloth soaked in equal mixture of
witch hazel and rosewater.*

Rich Moisturising Cream

> Rich and heavy, applied to face
> before a bath. (**Adapted for
> modern use.)

1 tablespoon emulsifying wax
1 ½ tablespoons white beeswax
2 tablespoons anhydrous lanolin
5 teaspoons avocado oil
1 teaspoon glycerine
6 tablespoons water
2 tablespoons rosewater
** 2 vitamin E capsules
½ teaspoon borax

*Melt waxes and lanolin separately. Measure them into a basin over pan of simmering water.
Blend in avocado oil and glycerine. ** Prick capsules, and shake out the oil. Remove from the
heat. Stirring continuously, slowly add water, rosewater, and borax. Keep stirring (over cold
water) until mixture thickens. Store in screw-topped jar.*

Orange Flower Bath Oil

> Easy to make fragrant bath oil.
> (Turkey Red Oil is caster oil
> specially treated to disperse
> in water.)

4 tablespoons Turkey Red Oil (castor oil, specially
   treated to disperse in water)
3 tablespoons orange-flower water*
½ teaspoon essential orange-flower oil*

*Put the three ingredients into a basin. Beat until combined. Pour into pretty corked or stoppered
bottles and store in the bathroom. Use 1 tablespoon per bath. (If floating bath oil is preferred, use
avocado, almond, olive, or sunflower oil instead.) *Any flavour can be used.*

Honey Recipes for the Face

Honey Face Pack -- honey and egg white *(for pores)*
Honey Astringent -- honey and witch hazel *(face tonic)*
Honey Skin Soother -- honey and cider vinegar *(for spots)*
Honey Night Healer -- honey and comfrey *(antiseptic)*
Honey & Pollen -- pollen and natural honeycomb *(for spots)*

Honey Refresher

Honey wax
Witch hazel
Lanolin
Cucumber

Mix the ingredients until creamy.

A Glimpse Into The Old-Fashioned World of the Footman and the Carriage Postillion

For Cleaning Carriage Lining

I part fullers earth
I part pipe clay

Wet, and mix together. Apply to leather. When dry, rub it off well.

For Cleaning Harness

¼ lb of ivory black (black pigment from calcined ivory)
I pint of bullock's blood
I oz of oil

Mix well. Put it on the harness with a sponge, and leave it. When dry, the polish will appear beautiful.

To Make Ink for Writing

4oz of blue gall (insect excrescence on oak trees)
2oz of green coppers (sulphate of iron, green vitriol)
1 ½ oz of gum arabic
1 quart of rainwater

Shake it all together. Keep for at least one week before use.

To Take Out Ink Stains

Spirits of Salts (hydrochloric acid).

To Stain Leather Black

Salts of Tartar (pink and red deposits from completely fermented wine).

To Polish Boots

2 or 3 eggs
¼ lb of ivory black
¼ lb of treacle
1oz sweet oil
1 ½ pints of vinegar or beer

Beat up finely the whites of 2 or 3 eggs. Mix the blacking and the treacle, and then the eggs. And finally mix in the oil with the vinegar or beer.

To Refresh Stale Beer

Spirits of Woodworm (a perennial herb with bitter tonic stimulating qualities)

Put a little into the jug of stale beer.

To Remove Grease from Silk

Light brown paper rubbed onto any greasy spot on silk. Use ether on delicately coloured silks.

To Recover Faded Scarlet

Wash the cloth in Spinach water.

To Clean Carpets

Fresh tea leaves
Sprinkled over carpets to help collect and fix the dust.

To Make Polish

Used tea leaves

Keep for several days. Infuse with boiling water, strained, and use to polish mirrors, windows, glasses, and varnished woods.

To Remove the Smell of Cooking Fish

Put used tea leaves into the fish pan with the cooking fish, this relieves the odour.

To Remove Tea Stains

Tablecloths and other linen stained by tea should be soaked in a mixture of borax and water.

From the Medicine Cupboard

To Remove Thorns

A marrow bone of ham will draw out a thorn from your finger immediately.

To Ease Stings

Rub a common washing blue to cure the sting of wasps immediately.

For the Relief of Asthma

Blotting Paper
Saltpetre

Get blotting paper. Soak it well in a strong solution of Saltpetre. Dry it outside in the air. At bedtime, light it, and lay it upon a plate in the bedroom. A good night's sleep is obtained.

Mrs Murphy's Hints

To Revitalise a Lettuce *(in the days of plentiful coal)*

Place you lettuce in a large bowl of very cold water. Add a good-sized piece of coal. Leave for a couple of hours in a cool place. Magic! (You can only use a piece of coal once.)

A Tip on Making Mayonnaise *(modern)*

When making mayonnaise in a mixer, always add lemon juice first. That stops the sauce from curdling.

White Sauce

Always add a few drops of Worcester sauce and ½ teaspoon of Mustard ... Greatly improved!

Appendix 4

A Selection From *The Castletown Cookbook*

✧ Breakfast ✧

Breakfast Kedgeree *(With optional Cheese)*

8oz rice
8oz smoked haddock
1oz butter
2 hard-boiled eggs
1 tablespoon chopped parsley
6oz grated cheese (optional)
1 lemon.

Cook the rice in light stock. Cook the smoked haddock in milk and butter. Add the rice and butter to the fish, flaked and free from skin and bone. Heat slowly, stirring until quite hot. Add 1 sliced egg, parsley, cheese (optional), and seasoning. Pile onto a serving dish, and decorate with remaining egg. Serve with wedges of lemon.

Breakfast Boxty

1lb raw floury potatoes, peeled
1lb cooked floury potatoes, mashed and kept warm
4oz plain white flour
Salt
A little bacon fat for frying.

Cook the mashed potatoes first. Then grate the raw peeled potatoes into a clean cloth. Hold the cloth over a bowl, and twist the ends together tightly, thus wringing out all the starchy liquid from the grated potatoes into the bowl. Place the wrung-out potatoes into another bowl, and cover with the warm mashed potatoes (preventing the grated potatoes becoming black). As the squeezed liquid in the first bowl settles, the starch drops to the bottom. Carefully pour off the clear liquid at the top. Then mix the starch thoroughly with the grated and mashed potato mixture. Sift the flour, and mix in a good pinch of salt. Then knead the flour and salt into the potato mixture. Roll out onto a floured board, and cut into triangles about ½" thick. Slowly fry in the bacon fat until well browned on both sides. Keep hot.

✧ SOUPS ✧

Potato & Onion Soup (with leeks)

2oz butter
2 leeks – peeled and sliced
2 med. onions – roughly chopped
2lbs potatoes – roughly diced
3 pints of stock (½ chicken stock and ½ milk)
1 cup light cream
Chives – chopped
Parsley – chopped (for garnish)
6 rashers bacon – crumbled or chopped Dublin Bay prawns

Melt the butter. Cook sliced leeks and onions slowly (do not let them brown). Add diced potatoes. Season. Add the milk and stock. Cover with tight lid, and cook for 1 hour gently. Puree. Add the cream. Reheat gently (do not let it boil).

Serve with either chopped chives or chopped parsley, and with either crispy fried bacon rashers or chopped Dublin Bay Prawns crumbled on top.

Thirlestane Castle Bullshot Soup – For Shooting

Any Game carcasses (or pigeons etc.) to hand *(including those left on the plates after a meal – grouse are the best)*
Plenty of chopped carrots, turnips, lots of onions, and celery
Red currant jelly
2 glasses of Port
And any wine left over (dregs etc)
Pepper and salt

Put into a large boiling pot, and cover the contents with water. Cover the pot with a lid and bring to the boil. Simmer for 3 hours. Strain to make a clear Consommé. This freezes well until required. Reheat into thermoses. During serving, add Sherry or Vodka, or both to individual taste.

✦ MAIN COURSE ✦

Castletown Irish Stew

(Casserole method with carrots and Guinness)

2lbs Large neck or shoulder lamb chops
    (*or* mutton *or* stewing lamb)
2lbs Thickly sliced potatoes
2 Large onions, sliced into rings
2 Large carrots, sliced
7fl oz Lamb stock *or* water
7fl oz Guinness
Pepper and Salt
1 dessertspoon finely chopped parsley.

Preheat oven 140°c. Wipe the meat, and remove surplus fat (but not all the fat). Arrange a layer of lamb and vegetables in a flame-proof casserole dish. Sprinkle half the parsley and some seasoning on top of 1ˢᵗ layer. Add the second layer, and finish with some of the potatoes on the top. Mix the Guinness with the stock or water, and pour over the top. Use buttered greaseproof paper to cover the dish tightly, top this with foil, and lastly put on a tightly fitting lid. Bring to simmering point, and skim. Transfer the casserole to the oven. After a quarter of an hour, check it is still simmering gently. Cook until the meat is tender (about 2 hours). To thicken the juices, remove a few of the potatoes, mash them, and return them to the casserole. Add the remaining parsley, and check the seasonings.

Edward VII Lamb Cutlets

8 lamb cutlets
2 slices of ham
Salt and pepper
1 egg, beaten with 1 tablespoon of water
3oz of breadcrumbs
1oz of butter
1 tablespoon olive oil.

Trim the cutlets. Cut the slices of ham into quarters and put a piece of ham on each cutlet. Season. Paint the cutlets with the beaten egg (using pastry brush). Dip them in the breadcrumbs. Heat the butter and oil in strong pan. When it starts to brown, put in the cutlets, ham side up. Cook for 4-5 minutes, and then carefully turn them for a further 4-5 minutes. Serve at once with mayonnaise, sauté potatoes and buttered broccoli.

Cauliflower Cheese

Preheat oven to 200°c

1 medium cauliflower
½ pint white sauce
4oz cheddar cheese, grated
1½ oz stale breadcrumbs
Generous pinch dry mustard
Salt and pepper.

Trim cauliflower, and cut into florets. Cook in boiling water for 15 minutes, and drain well. Into the newly prepared White Sauce, stir in most of the cheese, the mustard, and the salt and pepper to taste. Carefully lift the drained cauliflower into an oven dish. Cover with the cheese sauce, and sprinkle the breadcrumbs and remaining grated cheese on top. Bake in the oven for 20 minutes, till the top is golden and crunchy.

Blackened Seasonings

Good with chicken or fish

1 teaspoon sweet paprika
2½ teaspoons of salt
1 teaspoon of compressed onion
1 teaspoon garlic
1 teaspoon cayenne pepper
¾ teaspoon white pepper
¾ teaspoon black pepper
½ teaspoon dried thyme leaves
½ teaspoon dried oregano

✧ DESSERT RECIPES ✧

Flummery

Rich dessert for dinner parties, serve in individual dishes

1 level tablespoon of oatmeal
½ pint of heavy cream
3 tablespoons honey (running)
4 tablespoons of Drambuie
Juice of ½ a lemon.

Heat the dry oatmeal in a heavy-based pan until brown. Set aside to cool. Beat the cream until smooth, but not stiff. Melt the honey over gentle heat until it runs easily (do not allow it boil). Fold the honey into the beaten cream, and finally stir in the Drambuie and lemon juice. Serve the mixture in individual glasses or dishes, and sprinkle oatmeal on top.

Glazed Rice Pudding

1 pint milk
1 ½ oz rice
1 tablespoon sugar
Plus sugar for sprinkling on top.

Put rice and milk in a pie dish, and add the sugar. Cook in a slow oven for 2½ - 3 hours, stirring once or twice in the first hour. When creamy, but not stiff, take it out. Cool, and remove skin. Dust gently with fine sugar, and slide under a hot broiler (to grill). When the sugar melts to a caramel, remove carefully.

Irish Coffee

1 double Irish whiskey
1 heaped teaspoon sugar
1 cup hot strong black coffee
1 tablespoon double cream

Warm a stemmed glass. Put the sugar in the bottom, and enough coffee to just dissolve the sugar. Stir well. Add the Irish whiskey to within an inch of the top of the glass. Carefully hold a teaspoon upside down across the rim of the glass. Pour the cold cream into the coffee. It floats on top, and the hot Whiskey coffee is drunk through the cream.

Castletown Cream Cheese

2 pints fresh cream, unpasteurised, at body temperature
1 tablespoon lactic acid (or unpasteurised sour cream)
1 Teaspoon of rennet

Mix together at body temperature. Place the mixture in muslin, and leave to drain the Whey overnight in cool place (the Whey should not be thrown away, it helps to make excellent brown bread).

The next day, add salt to the cheese to taste. Chives may be added (but not at Castletown).

✧ CASTLETOWN TEA-TIME ✧

Cinnamon Toast

Thin slices of white day-old bread (crusts removed)
1½oz softened butter (not too salted)
5 tablespoons icing sugar
1 teaspoon cinnamon

Combine butter, sugar, cinnamon. Beat with a wooden spoon till smooth. Spread the mixture on the thin slices of white bread. Cut the slices into 2in wide fingers. Place on a baking tray. Bake in a hot oven for about 8 minutes.

Chocolate Biscuit Cake

> For tea after shooting or hunting

3oz butter or margarine
2 tablespoons golden syrup
3 level tablespoons cocoa
A little dark chocolate
8 digestive biscuits (ginger, or any left over biscuits)

Melt butter and syrup over low heat. Add 2 tablespoons golden syrup and 3 level tablespoons of cocoa, melted chocolate, and the biscuits in crumbs. Mix and put in lightly greased tin. Chill in fridge, and cut into pieces.

Irish Soda Bread

> To be eaten fresh
> Preheat oven 200°c

1lb flour
½ teaspoon bread soda (bicarbonate of soda)
½ teaspoon salt
1-2oz caster sugar
½ pint of sour milk *or* buttermilk.

Put bread soda into palm of the hand, and press out the lumps. Sieve the flour, soda, and salt into a bowl. Make a well in the centre of the flour, and pour in nearly all the milk. Mix to a loose dough with a wooden spoon. Turn onto a lightly floured board, and knead until the bottom is smooth. Turn smooth side up, and flatten out. Cut a cross on top with a floured knife. Put it into a lightly floured shallow tin, leaving the surface rough, and sprinkle flour on the top. Put in the oven for about ¾ of an hour. Cool on a wire tray, and serve the same day.

Scones

Preheat oven 200°c

½lb flour
¾ teaspoon salt
¼ teaspoon bread soda (with raising agent) or 1 teaspoon baking powder
1 pint sour milk
¼ pint fresh milk
1-1½oz butter
½oz sugar

Sieve the flour and salt into a bowl. Cut butter with a knife and rub into the flour. Add the raising agent (free from lumps) and the sugar. Mix all dry ingredients well together. Make a well in the centre of the flour, and pour in the milk. Mix to soft, light dough with wooden spoon, adding a little more milk if needed. Divide into two parts, knead lightly; and turn the smooth side up. Flatten it into a circle – ½in thick. Divide into 6 or 8 triangles; Repeat with other half of the dough. Place on greased baking sheet, and put into a hot oven for 15-20 minutes. Serve at once, split and buttered.

Barm Brack

Preheat oven 160°c

9oz sultanas
9oz raisins
8oz soft dark brown sugar
16fl oz strong black tea
½ oz butter, melted
12oz plain flour
2 teaspoons mixed spice
2 eggs, beaten.

Put fruit and sugar in large bowl, and pour on hot tea. Stir to dissolve the sugar, cover and leave overnight to swell. Line all around an 8in x 3in cake tin with greaseproof paper and grease lightly with the melted butter. Sieve the flour, baking powder, and spice together, and mix in the fruit mixture alternately with the eggs, beating well each time. Pour into the prepared tin, smooth over the top. Bake for approx. 1½ hours. Leave to cool in the tin, before turning out onto a wire rack. Store in airtight tin.

Serve buttered or plain.

✦ DRINKS ✦

Orange Brandy

The rind of 3 bitter oranges (Seville) cut very thin

Put the rind into a bottle of best brandy. Let it stand for 4 days. Take out the rind. Make syrup of ½lb of Sugar to ½ pint water, plus the juice of two sweet oranges. When cold, add it to the brandy. Let it stand 2 days before corking it very tight.

Elderflower Cordial

1 bucket elderflower heads
Cold water, to cover
Sugar
Citric Acid

Fill a bucket with elderflower heads. Cover with water. Leave to stand for 36 hours. Strain the liquid through muslin into a large saucepan. For every pint of liquid, take 12oz sugar and ½oz citric acid, and place separately in a large container. Bring the liquid in the saucepan to the boil. Pour it over the sugar and acid. Stir to dissolve. Cool and pour into screw-top bottles. Dilute to taste.

Christmas Pudding

We loved the family tradition of stirring the Christmas Pudding, closing our eyes and making a wish – usually on my birthday in early November. (It was the one time in the year we were officially allowed in the kitchen.)

> Makes two 3½ pint pudding. For half this amount, follow the weights given in brackets. *Can keep for a year*

1lb each of raisins and sultanas (8oz each for only one pudding)
½lb currants (4oz)
8oz mixed peel (4oz)
6oz glace cherries (3oz)
4oz figs (2oz)
4oz dates (2oz)
4oz blanched almonds (2oz)
1 large cooking apple, peeled and chopped (1 medium)
Grated rind and juice of 1 lemon (½ lemon)
4oz butter *or* suet (2oz) *(could use margarine)*
4oz breadcrumbs (2oz)
8oz brown sugar (4oz)
8oz flour (4oz)
2 level teaspoons mixed spice (1 level)

½ level teaspoon salt
½ pint stout
5-6 large eggs (3)
1 glass whiskey
1 tablespoon treacle (½ tablespoon)
1 level teaspoon each of nutmeg and cinnamon. (½ teaspoonful)

Use two 3-3½ pint bowls, or use 2 pudding cloths, each about ½ yard square (for 1 large pudding use cloth 1 yard square).

Prepare the fruit into 1 bowl. Make the breadcrumbs (do not use very stale bread – not nice to taste). Mix the fruit, nuts, lemon (rind only) into a bowl. Sift the flour, spices, and salt into a separate bowl. Mix the suet and sugar into the flour mixture (If using butter, rub it in like breadcrumbs). Add flour mixture to the fruit mixture. Warm the treacle, and add it, with the stout, whiskey, and lemon juice, to the beaten eggs. Add the liquid ingredients to the dry ones – and mix well.

(Time for the family to stir the pudding, and make their wishes!)

Divide the mixture between well-greased bowls. If there is no lid to fit the bowl, cover it with a double thickness of greaseproof paper (pleated across the centre to allow for expansion of air during cooking). Tie securely with string around the lip of the bowl.

If using a pudding cloth, first scald it in boiling water, and when cooled, spread thickly with butter (no need to butter right to the edges). Pile the pudding mixture in the centre of the cloth, and draw up the edges of the cloth. Tie tightly with a long piece of string; put a few tablespoons of flour in the neck of the cloth, and tie again with string just above (this is to make the neck airtight). Allow some string for hanging the pudding.

To steam the pudding in a bowl:
Place it in a steamer over a saucepan of boiling water. Allow about 7 hours steaming. The water must be kept at a steady boil, top up with boiling water frequently.

To boil the pudding in a bowl:
Place bowl in a saucepan of boiling water, which should come three-quarters of the way up the side of the bowl. (You can stand the bowl on a pastry cutter, of a bit of wood, so it is not in direct contact with the bottom of the saucepan.)

If the pudding is in a cloth:
It must hang into the saucepan, preferably from something overhead. The pudding must be completely covered with water, and yet it must not touch the bottom, as it will scorch. Boil the puddings for about 7 hours. (If all the ingredients are used in one super-pudding – it must be boiled for 12 hours.) At all times the water should be gently boiling, and should be topped up frequently with boiling water.

Lift out the pudding(s). While still warm, replace the greaseproof paper lid with foil to prevent damage during storage. Store puddings in a cool dry place. (A cloth pudding must be kept hanging.)

✦ SPECIAL TIPS FROM CASTLETOWN ✦

Elephant Stew

For mass caterers, follow the instructions carefully

1 medium elephant
1 ton salt
1 ton pepper, freshly ground
5,000 bushels of potatoes
200 bushels of carrots
4,000 sprigs of parsley
2 small rabbits (optional)

Cut the elephant into bite-sized pieces (this takes 2 months). Cut vegetables into even-sized cubes (another 2-3 months). Place meat in a pan, and cover with 4,547 litres of brown gravy. Simmer for 4 weeks. Shovel in the seasonings to taste. When meat is tender, add vegetables (a steam shovel is useful for this). Simmer slowly for another month. Garnish with parsley.

This will serve 3,800 guests. If more guests are expected, add the two rabbits.

Recipe for Preserving Children

1 green grass field
¼ dozen or more children
Several dogs
1 brook
Pebble

Pour the children and dogs into the field. Allowing them to mix well. Pour the brook over the pebbles till slightly frothy. When the children are nicely brown, cool in a warm bath. When dry, serve with milk and fresh gingerbread.

NOTES

1   Tom Kelly's letter and telegram are in the Joyce Collection at Cornell University, in the USA.

2   Ted Conolly had copies made by Hicks of Dublin.

3   Tea tasting and the mixing of blended tea was regarded as an important profession; much like wine tasting, they both took years of training. A good taster would have a 'nose' for flavour, even though he might have to taste 200-300 teas in the course of a day. Gerald Shapland Carew had first been a tea planter with his cousin, Henry Shaw, in India.

4   Sadly, neither he, nor his father ever had the chance to live in the Carew family seat at Castleboro, in Co. Wexford (built in 1770 by the 1st Lord Carew), as it was destroyed during the Troubles of 1922/3. Even earlier, in 1840, an accidental fire destroyed all but the west wing of Castleboro; and the Kilkenny (and Oxford) architect, Daniel Robertson, was asked to design a new classical house, (central block and two wings) incorporating the surviving wing; and to create terrace gardens, and a lovely lake. Its triple terraced garden, with three fountains and magnificent water features, were reputed to be second only in Ireland to those at Powerscourt House, Co. Wicklow, which were designed by the same architect.

    A relation of William Adams, Daniel Robertson had redesigned All Souls' College, Arial College, as well as St Clement's Church, in Oxford, but had left England under a financial cloud. Years later, he worked on the designs for the gardens at Powerscourt, but became so befuddled while imbibing the 'hard stuff' that he had to be transported about in a wheelbarrow. According to contemporary reports, unwary visitors were greeted with the incongruous sight of this rather large folded-up person with ginger whiskers, waving his arms about attempting to direct the workmen.

5   She also lived at Westport House, Co. Mayo.

6   Castletown can be very cold if no fires are lit. Even with the house full of servants to light the fires, we used to put coats on to run along the passages from room to room.

7   Leixlip was bought by Lord Decies, who installed a new front door with his family coronet and a large 'D' carved on it.

8   For short history of Dongans, see *Dongans, Earls of Limerick* in the appendix.

9   These copied a line of lime trees that Speaker Conolly planted, in the late 1600s, at his previous house at Rodanstown, Kilcock, 8 miles away.

10   The Number 1 high hurdler was (later) Lord Burghley, from Burghley House, who went on to win an Olympic Gold Medal.

11   Ralph Vaughan Williams was a composer of sublime classical music, as well as hymns like 'For all the Saints'.

12   That privilege has continued to this day. Patrick and his wife, Celia, hunted army horses when he served in the Household Cavalry in London in the late 1950s and '60s.

13   There is a shorter route from the old kitchen, if you climb the stairs at the side. But this led through the servants' private quarters above, and would not have been used for the transport of food.

14   Later, Lady Athlumney became godmother to Diana.

15   Zonda – a little horse Peggy later lent to Bunny, to race as a schoolmaster.

16   The Larder was moved in 1938/9 to the bottom of the backstairs in the main house. The wash room and larder were lined with white tiles to keep food cool.

17   Rosie, Marchioness of Headfort, was previously called Rosie Boote and was brought up in Ireland. Her father was a comedian in England, and Rosie joined the Bluebell Girls dancing troupe in London (who were considered respectable and well chaperoned), many of whom married into titled families. It was said that these lovely ladies managed to 'stiffen up the over thin blue blood.' This meant that too many aristocratic family members showed signs of being too closely related to each other. Rosie was a strong character, and she and her husband were great family friends.

18   Shortly after Castletown was finished, around 1730, the MP architect Lovett Pearce, who had overseen the building of the house, petitioned Parliament to request the standardising of Irish-made bricks because they were too soft. He mentioned Dutch bricks as being a better alternative.

19   We still wonder if some of the gardens of the new houses are still turning up red-brick dust?

20   When the house was open to the public, Diana used to enjoy playing a trick on the visitors, by pointing out the pet cemetery and telling them that the graves were for servants secretly buried, because one Conolly had killed them in a drunken rage! She did confess the truth immediately afterwards, but no doubt she spooked a few.

21   Serving the Dongans (later the Earls of Limerick) in the days of the old secret castle, long before the present Castletown was built. See *The Dongans* in the appendix.

22   In the 1950s, there were still the remains of wooden stalls for polo ponies along the Big Wood edge of the polo field.

23   Eventually, a tractor and trailer took over these duties.

24   The Gate House was built in 1783 as a three-bay, two-storey cottage, and separate from the existing Round House. The space between the two buildings was later filled in to create a terrace of three. The central lodge was called The Pottery.

25   Helen McDonald now has two children. Susanne is a paediatric nurse at Portloise

Hospital; and Alan, who farms part-time, and works in the Midland Veterinary in Tullamore.

26   In time, Summerhill became known as the most beautiful ruin in Ireland. The owner disliked so many intruders coming to see its romantic setting; she pulled it down, and sold the stones in the early 1950s. They were reputedly used to build a convent.

27   Another attack by the IRA was on a house called Curraghmore. This had a happier outcome. The men with burning torches approached up the drive with petrol at the ready, when a full moon appeared suddenly from behind the midnight clouds, and shone onto the Beresford family Crest, which was situated high up above the house. The crest was a cross between the antlers of a stag. The effect was so eerie, they thought it was a holy message, and took off in fright, and left the house alone.

28   Castletown Kedgeree recipe at the back.

29   For the Story of the Devil, see chapter 18.

30   Mother's bed had been a four-poster, but her mother, Granny Lauderdale, insisted on getting the four posts sawn off short ... even though it wasn't her bed! Perhaps it got the woodworm. Granny also beheaded another four-poster bed in the main guest room, the blue bedroom, which had been beautifully draped in blue silk.

31   'Grandpa's going hunting!' said one grandson, years later, when he spotted the long white (all-in-one) combinations, worn with long black socks, fresh out of bed.

32   It was decided to send Patrick and Bunny to different prep schools, because of the rowdy reputation of our father and his two brothers in their day.

33   In a somewhat unlikely turn of events, I became the Greek Dancing Champion of Ireland; quite splendid at standing still and looking like Apollo, or Aphrodite, pretending to release an arrow towards a far-off foe. But distinctly un-useful in later life!

34   The chest is now owned by Tim and Frank Foley, architects, Dublin.

35   This desk and matching cabinet are still in the family.

36   The boys from the school behind the church would last about two years as 'pumpers'. He had to be small and strong. The organist had to give him something out of his own pocket.

37   Your author, despite growing up at Castletown between the 1940s and the '60s, saw the inside of the servants' wing for the first time, only three years ago on a public tour.

38   In the days before our parents arrived at Castletown, the old kitchen was still in use. Opposite the old kitchen there was a big glass Scullery, with long glass windows, and sinks like baths; a structure that was built out into the kitchen yard. It had been used for generations for the washing up. This was removed when a more modern kitchen was built in the basement of the main house.

39   Diana particularly hated baked custard, was unwise enough to say so and for weeks it appeared just for her at lunch in the dining room.

40   Other Castletown workers moved into Council Houses close by, including Paddy McGarry, Mr Cummins, Paddy Baggeley, and Mick McCarthy.

41   This was painted by a neighbour, John Jobson.

42   We grew up appreciating a bath as a very great luxury. Our parents had an
      immersion heater in their private bathroom, and wonder upon wonder, they could
      have a bath every day!

43   This brought the total in the stable yard to twelve stables for horses, and six pony
      boxes. There was also some hay and straw taking up space in the lower stables. (The
      main body of hay and straw were stored in a large barn beyond the garage.)

44   Patricia later married Patrick Ellis, Diana's Joint Master of Hounds.

45   This method of passing on old family favourites, gave other lucky children of
      friends, the chance to ride really experienced ponies. We also did it with Copper Top
      in later years.

46   Diana was very slight, well under 9 stone, which made life difficult for her horses,
      who were required to carry 11stone 11lbs (75 kilos) in international competitions.
      They carried pockets of lead weights under the saddle. It was a definite disadvantage,
      because the lead was static and could not move forward over the horse's neck to
      assist the horse's balance while jumping.

47   To us, Nan was quite mad, but in truth, there was certainly a perception there that
      was out of the ordinary.

48   The same rhyme in the nursery.

49   By this time we were all on the Sunday Show circuit, held most Sunday afternoons
      in the summertime. These were competitions held at Dublin venues such as
      Terenure College, Galloping Green, Stillorgan, Bray etc.

50   We once had fun rounding-up stray cattle along beside the river after they made
      wild escapes from the meat factory next door. As we herded them, they freely
      jumped part of our cross country course, most of the ditches and obstacles along
      the way, and memorably, over a low part of the estate wall and back into their own
      field.

51   Other tunnels have been recently discovered. One of them has an entrance at the
      village end of the front avenue, and is still to be fully investigated.

52   The gates were decorated with the back-to-back initials 'C.C.', for Catherine Conolly,
      wife of Speaker Conolly who created the Garden in the early 1700s.

53   The print room next door was originally its dressing room.

54   Long gone were the days when the local IRA planned to ambush a train near
      Hazelhatch station (during the Troubles of 1922). Word had reached them that
      British soldiers were due to travel by train from Dublin to Cork. Unfortunately,
      several of the local men had sisters working as maids in the big houses, who talked
      about the planned ambush to others. The British Army was told, and turned the
      tables on the IRA, who were surprised and captured without injury.

55   Nowadays, before competing, every horse or pony is blood tested, micro chipped,
      and every marking recorded.

56   One groom at Castletown was given a half-share in a young horse. 'What
      name?'
      'Well, one name you see a lot is Cul de Sac.'

'That means "Dead End", that's not a good name for a horse!' Eventually it was named after a local pub.

57   Col. Dudgeon had been a well-known show jumping rider in the 1930s, and had such a bond with his old horse Sea Lion, that he still gave jumping exhibitions on him at the RDS, without a bridle!

58   Father first attempted to hunt a horse called Sergeant Major, which he had brought over from England with him, but it proved to be hopeless at jumping ditches. He was forever being left in the bottom. It became a great plough horse instead. Later, Father hunted a huge horse, Mr Jones, with giant feet.

59   In the early days, Christy Murphy did the hand milking, followed by Stanley. Originally, the milk was skimmed for the cream. Later, they used a separator; then a lot of the cream was put in the hand churn (which was a monotonous back-breaking machine that looked like a biggish barrel) to make the butter.

60   Our own dresses were made for us by a dressmaker in her house in White City, off the Dublin Road. Our riding clothes were made by a tailor living on the old Lucan to Dublin Road, beside the Liffey. His enchanting white cottage with a blue door and two windows was in a row of six; and they still look the same today. It backed onto the strawberry beds, where fashionable carriages once drove out of Dublin through Phoenix Park, on their way to Lucan on a Saturday afternoon.

61   Josie Darlington was a superb blacksmith, and when he lost his licence for drink driving and causing an accident, Mother went to court to plead, 'He is needed to shoe Barrymore', and his licence was returned!

62   Susie Lanigan O'Keefe and her family have been lifelong friends, through ponies and horses. Her own quick reactions saved herself from being decapitated one year at the Dublin Show. Competing in the main arena, her horse decided the next jump was the large decorative hedge around the outside of the arena. This was extremely dangerous. The horse took off, and landed in the Competitors' Stand, which had a very low overhanging roof. Susie had the presence of mind to take her hands from the reins in mid-air, and grab at the edge of the roof. No rider could have fitted under there. Susie now breeds Irish Draughts.

63   Weston Aerodrome was a flying club owned by the Kennedys, with many double-winged aircraft. The film *The Blue Max*, depicting aerial combat during the First World War, was filmed there, using their Tiger Moths.

64   Alas, the Castletown children were never taught to play chess.

65   John Drummond had been the Prince of Wales's (Edward VIII) pilot out hunting in England, always leading the way over the obstacles.

66   For the story of Castletown's Devil, *see* chapter 18

67   Meeting in the green and red drawing rooms, and walking out down the garden path, were reputedly where a young Arthur Wellesley, the future Duke of Wellington, wooed and won Catherine Pakenham, a Castletown niece.

68   Later, Van and Peter broke off their engagement.

69   Squire Conolly's wife was Lady Louisa, great-granddaughter of Charles II. His pack of hounds are thought to be the origin of the Kildare Hounds.

70   The poem is several pages long, and is due for re-publication next year in the sequel
      Castletown Book, with its Fitzgerald, Dongan, and Conolly family histories from the
      year 1460.

71   Mother had a big old car to tow the trailer, and Father had a small run-around,
      which he changed every two years.

72   Col. Guy Cubitt started the Pony Club in England.

73   Barrymore himself had only cost £240.

74   Alas, they found out later that several suitcases left behind in the plane had been
      opened, and Diana's family pearls had been stolen. The Embassy of each European
      competing country held a smart reception for the Ladies European Championships;
      all except the Irish Embassy. Ireland was not a rich country, and the Ambassador
      was suspected of staying away that week, a wise move to save the costs. Though, to
      Marion and Diana's delight, he did turn up on the last day, and obviously brought
      Barrymore luck when he won.

75   Around a £500,000 now.

76   The family were especially upset at the necessity to sell the 20 acres around Batty
      Langley Lodge, which included the Leixlip Entrance, and the Ice House area.

77   When he was in hospital, and his cigarettes were taken away from him, towards the
      end of his life, they had to give his cigarettes back, because his body was so used to
      them. When he died in 1994, he was buried with a packet of cigarettes in his breast
      pocket. He was affectionately known as 'Puffing Billy'.

78   In recent years, Donacomper was sold for £73million for a small town. It had once
      been a Conolly/Packenham house.

79   At the time, we dreaded the new houses and what they might look like. Happily they
      have matured, and now look really nice. Our historic and unique six-sided garden
      potting shed became a useful newspaper shop (but has since been pulled down,
      against the wishes of the local authorities, who wanted it preserved).

80   Eventually the whole of Carton Estate was sold.

81   Top level fundraising societies in the USA.

82   The double desk in the middle of the Long Gallery was where generations of
      Conolly's sat and worked at their daily task of running the estates. This was where
      Squire Conolly, in the mid to late 1700s, struggled with endless lawsuits from his
      mother and sisters, trying to prevent him inheriting the vastly wealthy Wentworth
      Estates in Yorkshire on her death. Eventually, she succeeded in ruining him.

83   For stories of the Secret Castle, as well as for earlier family tales of the Castletown
      we know today, there is a sequel book due out.

84   The Dongan family now live in the USA, and have recently been advised that the
      title of the Earl of Limerick is still claimable.

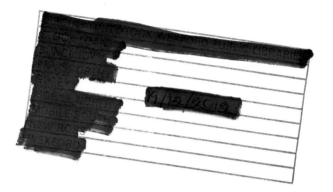